AF531699

Supply Chain Management in Services Industry

Supply Chain Management in Services Industry

An Introduction

Edited by

B V S Prasad

N Kalai Selvan

2010

Icfai Books

The Icfai University Press

SUPPLY CHAIN MANAGEMENT IN SERVICES INDUSTRY: AN INTRODUCTION

Editors: B V S Prasad and N Kalai Selvan

First Edition: 2010
Printed in India

Published by

The Icfai University Press
52, Nagarjuna Hills, Punjagutta
Hyderabad, India – 500 082
Phone: (+91) (040) 23430–368, 369, 370, 372, 373, 374
Fax: (+91) (040) 23352521, 23435386
E-mail: info@icfaibooks.com, icfaibooks@icfai.org, ssd@icfai.org

ISBN: 9788131407561

Editorial Team: Thiyagarajan D, Vellingiri D and G Srinivas Reddy
Quality Support: Kalyani R and Ramesh Ch

Contents

SECTION II

SCM APPLICATIONS IN SERVICE INDUSTRY

SECTION III

CASES

Overview

In today's competitive environment, services industries are facing the challenge of improving operational efficiencies and reducing costs, without negatively impacting customer service. Further challenges arise due to technology revolution, increasing customer expectations, frequently changing customer needs and a dynamic market scenario. In a highly competitive market scenario, the services industry has to reduce cost, turn into an innovative player and differentiate itself in the market in order to achieve sustainable bottom line growth. Customers expect more quality service from service providers such as on-time delivery and optimal price. The service industry has to provide and maintain its service reliability, consistency and on-time delivery across the globe. To increase the efficiency and effectiveness of service, service providers have to coordinate and control all the processes in their supply chain.

In the highly competitive environment of today, new product development, marketing and promotion costs are increasing constantly. Services providers are recognized, because only in that area it is possible to reduce costs in the supply chain. To meet these challenges, services providers are beginning to implement the Supply Chain Management practices (SCM), that create a balance between customer requirements and supply chain capabilities. The service supply chain must be more and more dynamic and flexible to successfully compete in the global market. SCM greatly improves customer service and creates synergy within the process. The SCM concept is a familiar one in the manufacturing industries but services industries are yet to fully realize the importance of SCM. The character of the services industry is different from that of the manufacturing industry as its products/services are intangible, and depend more on people's experience, reliability, flexibility and ethics.

The success of business in the services industry depends on good customer relationship, implementing new technologies, accurate forecasting, managing outsourcing and cost management. SCM is one of the best strategic tools to achieve success and competitiveness in this industry. SCM can bring reliability, responsiveness, consistency, flexibility, cost reduction and process efficiency. In recent years, the purpose of a supply chain has changed much more than ever before. Traditionally, organizations were implementing SCM with the purpose of achieving operational efficiency and cost cutting. In today's competitive environment with increasing customer demands, organizations are looking for leveraging competitive advantage to deliver better customer service. Integrated supply chain management fulfils the organization's requirement.

SCM concepts have been implemented successfully in the services industries like retail, financial services, transportation services, postal and courier services and logistic providers. When the internet and RFID (Radio Frequency Identification) technologies emerged, they brought a new dimension to SCM concepts. RFID technology provides a huge amount of information to the organization about the status of the product/service. Even though many software providers, such as SAP, Oracle and IBM offer SCM concepts to the organization, no one has a complete software package, which is suitable for any particular organization, because each industry and organization has its own unique business model and business process. The SCM software provider has to customize its software according to a particular organization.

The present book **"Supply Chain Management in Services Industry: An Introduction"** is divided into three sections – introduction, SCM application in services industry, and case studies. The first section contains eight articles which explain how service chains differ from the traditional supply chain, and elaborates on the challenges in implementing SCM in the service industry.

To increase the efficiency and effectiveness of service, service providers have to coordinate all the processes in their supply chain to bring reliability, responsiveness, flexibility, cost reduction and process efficiency in the services industry. SCM is one of the best strategic tools to achieve success and competitiveness in this industry. The first article of the first section titled **"SCM in Services Industry"** written by *B V S Prasad* and *N Kalai Selvan,* discusses various challenges in implementing SCM in the services industry. It also explains the strategies for implementing SCM in the services industry and benefits of using a supply chain in the services industry.

SCM continues to change as communication technologies improve, and as organizations experiment with strategic partnerships among suppliers, distributors, and other service providers. A great deal of importance is placed on supplier conformance and performance through an emphasis on quality and service. The second article titled **"The Impact of Supply Chain Management on Service Organizations"** written by *Linda L Stanley* and *Joel D Wisner,* explores the supply chain model from a service perspective. Specifically, the goals are to identify current practices, issues, and barriers associated with SCM. The article also discusses several key characteristics of successfully integrated service supply chains, including: a relentless focus on the customer, a drive to improve asset efficiency, recognition that collaboration between firms is critical, concentration on processes instead of functions etc.

Service chains resemble supply chains in basic aspects-both comprise three or more entities, both have common threads, and entities of both are dependent on other entities of their chains. The next article titled "**Where are Service Chains?**" written by *Sandeep Kayastha,* elucidates the concept of service chains which enable service firms to capture interdependencies between their various entities. They can, then, exploit the interdependencies to design and manage service chains. The concept of service chain can dramatically transform the performance of service firms in the same way supply chains have done for manufacturing and material-handling firms.

Various companies are using the Internet to efficiently link their premises with the consumer's homes. The continuous improvement of supply chain would always decrease the cost for the retailer. Many global companies like Amazon and Dell follow the famous supply chain strategy "Decoupled extended supply chain". The main thing about this is that the products are delivered by specialized third party logistics partners. The fourth article titled "**Extending the Supply ChainHow Cutting-Edge Companies Bridge the Critical Last Mile into Customers' Homes**" is a book summary by *P Sashikala.* It describes different types of decoupled extended supply chain, such as semi-extended supply chain, fully extended supply chain and centralized extended supply chain.

Living Supply Chains is a new model for understanding customers and practically allocating resources to the customers effectively. Dynamic alignment treats the supply chain as a living being. The liberal view of supply chain is any combination of processes, functions, activities, relationships and pathways along which products, services, information and financial transactions move and in between enterprises. The succeeding article titled "**Living Supply Chains: How to Mobilize the Enterprise Around Delivering What Your Customers Want**" is a book summary by *J Venkataraman.* It deals with the four types of supply chains – Continuous Replenishment Supply Chains, Lean Supply Chains, Agile Supply Chains and Fully Flexible Supply Chains. The author quotes the examples of Dell,

Supply Chains, Lean Supply Chains, Agile Supply Chains and Fully Flexible Supply Chains. The author quotes the examples of Dell, Nokia, Zara, Li & Fung as companies with outstanding supply chain management systems, which can deliver products and services to their customers smoothly at breakneck speed.

The next article titled "**Innovating the Service Chain (Beyond Repair and Replace)**" written by *Steven Titch,* emphasizes that manufacturers should focus their efforts on innovating the warranty management process into three phases such as overhaul of transactional processing, supply chain integration and reengineering model. Warranty management functions can be spread out among different systems from different vendors, beginning with enterprise resource planning (ERP) systems and customer relationship management (CRM) systems and extending to more specialized warranty systems. Parts supply is another aspect of post-sales support, and warranty management systems can be used to create the supply models for warehouses, depots, and distribution centers.

The structure and dynamics of service chains that do not process or handle physical goods is different from that of supply chains. Some of the factors that researchers will have to consider for modeling service chains are Material balance equations, Performance drivers and metrics, Bullwhip effect, Pricing and revenue sharing, and Customers on either side. The next article titled "**Issues in Modeling Service Chains**" written by *Sandeep Kayastha,* suggests that to build models of service chains, researchers will have to identify relevant drivers and metrics of service chain performances. This paper concludes that the dynamics and structures of service chains and supply chains differ in several dimensions.

The following article titled "**SOX (Sarbanes Oxley Act) and Its Impact on Retail Supply Chains**", written by *Kannan Natarajan* and *Satish Panchapakesan,* discusses the supply chain risk areas, where the Act can have a significant impact. Supply chain risk points are identified and a framework is suggested to eliminate these risks. The article discusses the step-by-step framework towards achieving compliance in supply chain activities. The '58' philosophy is a 'low cost' and 'high employee involvement' starting point or guidance framework for improving supply chain visibility. Retailers should look out for solutions, which will increase visibility and reduce inventory through better forecasting or best practices, control or lower liabilities resulting from agreements with partners, and strengthen the bonds with partners across the supply chain.

The second section contains eight articles which are focused on benefits of using supply chain in services industries like financial services, health care, postal and courier, retail industry, entertainment industry and tourism industry.

The first article of the second section titled "**Financial Supply Chain Management**" written by *A Lakshminarasimha* and *Jyothi G Rao* proposes the use of the Financial Supply Chain Management (FSCM) solution to enable the Chief Financial Officers (CFOs) to effectively manage their receivables and payables, forecast their company's financial future, and reduce their working capital needs. It introduces the basic concepts of supply chain management and proposes the benefits of optimization of FSCM, deals with the integration of Physical Supply Chain Management (PSCM) and FSCM, and discusses the possible limitations of FSCM. The article explains that Financial Supply Chain Management (FSCM) relates to all the activities involved in the flow of cash, from the end buyer's initial order to the final reconciliation of payments across the entire supply chain.

The general framework for SCM in the service domain suggests that the level of intangibility of services has an effect on the anatomy of a supply network, the strength and behavior of the IORs between a service user and a service provider, and the activities involved in the provision of the service. The second article titled "**SCM in Banking Services**" written by *Y G Sivaram* and *Jangaiah Paladi* elucidates that SCM in services involves corporate strategy decisions, business strategy decisions and operations strategy. The article explains the key elements

Supply Chain Finance (SCF) solutions are designed to adapt to today's rapidly changing environment. The SCF product umbrella offered by the banks covers the entire supply chain cycle from supplier finance to buyer finance – all on an open account basis. The SCF models are also extremely flexible, designed to be aligned with seasonal peaks and changing country risk profiles and seamlessly fit in with companies' existing trading relationships. SCF can put the foot into the door for a relationship between a bank and a large corporate by providing a product which offers a predominantly off-balance sheet solution. The third article titled "**Supply Chain Finance – A Win-Win Situation**" written by *Sameer Sawhney,* emphasizes that SCF solutions create a multitude of benefits and a win-win situation for companies and their trading partners.

Today, postal operations have implemented RFID in various closed-loop systems to measure, monitor, and improve operations. For example, RFID is being used to monitor international mail service between major hubs. The fourth article titled "**RFID in Postal and Courier Services**" written by *Libor Švadlenka* explains that RFID (Radio Frequency Identification) can help postal and courier services by tracking and tracing, workload and transportation planning, and asset management and security. RFID (Radio Frequency Identification)-tracked mailbags, which provide delivery status, have already been created for priority mail services. Tagged mailbags are automatically read at specific points in the network to provide this automated track-and-trace capability.

The next article "**SCM in Healthcare Industry**" written by *Sathish Kumar Nagarajan,* describes how SCM improves patient care through a centralized database, that can be accessed from different locations with less time consumption. Supply chain improves inventory management with accurate medical supply and equipment orders, tailored to the patient's needs, and delivered on-time. This article discusses ways to improve the procurement process by automating the complete procure-to-pay process and analyzing purchase transactions to further drive continuous processes improvement through tailored to the patient's needs, and delivered on-time. This article discusses ways to improve the procurement process by automating the complete procure-to-pay process and analyzing purchase transactions to further drive continuous processes improvement through SCM. Finally, the article emphasizes improved efficiencies and streamlines operations to generate significant cost savings through SCM.

The article titled "**Supply Chain Management in the Entertainment Industry**" written by *R Santhana Krishnan* and *D Thiyagarajan,* states that Service Supply Chain Management framework can be used to assess and improve the performance of the demand and supply chain operations in Media and Entertainment companies. The framework includes increasing the accuracy of demand planning, improving the flexibility and cost structure of the supply chain, and wielding, greater control and ability to manage content distribution across markets and distribution channels. The article also discusses how SCM enables fighting piracy and free consumption of content by consumers, and improves decision support and analytical capabilities to serve the mass retailers, online retailers and digital distribution services by managing entire categories for them.

To meet the expectations of consumers, like consistent food supply chain of top quality, and hygienic and nutritious foods, and to gain customer satisfaction by rebuilding consumer confidence, a measurement system has to be introduced into the food supply chains. The seventh article titled "**Measuring Food Supply Chains**" written by *Venkata Nimeesha Posa,* has identified four key elements for developing a Food Supply Chain Network (FSCN). These are: The Network Structure, Chain Business Processes, Network and Chain Management, Chain Resources. The purpose of the food supply chain measurement is to keep track of the process right from the farmhouse or farmer till the food product reaches the customer.

The next article titled "**Poverty-Sensitive Value Chains in the Tourism Industry**" written by *Eugenio Yunis,* stresses that the supply chain of tourism, and especially that of hotel companies, can be substantially improved in developing countries and LDCs, in order tourism companies. A first step is to gain awareness and accept that local suppliers can offer goods (such as food and furniture) as well as services (guides, transport or laundry).

The third section contains case studies of Dell Inc, FedEx, Mumbai dabbawallahs and the construction industry.

Nowadays, the market is compelling the setting up of Virtual Enterprises (VE) with a customer-oriented policy to facilitate management, and to improve the efficiency of the construction project. Based on this context, the case titled "**Supply Chain Management in the Construction Industry: A Case Study in Spain**" written by *Josep Capó-Vicedo, José V Tomás-Miquel* and *M Expósito-Langa,* analyzes the case of a Spanish construction Small and Medium Enterprise (SME), which acts as the broker of the VE corresponding to each construction project. The case study examines the characteristics of this enterprise, the advantages for the customer, the difficulties in its creation, which occur due to the necessity of a cultural change in customers and suppliers, as well as the processes established to solve the problems.

The case titled "**The Mechanics and the Method**" written by *Nasreen Taher* describes how dabbawallahs have evolved a unique coding system of their own, which is used to track the flow of dabbas within the entire delivery network. The system relies on the hub-and-spoke concept comparable in many ways to the postal mail delivery system, where mails are sent to a central sorting facility for consolidation, subsequently being redirected to various destinations. From the customer's house to his office or factory, the dabba is handled by at least three different dabbawallahs, up to a maximum of 12 men, depending entirely on the place of pick-up and the place to which it has to be delivered.

The case titled "**E-procurement Excellence – Behind the FedEx's Success**" written by *Mohammed Naved Khan,* discusses the selection, implementation and the architecture of E-procurement and supply chain solution at FedEx, while highlighting the reasons for

The case titled "**E-procurement Excellence – Behind the FedEx's Success**" written by *Mohammed Naved Khan,* discusses the selection, implementation and the architecture of E-procurement and supply chain solution at FedEx, while highlighting the reasons for implementation. FedEx recognized service reliability as the most important piece of the picture—believing that, if the delivery did not reach its destination on time, all other issues simply faded away. E-procurement systems consist of three parts: Server-based software at the buyer's end, the supply side, which is effectively a mirror image of the buyer's end, and in between these two applications, the most powerful feature of the e-procurement market – the trading portal.

Michael Dell's innovative direct-sales strategy together with efficient supply chain management has been successful in allowing his company to sell computers at competitive prices. Dell Inc. bought components from its suppliers on credit; it sold most of the computers directly to end-users on cash payment. The main idea behind this direct-sales model was to bypass the intermediary distribution network such as retail stores and system integrators, and, thereby, offer products at lower prices compared to competitors. The case study titled "**Dell Inc.: Time to Discard its Direct-selling Model?**" written by *Ramamurthy Nambi,* describes how Dell has successfully implemented supply chain management to sell computers to the customer. Each customer order may be distinctive in terms of manufacturing, procurement, packaging, and logistics requirements, but Dell's system has ensured that customers get what they ask for.

Section I

Introduction

1

SCM in Services Industry

B V S Prasad and N Kalai Selvan

To increase the efficiency and effectiveness of service, service providers have to coordinate all the processes in their supply chains to bring reliability, responsiveness, flexibility, cost reduction and process efficiency in the services industry. SCM is one of the best strategic tools to achieve success and competitiveness in this industry. The article discusses various challenges in implementing SCM in the services industry. It also explains the strategies for implementing SCM in the services industry and benefits of using a supply chain in the services industry.

Introduction

Today, most of the industrialized nations continue to move towards service-based economies as this sector is the largest contributor to the economy of most developed as well as developing countries. The recent *Fortune* 500 companies contain more service based companies and less manufacturing companies than the last decade[1]. The services industry has been facing huge challenges due to the technology revolution, increasing customer expectations, frequently changing customer needs and a dynamic market scenario. In a highly competitive market

[1] *http://money.cnn.com/magazines/fortune/fortune500/*

scenario the services industry has to reduce cost, turn into an innovative player and differentiate itself in the market in order to achieve sustainable bottom line growth. Customers are expecting more quality service from service providers such as on time delivery and at optimal price. In this competitive environment, the services industries are facing the challenge to improve operational efficiencies and reduce costs without negatively impacting customer service. Moreover, the services industry has branches nationally and internationally to provide service to its customers. The service industry has to provide and maintain its service reliability, consistency and on-time delivery across the globe. To increase the efficiency and effectiveness of service, service providers have to coordinate and control all the processes in their supply chain. In the highly competitive environment of today, new product development, marketing and promotion costs are increasing constantly. Services providers are recognized because only in that area it is possible to reduce costs in the supply chain. To meet these challenges, services providers are beginning to implement the Supply Chain Management (SCM) practices which create a balance between customer requirements and supply chain capabilities. The service supply chain must be more dynamic and flexible to successfully compete in the global market. SCM greatly improves customer service and creates synergy within the process.

The SCM concept is a familiar one in the manufacturing industries but services industries are yet to fully realize the importance of SCM. The character of the service industry is different from the manufacturing industry as its products/ services are intangible, and depend more on people's experience, reliability, flexibility and ethics. We need a different approach and framework to implement SCM in the services industry. E-commerce, Globalization and Customer Expectation are key factors which force the implementation of SCM concepts in the services industry. The success of business in the services industry depends on good customer relationship, implementing new technologies, accurate forecasting, managing outsourcing and cost management. The SCM is one of the best strategic tools to achieve success and competitiveness in this industry. SCM can bring reliability, responsiveness, consistency, flexibility, cost reduction and process efficiency in the services industry.

Service Supply Chain

Service Supply Chain Management is a tool for forecasting, planning, implementing, and controlling the process of the supply chain with the objective to satisfy customer requirements in an efficient manner[2]. It involves coordinating, integrating and controlling the product, information and finance flows both within the organization and among the partners. Figure 1 Shows Multi-Echelon Service Supply Chain Material Flows and it explains how these flows have been coordinating from supplier to end user with efficiency. SCM enables the service organization to have a clear view of the entire process. In the recent years, the purpose of supply chain has changed as never before. Traditionally, organizations were implementing SCM with the purpose of achieving operational efficiency and cost cutting. In today's competitive environment and increasing customer demands, organizations are looking for leveraging competitive advantage to deliver better customer service. The integrated supply chain management fulfils the organization's requirement.

Figure 1: Multi-Echelon Service Supply Chain Material Flows

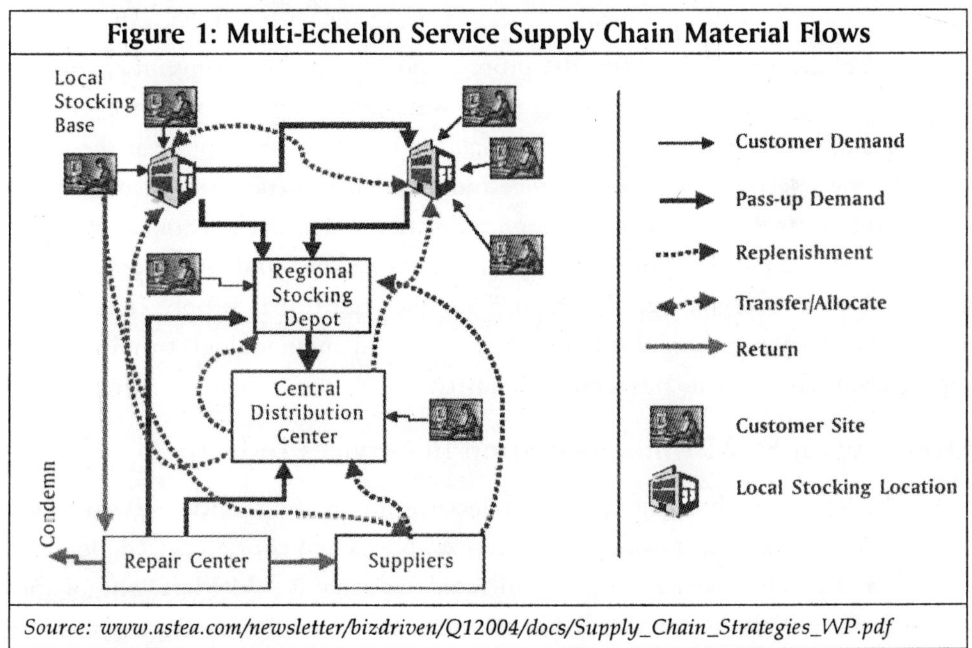

Source: www.astea.com/newsletter/bizdriven/Q12004/docs/Supply_Chain_Strategies_WP.pdf

2 *en.wikipedia.org/wiki/Supply_chain_management*

Uniqueness of Service Supply Chain

Service chains are similar to traditional supply chains in fundamental aspects such as containing more than two entities, having common threads and entities dependent on other entities of their chains (*Sandeep Kayastha, 2004*). Service supply chain is different from traditional supply chain mainly due to product that it offers i.e., service is intangible. For instance, identifying the common thread is not easy in financial service. The purpose of the supply chain in a manufacturing industry is reducing cycle time, inventory and logistic costs. In the service industry, most of this purpose is irrelevant as the service provided is intangible or intransferable. The service industries are keen on increasing supplier responsiveness and better customer service delivery. Most of the service industries deliver the service directly to the customer with out the distributor and logistic partner. The traditional supply chain deals only with the flow of materials from suppliers to end users whereas service chains deal with flow of resources which require managing processes. In addition, the traditional supply chain entities process the material within a short duration whereas service chain process takes a longer time. For example, bank deposits and leasing take a long duration of time. In traditional supply chain, the material moves from one entity to another after the process and it is stored as inventory. In the service industry, the operation takes place simultaneously. For instance, in the banking and telecommunication industry, all the operations take place at the same time. In the telecommunication service industry, customers are located in both ends as the receiver and sender. The service organizations need to equip themselves well to deal with the frequent changes in customer demand. All these aspects differentiate the service supply chain from the traditional supply chain. The organizations need to take a different approach and methodology to implement supply chain concepts in the services industry.

Overview on SCM Implementation in Services Industry

SCM concepts have been implemented successfully in the services industry like retail, financial services, transportation services, postal and courier services, logistic providers, etc. The classical example in retail industry is Wal-Mart, one of the largest retail players in the US. It has provided better service to its customer by collaborating the entire operation using SCM. P&G also implemented the SCM concept which has earned the company competitive advantage in the market.

When the internet and RFID (Radio Frequency Identification) technologies emerged, it brought a new dimension to SCM concepts. The RFID technology provides huge amount of information to the organization about the status of the product/service. This would revolutionize industries like retail, postal and courier, logistic provider, transporter, etc. For example, FedEx has implemented SCM concepts, which enables the organization to collaborate with the entire global operations. Even though many software providers such as SAP, Oracle and IBM offer SCM concepts to the organization, no one has a complete software package which is suitable for any organization because each industry and organization has its own unique business model and business process. The SCM software provider has to customize its software according to the particular organization.

Issues in Modeling Supply Chain Framework for Services Industry

There are many issues and obstacles in creating the supply chain framework for the services industry. Naturally, the service industry has a wide range of industry sectors such as retail, transportation, healthcare, financial services, courier service etc. and each differs from the other. Each sector has its own operation and business processes. Hence, the industry needs a customized framework for each sector. In a manufacturing industry, the product quantity that enters a supply chain is equal to the product that goes out of it. But, the service industry's quantity of inflows and out flows may not be the same as in the television broadcasting industry. Today, most of the organizations practice a performance-driven business model while implementing best practices. Traditionally, the SCM performances are measured by cycle time, inventory control, cost of production etc. But in the services industry, organizations can measure their performance in terms of number of customers serviced, based on customer satisfaction, responsiveness and quality of services. The services industry like financial services, telecommunications, etc., is practicing a revenue sharing model rather than sales agreement. Hence, the organization's revenue depends on the other partner's operational efficiency[3].

Benefits of Supply Chain in Service Industry

Supply chain management offers huge benefits to the services industry. This will enable the organization to achieve greater customer satisfaction and loyalty. Using

[3] Sandeep Kayastha (2005), "Issues in Modeling Service Chains", published in *The Icfai Journal of Services Marketing*.

SCM in the services organization carries greater competitive advantage in the market place and increases the bottom line growth. It also enables the organization to reduce the cost, helps in a better delivery system, forecasts the customer demand, etc.

The major benefits of SCM in the service industry are as follows:

- Competitive advantage
- Improved quality of service
- Increased visibility of processes
- Increased bottom line growth
- Better customer service delivery
- Reliability
- Responsiveness
- Consistency
- Flexibility
- Cost reduction
- Improved operational efficiency
- Improved ability to implement best practices
- Better ability to control the process
- Understanding customer through customer database
- Efficient resource planning
- Collaboration with the business partners.

Strategies to Implement SCM in the Service Industry

Management Commitment

This is a very important factor while implementing SCM in the services industry. The top management must provide adequate resources and support to implement SCM in the organization. The organization must have a common goal and objectives to facilitate a smooth and successful implementation process.

Organization Culture

While implementing SCM in the service industry, there may be some resistance from within the organization. The organization must change the attitudes and behavior of those engaged in the system. Employees must be innovative and willing to make changes.

Organization Structure

The organization structure must be changed according to the SCM framework. The organization structure must support and coordinate the SCM implementation and application process.

Understanding Business Partners

Before implementing SCM, the organization must understand deeply its business partners. The success of SCM depends on how it is collaborating with all business partners. Hence, SCM should be implemented within an organization as well as its business partners. Without understanding the business partner's business model, it is very difficult to implement SCM in the organization.

Financial Support

The organization needs to allocate adequate financial support to the project team for implementing SCM. The organization needs capital support to overcome the hurdles, because while integrating business process within an organization, the partner's organization may face a short-term crisis.

Select Right Software and Consultant

The success of SCM depends on how the organizations choose the right SCM software which rightly fits its business model. The organization also must choose the right consultant for SCM implementation. Before implementing SCM, the consultant has to study the entire business model and the customized SCM software which is suitable for a particular organization.

Customer Focused

Customer must be the centre stage of SCM implementation. The organization and consultant must keep in mind the customer during SCM implementation. In the services industry, customer satisfaction is the primary objective of an organization.

Training and Motivation

The Organization must provide appropriate training to all employees within and outside it. For successful SCM implementation, business partners need proper training. Organization must motivate all employees and business partners with right reward system.

Performances Measures

The organization must measure its performance periodically during implementation. This will provide great motivation to top management and employees.

Challenges to Implement SCM in the Service Industry

Partner's Involvement

Partner's involvement is a huge challenge to implement SCM in the services industry because SCM implementation requires cultural changes, initial investment, commitment, etc. If one partner is reluctant to follow SCM system, the entire effort will go in vain.

Initial Cost

The services organization must invest a huge amount of money initially, for implementing SCM. Hence, small players may not be able to invest adequate money on SCM. In order to provide better customer service, an organization must have distributed physical infrastructure of service centers, depots, and field staff closer to the customers.

Sharing Data and Information

SCM provides transparency within the organization and among the partners. Problems arise if any supplier does not wish to share the information with others.

Interrupt Business

When SCM is implemented, the organization must make sure that it will not disturb the existing business process and customer satisfaction.

Conclusion

In a highly competitive market environment, services organizations are facing huge challenges to satisfy customers and retain them. A SCM concept gives competitive advantage and bottom line growth to the services organization. The character of the services industry is different from the manufacturing industry as its products/services are intangible. So the services organization must draw a new framework for implementing SCM.

(B V S Prasad is a Senior Faculty Member at Icfai Business School Research Center, Chennai. He can be reached at bvsprasad129@yahoo.com and

N Kalai Selvan is a Faculty Associate at Icfai Business School Research Center, Chennai. He can be reached at kalai_gems@yahoo.com).

References

1. Morris Cohen, "Supply Chain Strategies to Increase Corporate Profitability" an MCA Executive White Paper Passed on *www.mcasolutions.com*
2. Gina Paglucia Morrison and Anca van Assendelft (2006), *"Charting a new course: The retail merchandising-supply network"*, published in IBM Corporation.
3. Morris A. Cohen , Narendra Agrawal and Vipul Agrawal (2004), "Achieving Breakthrough Service Delivery Through Dynamic Asset Deployment Strategies" published in Wharton publication.
4. Sandeep Kayastha (2005), "Issues in Modeling Service Chains" published in *The Icfai Journal of Services Marketing*, The Icfai University Press.
5. Yunus Kathawala, Khaled Abdou (2003), "Supply chain evaluation in the service industry: A framework development compared to manufacturing" published in *Managerial Auditing Journal*, MCB UP Ltd.
6. Charlie Hawker, John Nelson and Simon Terry (2004), "Building the supply chain of the future consumer-driven supply chain networks", published in IBM Corporation.
7. Ben Worthen (2006), "ABCs of Supply Chain Management", posted on *http://www.cio.com/research/scm/edit/012202_scm.html*
8. Manhattan Associates, Inc. (2006), "The Service Oriented Architecture in the Supply Chain—Benchmark Report: What Supply Chain Managers Need to Know", Business Value Research Series.

9. A T Kearney, Inc. (2004), "How Many Supply Chains do You Need? Matching Supply Chain Strategies to Products and Customers" published in *The Icfai Journal of Supply Chain Management,* March 2006

10. Korrakot Yaibuathet, Dr.Dario Toncich and Choon NG, "The Development of a Supply Chain Measurement Framework for the Milk Products Industry" posted on *www.swin.edu.au/iris/pdf/profiles/KorrakotYaibuathet.pdf*

11. Linda L Stanley and Joel D Wisner (2005), "The Impact of Supply Chain Management on Service Organizations" published in *The Icfai Journal of Supply Chain Management.*

12. Sandeep Kayastha (2004), "Where are Service Chains?", published in *The Icfai Journal of Services Marketing.*

2

The Impact of Supply Chain Management on Service Organizations

Linda L Stanley and Joel D Wisner

Supply chain management has been used to describe the integration of purchasing, operations, and distribution activities among a network of interdependent organizations. Most of the research to date focuses on manufacturing practices within the supply chain with little emphasis on the service sector. This paper presents exploratory findings of a comprehensive survey of US and European organizations to study the practice of supply chain management in services. Respondents who practiced supply chain management were asked a number of questions regarding their supply base including logistics, partnership, certification, supplier selection and performance, and customer relationship issues. Their responses form the basis for this paper.

Introduction

The United States and other industrialized nations continue to move toward more service-based economies. For example, services now account for more than 60% of the GNP and close to 80% of employment in the US (Heizer and Render, 2001).

Source: The Icfai Journal of Supply Chain Management, March 2005.

The world is also changing as more services are exported, with US service sales representing approximately 30% of all exports in 2003 with a trade surplus (Bureau of Economic Development, 2004). As services continue to gain importance and are exported internationally, similar to manufactured goods, a need for a Supply Chain Management (SCM) perspective is warranted. While trade journals and academic research have addressed manufacturing's SCM practices to a great extent, less attention has been paid to the service sector (for trade journal examples, see Benchley, 2004; Tobin and Osyk, 2004). Specifically, limited prior attention has been paid to supply chain participation, integration of processes, or successful logistics strategies (Lambert *et al,* 1998). Differences do exist between manufacturing and service operations, however, which make further exploration necessary and constitute the basis for this research.

Thus, the objective of this study was to explore the supply chain model from a service perspective. Specifically, the goals were to identify current practices, issues, and barriers associated with SCM. We believe the findings here begin to offer a snapshot of SCM within service organizations and will hopefully lead to further research in this area.

The following section describes the existing SCM literature relevant to the study of service organizations. Subsequent sections present discussions of the research methodology, demographic characteristics of the respondents, logistical activities and strategies and their relationships to SCM, and the managerial or strategic implications of the study. Future research directions are also presented and discussed.

Review of Relevant Supply Chain Management Literature

A number of definitions have been used to describe Supply Chain Management (SCM), including:

- "...firms collaborating to leverage strategic positioning and to improve operating efficiency (Bowersox *et al.,* 2002)."
- "An integrating philosophy to manage the total flow of a distribution channel from supplier to ultimate customer (Ellram and Cooper, 1993)".
- "...the integration of (all activities associated with flow and transformation of goods from raw materials stage through to the end user as well as the

associated information flows) through improved supply chain relationships, to achieve a sustainable competitive advantage (Handfield and Nichols, 1999)."

The above definitions and others (Christopher, 1998; New and Payne, 1995; Scott and Westbrook, 1991) generally describe the coordination and integration of logistical, operations, and marketing activities among a network of interdependent organizations—including manufacturers and service industries—to control and improve the flow of materials, products, and information from original suppliers to end users. Most of the research to-date has focused on the upstream SCM roles and activities of OEM manufacturers and their suppliers, which is fairly clear-cut. However, services can be somewhat complex and deserve attention.

Service organizations, for example, fall into several categories including (Guile and Quinn, 1988):

- Value-added services, including insurance, financing, and leasing companies.
- Business services that support manufacturing, including consulting, auditing, and advertising firms.
- Distribution services, including wholesalers, retailers, and distributors.
- Infrastructure services, including transportation, utilities, and banking.
- Personal services, including healthcare, restaurants, and hotels.
- Government services.

Service organizations also serve multiple roles in the supply chain, as buyers of finished goods from manufacturers; facilitators, such as distributors or wholesalers; service providers to other businesses, including transportation companies, insurance companies, universities, and web-based services; or suppliers directly to the consumer, including utilities and banks. An individual service organization may also serve in multiple roles. For example, insurance companies may buy printed policies, office equipment and computers to meet operational requirements, and sell policies directly to both HR departments through agents or individual brokers, and to individual consumers.

The question has been raised whether service and manufacturing organizations are similar in their approaches to SCM. While there may be some similarities in tasks related to purchasing and supply management (Fearon and Leenders, 1996), Smeltzer and Ogden (2002) found the perceived complexity of purchasing services to be greater than that for materials due to the intangibility of services and the difficulty of assessing financial and other benefits of the purchase. Service organizations also need a vehicle to adjust to frequent changes in customer demand and reduce inventory levels due to the bullwhip effect (Lee *et al.,* 1997). Although consumer sales may not seem to vary much, there is significant variability in retailers' orders to wholesalers.

Supplier development practices also differ in service organizations, according to Krause and Scannell (2002). For example, service firms place more emphasis on the financial strength of suppliers when assessing their strategic goals. They also rank the importance of reduced cost, increased supplier responsiveness, and improved delivery significantly higher than manufacturers.

Another issue relates to position, size, and relative power in the supply chain, all affecting the degree SCM impacts the service organization. Additionally, the type and importance of material flows can vary in importance. As shown in Figure 1, some service organizations, such as distribution services and transportation companies are as concerned with physical inventory management issues as manufacturers. To consultants and auditors, on the other hand, "materials" more often are flows of information between supply chain partners.

Other challenges face service organizations. For example, there is the issue of "customer-supplier duality" according to Sampson (2000). In manufacturing, production flows in one direction (toward the customer). For service providers, however, production flows in both directions between customer and supplier because the customer is an integral part of the process. Another challenge is found in the complexity of the supply chain itself. Spens and Bask (2002), for example, discovered that the framework to map the supply chain for a blood bank was extremely complicated with many levels and components that had to be considered simultaneously.

Figure 1: Change in Outsourcing Practices

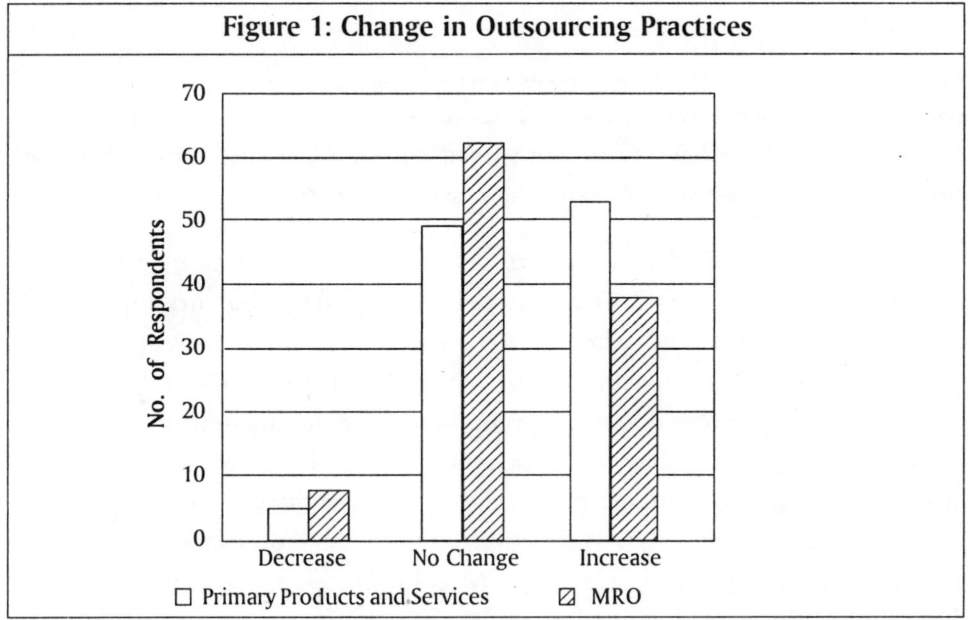

Lastly, collaboration has been found to improve logistical effectiveness in the supply chain and the best service firms practice both internal and external forms (Stank *et al.,* 2001). In the retail sector specifically, relationships with suppliers seem to be moving toward greater collaboration in planning and synchronizing inventory movements (Islei and Becker, 2001). The extent of collaboration in other service sectors has not been studied yet.

Practices important to collaboration in the service supply chain have been found to be (Frankel *et al,* 2002; Cuthbertson and Collet, 2001):

- A willingness to make changes and be innovative.
- An understanding of each supply chain partner's business.
- Commonality in goals and objectives.
- Information exchanges.
- Process integration.
- Capital investments to support integration.
- Application of appropriate performance measures and rewards.

Summary

The most recent SCM literature suggests that a set of "best practices" is still evolving for service organizations and there are a number of challenges. While most research efforts have focused on retail and/or distribution, little has been done to include other service sectors as described earlier.

The concept of SCM continues to change as communication technologies improve, and as organizations experiment with strategic partnerships among suppliers, distributors, and other service providers. Retailers, for example, have integrated their logistics functions with transportation partners to achieve direct store deliveries or cross-docking without the need for incoming inspections (St. Onge, 1996). SCM has also been practiced by wholesalers and retailers to integrate logistics functions and partnership with transportation and warehousing providers to more efficiently and effectively manage the movement and storage of materials. Today, a primary focus of SCM is on process integration throughout the supply chain, with the ultimate objectives being to create a balance between customer requirements and supply chain capabilities (Lummus and Alber, 1997). Despite its importance, and some mention in the business press, there has been limited empirical research in the service SCM area describing supply chain activities from a broader perspective. Most of the studies found were limited to issues of collaboration with some attention paid to differences between manufacturing and services. Thus, the limited research available suggests a need for further investigation of supply chain practices in service organizations as a whole.

This research begins to address some of these issues missing in the current literature by focusing on all service industries. The following sections describe the research methodology, the findings of our research, the conclusions, and suggested future research directions.

Research Methodology

To gain a better understanding of SCM practices, a survey was designed based on a thorough review of the SCM and related literature. The survey included sections regarding SCM strategies and sourcing practices. Additionally, a number of barriers to successful SCM were identified and included in the survey. These concerns included cooperation and trust among supply chain members, information sharing capability, competition from other supply chains, and geographical proximity between supply chain members. Finally, issues of importance to the respondents regarding their service to customers were explored. The survey instrument was designed based on these practices and barriers, and also included a number of general questions regarding SCM and its relationship to various elements within the firm.

For many of the survey questions, respondents were asked to indicate, using a five-point Likert scale (where 1 = low and 5 = high), the importance, impact, or success of the various SCM practices, issues, and terms. The Appendix contains summary information of actual questions asked in the survey. A number of other questions required simple yes or no answers, and several demographic questions were also included in the questionnaire. The survey instrument was then pre-tested for content validity based on the feedback from 30 purchasing managers. Where necessary, questions were re-worded, added, or discarded to improve validity and clarity. The pre-test questionnaires were not used for subsequent analyses.

The questionnaire was mailed in three phases to senior managers in US and European manufacturing and service organizations using a modified version of Dillman's (1978) total design method. In each phase, three mailings were conducted, consisting of the survey with a cover letter, a reminder post card, and finally, a second survey with a follow-up letter. In the first phase, the survey was mailed to 1500 US manufacturing firm supply and materials managers, randomly selected from the Institute for Supply Management (ISM) membership database. The second phase of the study involved mailing surveys to 3000 senior US managers randomly identified from the American Production and Inventory Control Society (APICS)—the Educational Society for Resource Management membership database. This sample included 1000 manufacturing firms and 2000 service firms. The third phase involved sending 970 surveys to senior European firm managers, also randomly identified from the APICS membership database. Care was taken to delete multiple listings for firms with more than one ISM or APICS membership listing. A total of 527 useable surveys, consisting of 411 US firm responses and 116 European firm responses, were received, for a combined response rate of 9.6% (9.1% for the US firms and 12.0% for the European firms). Of the 527 usable surveys, 192 responding firms—149 US and 43 European—were service organizations and these formed the sample frame for the purposes of this study.

Testing for non-response bias was considered warranted and the responses of early and late waves of returned surveys were compared based on tests for statistically significant differences (Lambert and Harrington, 1990; Armstrong and Overton, 1997). The sample was split into two groups on the basis of early and late survey return times with the last wave of returned surveys considered representative of non-respondents. T-tests were performed on the responses of the two groups and yielded no statistically significant differences among the survey items tested. These results suggested that non-response bias did not significantly impact this study.

Because most of the data included in the tables was generated from scaled responses, reliability was also a concern and testing for internal consistency was deemed necessary. Reliability tests were performed through the calculation of Cronbach's coefficient alpha for each set of scales. As shown in Table 1, all alpha results ranged from 0.7508 to 0.9123, indicating internal consistency of the scales (Nunnally, 1978).

Respondent Firm Characteristics

General demographic information of the respondent firms is presented in Table 2. The firms represented multiple types of organizations, including retailers, wholesalers/distributors, banks, hospitals, and schools. A wide variety of firm sizes was also represented in the sample. Almost 40% had fewer than 500 employees, while over 43% of the respondent firms had over 1000 employees. Similarly, firm size based on annual sales was also well-represented. Almost 17%

Table 1: Summary of Reliability Analysis

Scale	Number of Questions	Cronbach's Alpha Reliability Coefficient
Logistical Strategies	16	0.8307
Logistical Barriers	9	0.7508
Strategic Alliance Performance	6	0.7950
Key Supplier Selection Criteria	11	0.8067
Key Supplier Performance Criteria	13	0.8265
Supplier Conformance Issues	12	0.9099
Customer Relationship Issues	12	0.9123

had annual sales of less than $25 mn, while almost 20% had sales of greater than $1 bn annually.

Of the useable surveys, 57%, or 93 US and 17 European respondents, noted they practiced SCM. These surveys were used in the remainder of the analysis for the purposes of this study, as noted earlier. To determine the breadth of supply chain practices, the 110 respondents were asked to name those members of the supply chain targeted in their organization's SCM efforts. A schematic representation of the supply chain, from raw material extractors to end product recycling was included in the survey, and respondents were instructed to circle all elements considered part of their SCM efforts. As shown in Table 2, the breadth

Table 2: A Description of the Service Firm Respondents and their Supply Chains

Business Description	Percent	Number of Employees	Percent
Wholesaler/distributor	22.4	500 or fewer	39.6
Retailer	8.9	500-1000	8.3
Other services[a]	68.8	1000-10,000	29.7
		Over 10,000	13.5
Practice SCM?	**Percent**	No response	8.9
Yes	57.3		
No	42.7	**Annual Sales**	**Percent**
		$25 MM or less	16.7
Supply Chain Description	**Percent**	– $25 Mn-$100 MM	11.5
Supply chain includes[b]:		– $100Mn-$500 MM	17.7
1st tier suppliers	69.1	– $500 MM-$l B	8.3
2nd tier suppliers	34.5	Over $1 B	19.8
1st tier customers	42.7	No response	26.0
2nd tier customers	17.3		
End customers	33.6		
Transportation function	50.0		
Warehousing function	53.6		
Recycling	11.8		

[a] Includes banks, hospitals, school, consultants, utilities, and others.

[b] Refers to the percentage of the 110 respondents stating they practiced supply chain management.

of the supply chain varied widely. More than 69% of the respondents reported that their supply chain efforts were focused on their immediate suppliers at the time of the survey, while almost 43% of the respondents included immediate customers in their supply chain efforts. Transportation and warehousing were targeted at least 50% of the time. As expected, less involvement occurred as firms looked outward toward second and third tier suppliers. Interestingly, recycling was mentioned by almost 12% of the respondents.

Importance of Logistics Strategies

Respondents were initially asked to rate the importance of 16 logistics strategies considered important to successful SCM efforts, based on a five-point Likert scale (1 = low importance and 5 = high importance). These strategies included multiple aspects of logistics, including response time reduction, integration and communication, with issues related to both suppliers and customers. As shown in Table 3, mean responses ranged from 2.14 to 4.31.

The five logistics strategies considered the most important indicators of successful SCM were:

- Reducing response time across the supply chain.
- On-time delivery of purchased materials to points-of-use.
- Improved integration of activities across the supply chain.
- On-time delivery directly to customers' points of use.
- Searching for new ways to integrate supply chain management activities.

Based on Bonferroni's tests for multiple comparisons, the means were not significantly different between the top five indicators. Recurring themes were evident, including integration, timeliness, and meeting customer needs. Of least importance to successful supply chain management were the location of suppliers and customers and involving third-party specialists.

Barriers to Supply Chain Management Efforts

Respondents were also asked to assess several logistical barriers that might prevent them from attaining SCM objectives, based on a five-point Likert scale

Table 3: Importance of Logistical Strategies to Supply Chain Management[a]

Issue	Importance[b,c] (Std. Dev.)
1. Reducing response time across the supply chain	4.31 (0.90)
2. On-time delivery of purchased materials directly to point of use	4.17 (1.10)
3. Improving integration of activities across the supply chain	4.15 (1.00)
4. On-time delivery directly to customer's points of use	4.11 (1.23)
5. Searching for new ways to integrate SCM activities	4.06 (0.98)
6. Communicating future strategic needs to suppliers	3.93 (1.00)
7. Establishing more frequent contact with members of your supply chain	3.83 (0.83)
8. Use of informal information sharing with suppliers and customers	3.70 (0.93)
9. Use of formal information sharing agreements with suppliers and customers	3.66 (1.03)
10. Communicating customers' future strategic needs throughout the entire supply chain	3.66 (1.18)
11. Creating a compatible communication/information system with your suppliers and customers	3.61 (1.16)
12. Creating supply chain management teams that include members from different companies	3.12 (1.16)
13. Extending your supply chain to include members beyond immediate suppliers and customers	2.95 (1.24)
14. Locating closer to customers	2.66 (1.36)
15. Use of third-party SCM specialists	2.37 (1.23)
16. Requiring suppliers to locate closer to your firm	2.14 (1.10)

[a] The information shown is compiled from the 110 respondents stating they practiced supply chain management.

[b] Scale: 1 = low importance, 3 = moderate importance, 5 = high importance.

[c] The vertical lines indicate insignificant differences between mean responses using Bonferroni multiple comparison tests at the 0.05 significance level.

(1 = low severity and 5 = high severity). These barriers were identified through an extant review of the literature. The list was then refined based on a review by several practitioners, with the addition of other potential barriers not identified in the literature. As shown in Table 4, three problems were rated the most severe by respondents based on a comparison of mean responses. The lack of a sophisticated information system that would allow information-sharing among supply chain members was perceived to be the most troublesome for respondents.

The inability to manage inventories more effectively throughout the supply chain was also a contributing factor. Lastly, the findings showed a lack of cooperation among organizations in the respondents' supply chains which was a problem. Geographical distance between respondents, customers, and suppliers was not considered to be a barrier, supporting the findings found in Table 3 which shows geographical distance to be the least important to respondents.

Key Supplier Management Issues in the Supply Chain

A number of initiatives designed to create closer relationships between buyer and seller and improve supply chain integration have been developed in recent years and are frequently mentioned in the SCM literature. Trends of increased outsourcing, supply base reduction, development of strategic alliances or partnerships, and supplier certification programs were of particular interest and explored in this study. Respondents were questioned on current practices and the value of these activities and the results are presented in the following paragraphs.

Table 4: Logistical Barriers to Effective Supply Chain Management[a]

Barrier	Severity[b,c]	(Std. Dev.)
Lack of sophisticated information system for information sharing among supply chain members	3.55	(1.13)
Lack of ability to manage inventories throughout the entire supply chain	3.33	(1.18)
Lack of cooperation among supply chain members	3.20	(1.00)
Lack of trust among supply chain members	3.10	(1.08)
Lack of interest by suppliers/customers to participate in the supply chain	3.05	(1.04)
Respondent's lack of leverage in the supply chain	2.93	(1.11)
Suppliers' geographical distance from respondent	2.53	(1.18)
Competition from other supply chains	2.52	(1.11)
Customers' geographical distance from respondent's facilities	2.25	(1.09)

[a] The information shown is compiled from the 110 respondents stating they practiced supply chain management.

[b] Scale: 1 = low severity, 3 = moderate severity, 5 = high severity.

[c] The vertical lines indicate insignificant differences between mean responses using Bonferroni multiple comparison tests at the 0.05 significance level.

As depicted in Figure 1, respondents experienced a significant increase in outsourcing activity over the past three years. During that same three-year period, however, respondents reported a small increase in their overall supply base. Based on Figure 2, this increase appears to be due to a large increase in the number of key/preferred suppliers while there was a slight decrease in the number of general/provisional suppliers.

Figure 2: Supply Changes Over Past Three Years

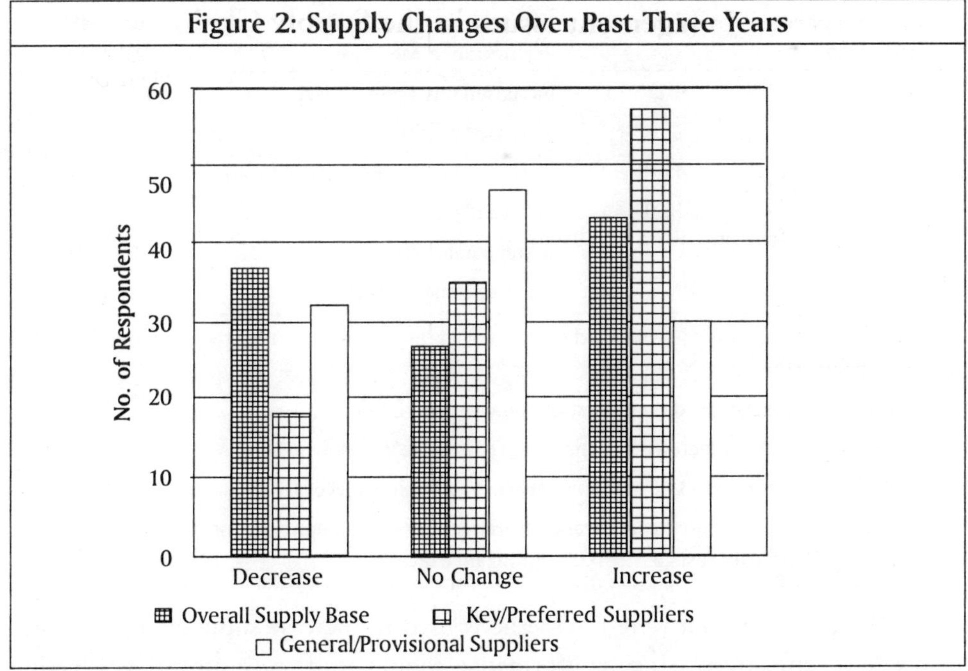

As shown in Table 5, close to 70% of all respondents reported the implementation of strategic alliances/partnerships. Respondents were asked to rate the success of their strategic alliances with suppliers in terms of a number of performance outcomes based on a five-point Likert scale (1 = low success and 5 = high success). The alliance programs were deemed successful in terms of increasing customer service, profits, buyer-supplier cooperation. However, respondents did not find as much success with increased market share or lower total costs.

Table 5 also provides results pertaining to supplier certification. More than 59% stated they had supplier certification programs in place. Almost 51% of all certification programs were either inhouse or self-reported while slightly more than 27% had implemented ISO 9000.

Table 5: Supplier Certification and Strategic Alliance/Partnership Programs[a]

Supplier Certification Program	Percent	Sig.[b]	Alliance Program	Percent	Sig.[b]
Yes	59.1	0.000	Yes	68.2	0.000
No	38.2		No	30.0	
Missing	2.7		Missing	1.8	

Type of Supplier Certification	Percent[c]	Alliance Performance Measure	Success[d,e] (Std. Dev.)
Self-reported	9.1	Increased customer service	4.07 (0.84)
ISO 9000	27.3	Increased profits	3.76 (0.98)
In-house program	41.8	Increased buyer-supplier cooperation	3.75 (0.91)
Others	10.0	Increased quality	3.74 (0.99)
		Lower total costs	3.65 (1.04)
		Increased market share	3.36 (1.16)

[a] The information shown is compiled from the 110 respondents stating they practiced supply chain management.

[b] Significance level is based on a t-test of equal yes/no response rates.

[c] Some respondents selected more than one type of certification method.

[d] Scale: 1 = low success, 3 = moderate success, 5 = high success.

[e] The vertical lines indicate insignificant differences between mean responses using Bonferroni multiple comparison tests at the 0.05 significance level.

Of particular interest were the methods used to increase supplier conformance to buyer specifications, since conformance should lead to improved satisfaction from the buyer's customers. Respondents were asked to rate the importance of a number of issues based on a five-point Likert scale. While all issues were rated more than moderately important, respondents rated nine issues equally important based on tests for significant differences in mean responses, as shown in Table 6. The results indicate that respondents want assurance that their suppliers will deliver products and services that conform to their specifications by implementing a documented quality system and taking corrective action when necessary. The top five in terms of importance were:

- Investigate any nonconformance issues and take corrective action.
- Ensure all purchased products/materials conform to purchasing's specifications.

Table 6: Supplier Conformance Issues[a]

Conformance Factor	Importance[b,c] (Std. Dev.)
Investigate nonconformance issues and take corrective action	4.25 (0.98)
Ensure purchased products/materials conform to specifications	4.12 (1.03)
Comply with all requirements of respondent's firm	4.11 (1.03)
Ensure quality policy is understood, implemented, and maintained	4.09 (1.02)
Establish and document quality system	3.94 (1.12)
Maintain adequate records of all inspections and tests performed	3.92 (1.24)
Maintain procedures to control and verify product design	3.85 (1.25)
Ensure crucial processes are carried out under controlled conditions	3.81 (1.22)
Has a comprehensive internal quality audit system	3.76 (1.15)
Verify whether quality activities comply with planned quality system	3.71 (1.17)
Provide their personnel with written inspection and testing instructions	3.68 (1.26)
Maintain adequate gauging and testing devices	3.66 (1.32)

[a] The information shown is compiled from the 110 respondents stating they practiced supply chain management.

[b] Scale: 1 = low importance, 3 = moderate importance, 5 = high importance.

[c] The vertical lines indicate insignificant differences between mean responses using Bonferroni multiple comparison tests at the 0.05 significance level.

- Comply with all requirements of buying firm.
- Ensure their quality policy is understood, implemented, and maintained.
- Establish and maintain a quality system.

Selection and evaluation of "key/preferred suppliers", those defined in the survey as "suppliers with strategic value to the firm, who have demonstrated a high level of commitment to our firm", was another area of interest in this study because of the supplier's importance to successful SCM, and the results are presented in Table 7. Respondents were asked to rate the importance of several selection factors for key suppliers based on a five-point Likert scale. Two selection factors rated equally and most critical were the ability to meet delivery due dates and a commitment to quality. Of less importance was the price of materials, parts, and services. The results indicate, for those service organizations practicing SCM, a relatively high level of importance placed on the suppliers' abilities to deliver high quality products and services on time as compared to price.

Table 7: Selection Factors and Performance Criteria for Key/Preferred Suppliers[a,b]

Selection Factor	Importance[c,d] (Std. Dev.)
Ability to meet delivery due dates	4.57 (0.81)
Commitment to quality	4.47 (0.77)
Technical expertise	4.23 (0.91)
Industry knowledge	4.15 (0.90)
Financial stability	4.12 (0.78)
Flexible contract terms and conditions	4.11 (0.87)
Price of materials, parts, and services	4.01 (0.80)
References/reputation of supplier	3.99 (0.94)
Strategic importance to respondent's firm	3.97 (0.97)
Ethical standards	3.95 (0.87)
Supplier's process capability	3.91 (0.89)
Performance Criteria	**Importance[c,d] (Std. Dev.)**
Service level	4.66 (0.60)
Quality level	4.62 (0.62)
Quick response time to emergencies or special requests	4.57 (0.76)
On-time delivery	4.53 (0.73)
Flexibility to respond to unexpected demand changes	4.30 (0.79)
Correct quantity	4.18 (0.86)
Price/cost of product	4.01 (0.86)
Willingness to change products/services to respondent's needs	3.99 (0.99)
Communication skills (phone, fax, e-mail, Internet)	3.97 (0.94)
Willingness to participate in new product development/value analysis	3.63 (1.10)
Presence of certification/other documentation	3.29 (1.21)
Willingness to share sensitive information	3.25 (1.02)
Use of EDI	3.11 (1.32)

[a] The information shown is compiled from the 110 respondents stating they practiced supply chain management.

[b] Key/preferred suppliers were defined as "suppliers with strategic value to the firm, who have demonstrated a high level of commitment to our firm".

[c] Scale: 1 = low importance, 3 = moderate importance, 5 = high importance.

[d] The vertical lines indicate insignificant differences between mean responses using Bonferroni multiple comparison tests at the 0.05 significance level.

When evaluating existing key/preferred suppliers, the respondents attached a high level of importance to a supplier's service and quality levels and their ability to quickly respond to emergencies or special requests. Least important were suppliers' use of Electronic Data Interchange (EDI), a willingness to share sensitive information, or the presence of certifications.

Table 8: Customer Relationship Issues in Supply Chain Management

Key Supplier to Customers	Percent	Sig.[b]
Yes	80.9	0.004
No	9.1	
Missing	10.0	
Customer Relationship Issue[a]		**Importance[b,c] (Std. Dev.)**
Quality of your firm's products and services		4.57 (0.70)
Successful resolution of customer complaints		4.54 (0.76)
Your firm's ability to meet delivery due dates		4.49 (0.84)
Being flexible to meet your customer's changing needs		4.39 (0.90)
Your firm's ethical standards		4.33 (0.94)
Your firm's effort in striving for continuous cost reduction		4.30 (0.88)
Your firm's financial stability		4.24 (0.97)
Making it easier for customers to seek assistance		4.18 (0.99)
Determination of key factors for improving customer satisfaction		4.10 (0.95)
Understanding how your customers use your products and services		4.09 (1.00)
Determination of customer's future customer expectations		4.05 (0.92)
Your firm's commitment to improvement in products and processes		4.04 (1.02)

[a] These questions were answered by the 110 respondents stating they practiced supply chain management.

[b] Scale: 1 = low importance, 3 = moderate importance and 5 = high importance.

[c] The vertical lines indicate insignificant differences between mean responses using Bonferroni multiple comparison tests at the 0.05 significance level.

Customer Relationship Issues

Lastly, the relationship between service organizations and their customers was considered important to complete the study of supply chain management practices. As shown in Table 8, slightly more than 80% of all respondents rated themselves as key/preferred suppliers to their customers. Respondents were also asked to rate the importance of 12 issues related to the responding firm's efforts to improve customer service and satisfaction based on a five-point Likert scale (1 = low importance and 5 = high importance). Mean responses ranged from 4.04 to 4.57, and eight issues were rated as equally important, based on Bonferroni multiple comparison tests for significant means at the 0.05 level. These issues included the quality of products and services, the successful resolution of customer complaints, ability to meet delivery due-dates, and flexibility to the customer's changing needs.

Conclusions

This study endeavored to identify current supply chain management issues and practices for service firms operating in the United States and Europe. An important contribution of this study is increased knowledge of the supply chain management from a service organization perspective and analyzing issues related to both supplier and customer. To date, most research has focused on manufacturing practices with respect to SCM while little was known on the general extent of supply chain management efforts in the service sector. This study provides solid exploratory analysis as a basis for further research on service organizations.

This ressearch specifically identified several important issues related to management of suppliers for those service firms practicing SCM and not found in previous studies. Two initial findings were insightful in that more than two-thirds considered first tier suppliers and 34.1% included second tier suppliers in their supply chain. Additionally, service organizations appear to be moving closer to an integrated approach to supply chain management based on the percentage of firms with strategic alliance/partnership (68.2%) and supplier certification (59.1%) programs, and the increase in the number of key/preferred suppliers over the past three years. The results suggest that service organizations are reducing their general supply base while focusing their recruiting efforts on key/preferred suppliers. A great deal of importance was placed on supplier conformance and performance through an emphasis on quality and service. The study indicates that their efforts are paying off based on respondent ratings of strategic alliances. However, there are a number of barriers preventing firms from fully practicing supply chain management, including a lack of sophisticated information systems and inventory management systems, and a need for more cooperation among supply chain members. These results confirm some of the work previously done by Fawcett and Magnan (1998) on supply chain barriers.

Central issues related to managing customer relationships were also found. Developing strong relationships with customers appears to be of importance to organizations that practice supply chain management, based on the finding that 80% of the respondents considered themselves key/preferred suppliers to their customers. The respondents' ranking of all relationship issues as more than moderately important also suggests service is a complex issue with multiple aspects required to please the customer. These results compare favorable with results from Fawcett and Magnan's (1998) study, identifying several key characteristics of successfully integrated supply chains, including:

- A relentless focus on the customer.
- A drive to improve asset efficiency.
- Recognition that collaboration between firms is critical.
- Concentration on processes instead of functions.
- Seeing open communication as imperative.
- Considering people in all decisions.
- Making the investment in information technology.
- An overriding concern with performance measurement.

These results lend themselves to the identification of some issues of importance to managers. First, firms practicing supply chain management realize price should be of secondary importance to other issues of delivery and quality. Supply chain management, as shown in this study, suggests organizations should refocus their efforts on response times based on the integration of activities across firms. Once firms improve communication and responsiveness within their supply chains, total costs across each chain as a result should decrease.

While there were a number of positive aspects among those firms practicing supply chain management, however, the results also suggest more can be done. The findings support the need for expansion of information systems to support supply chain management practices. Additionally, organizations need to develop and implement systems to management inventories more effectively. Lastly, cooperation is a key to support a fully effective supply chain and continues to be an issue.

This exploratory study, like all others, is not without limitations. The random sample for our survey was obtained from the NAPM and APICS membership databases; thus, the results are generalizable only to the extent that the NAPM and APICS membership lists resemble the population of all the US and European service firms and were knowledgeable about their firm's SCM practices. The response rate was also somewhat low; however given the length, complexity, and subject matter, we considered it reasonable. Readers should also be aware that much of the data reported here is based on management perceptions. Past research, however, supports the use of qualitative assessments and has found them to be a reliable alternative to actual performance data (Venkatraman and Ramanujam, 1986; Dess and Robinson, 1984). Future research efforts in this topic area should include a comparison of supply chain practices in manufacturing versus service organizations. Also, there appears to be a need for specific case studies on successful supply chain management efforts in the service sector. Additionally, studies that include linked respondents (firms, their suppliers and customers) could also lend new insights into the practice of SCM. Finally, the role of specific services such as transportation services and other third-party service providers in successful SCM needs to be further explored as firms become more experienced in SCM practice.

(Linda L Stanley is a Visiting Assistant Professor, Operations Management, Arizona State University, School of Global Management and Leadership, West Campus, Phoenix. AZ. E-mail: Linda.Stanley@asu.edu

Joel D Wisner is a Professor of Management, University of Nevada, Las Vegas. College of Business, Department of Management, Las Vegas. E-mail: wisner@ccmail.nevada.edu).

References

1. J Scott Armstrong and Terry S Overton, "Estimating Nonresponse Bias in Mail Surveys," *Journal of Marketing Research*, Vol. 15 (No. 8, 1977) 396-402.
2. Donald J Bowersox, David J Closs, and M Bixby Cooper, *Supply Chain Logistics Management*, Boston, (MA: McGraw Hill, 2002).

3. Bureau of Economic Development, "US International Trade in Goods and Services," Retrieved September. 1, 2004, on-line from *http://www.bea.doc.gov/bea/newsrelarchive/2004/trans403.htm.*

4. Martin Christopher, *Logistics and Supply Chain Management,* (Second Edition, Financial Times, Prentice Hall, New York, NY, 1998).

5. Richard Cuthbertson and Francois Collet, "Collaboration in the Supply Chain," *European Retail Digest,* Issue 32 (2001) 7-9.

6. Gregory Dess and Richard Robinson, "Measuring Organizational Performance in the Absence of Objective Measures," *Strategic Management Journal,* Vol. 5 (No. 3, 1984) 265-273.

7. Donald A Dillman, Donald A, *Mail and Telephone Surveys: The Total Design Method,* (Wiley, New York, NY, 1978).

8. Lisa M Ellram and Martha C Cooper, "Characteristics of Supply Chain Management and the Implications for Purchasing and Logistics Strategy," *International Journal of Logistics Management,* Vol. 4 (No. 2, 1993) 1-10.

9. Stanley E Fawcett and Gregory M Magnan, "Achieving World-Class Supply Chain Alignment: Benefits, Barriers, and Bridges," (Tempe, AZ: Center for Advanced Purchasing Studies, 1998).

10. Harold E Fearon and Michel R Leenders, "Purchasing's Organizational Roles and Responsibilities," (Tempe, AZ: Center for Advanced Purchasing Studies, 1996).

11. Robert Frankel, Thomas Goldsby, and Judith M Whipple, "Grocery Industries Collaboration in the Wake of ECR," *International Journal of Logistics Management,* Vol. 13 (No. 1, 2002), 57-72.

12. Bruce R Guile and James Brian Quinn, ed., *Technology in Services: Policies for Growth, Trade, and Employment,* (Washington D.C.: National Academy Press, 1988).

13. Robert B Handfield and Ernest L Nichols Jr., *Introduction to Supply Chain Management,* (Upper Saddle River, NJ: Prentice Hall, 1999).

14. Jay Heizer and Barry Render, *Principles of Operations Management,* (Upper Saddle River, NJ: Prentice Hall, 2001).

15. Gerd Isle and Johannes Becker, "A Close up View of Global Supply Chains," *European Retail Digest,* Issue 32 (2001) 15-16.

16. Daniel R Krause and Thomas V Scannell, "Supplier Development Practices: Product- and Service-based Comparisons," *Journal of Supply Chain Management,* Vol. 38 (No. 2, 2002) 13-21.

17. Douglas M Lambert and T C Harrington, "Measuring Nonresponse Bias in Mail Surveys," *Journal of Business Logistics,* Vol. 11 (No. 2, 1990) 5-25.

18. Douglas M Lambert, Martha C Cooper, and James D Pagh, "Supply Chain Management: Implementation Issues and Research Opportunities," *International Journal of Logistics Management,* Vol. 9 (No. 2, 1998) 1-19.

19. Hau L Lee, V Padmanabhan, and Seungjin Whang, "The Bullwhip Effect in Supply Chains," *Sloan Management Review,* Vol. 38 (No. 1, 1997) 93-102.

20. Rhonda R Lummus and Karen L Alber, "Supply Chain Management: Balancing the Supply Chain with Customer Demand," (APICS Educational & Research Foundation Research Paper Series, #07010, 1997).

21. Steven J New and Philip Payne, "Research Frameworks in Logistics: Three Models, Seven Dinners and a Survey," *International Journal of Physical Distribution and Logistics Management,* Vol. 25 (No. 10, 1995) 60-77.

22. Jum C Nunnally, *Psychometric Theory,* (Englewood Cliffs, NJ: McGraw Hill, 1978).

23. Scott Sampson, "Customer-Supplier Duality and Bi-directional Supply Chains in Service Organizations," *International Journal of Service Industry Management,* Vol. 11 (No. 4, 2000) 348-364.

24. Charles Scott and Roy Westbrook, "New Strategic Tools for Supply Chain Management," *International Journal of Physical Distribution and Logistics Management,* Vol. 21, (No. 1, 1991) 23-33.

25. Karen M Spens and Anu H Bask, "Developing a Framework for Supply Chain Management," *International Journal of Logistics Management,* Vol. 13 (No. 1, 2002) 73-88.

26. Larry R Smeltzer and Jeffrey A Ogden, "Purchasing Professionals' Perceived Differences Between Purchasing Materials and Purchasing Services," *Journal of Supply Chain Management,* Vol. 38 (No. 1, 2002), 54-70.

27. Theodore P Stank, Scott B Keller, and Patricia J Daugherty, "Supply Chain Collaboration and Logistical Service Performance," *Journal of Business Logistics,* Vol. 22, (No. 1, 2001), 29-48.

28. A St. Onge "New Concepts in Supply Chain Management," *Modern Materials Handling,* Vol.51 (No. 3, 1996) 33.

29. N Venkatraman and Vasudevan Ramanujam, "Measurement of Business Performance in the Absence of Objective Measure," *Strategic Management Review* Vol. 11 (No.4, 1986) 801-814.

APPENDIX

Survey Questions Used in the Study

- Does your firm practice supply chain management (circle one)? Yes / No

- Please indicate all the participants/elements included in your firm's supply chain management efforts

___	Immediate (1st tier) suppliers	___	3rd tier customers
___	2nd tier suppliers (immediate suppliers' suppliers)	___	transportation
___	3rd tier suppliers	___	warehousing
___	Immediate (1st tier) customers		
___	2nd tier customers (immediate customers' customers)	___	recycling

- How important are the following issues in your firm's supply chain management efforts?

	High Low
a) Locating closer to your customers	5 4 3 2 1
b) Requiring suppliers to locate closer to your firm	5 4 3 2 1
c) Use of a third-party supply chain management specialist	5 4 3 2 1
d) Use of informal information sharing with suppliers and customers	5 4 3 2 1
e) Use of formal information sharing agreements with suppliers and customers	5 4 3 2 1
f) Improving the integration of activities across your supply chain	5 4 3 2 1

g) Searching for new ways to integrated supply chain management activities 5 4 3 2 1

h) Establishing more frequent contact with members of your supply chain 5 4 3 2 1

i) Communicating your firm's future strategic needs to your suppliers 5 4 3 2 1

j) Communicating customers' future strategic needs throughout the supply chain 5 4 3 2 1

k) On-time delivery of your firm's products directly to your customers' points of use 5 4 3 2 1

l) On-time delivery of your purchased materials directly to your firm's points of use 5 4 3 2 1

m) Creating supply chain management teams that include members from different companies 5 4 3 2 1

n) Reducing response time across the supply chain 5 4 3 2 1

o) Extending your supply chain to include members beyond immediate suppliers and customers 5 4 3 2 1

p) Creating a compatible communication/information system with your suppliers and customers 5 4 3 2 1

- How much does each of these issues prevent your firm from achieving the full potential of supply chain management?

	High Low
a) Competition from other supply chains	5 4 3 2 1
b) Lack of trust among supply members	5 4 3 2 1
c) Lack of cooperation among supply chain members	5 4 3 2 1
d) Your firm's lack of leverage within your supply chain	5 4 3 2 1
e) Your suppliers' geographical distance from your facilities	5 4 3 2 1

f) Your customers' geographical distance from your facilities 5 4 3 2 1

g) Lack of ability in managing inventories throughout the supply chain 5 4 3 2 1

h) Lack of interest among your suppliers or customers to participate in the supply chain 5 4 3 2 1

i) Lack of sophisticated information system for information sharing among supply chain members 5 4 3 2 1

- Please circle if there has been an increase (+), decrease (-), or no change (nc) in your outsourcing over the last three years in:

  a) Primary materials, components, sub-assemblies and services ....(+/-/nc)

  b) Maintenance, repairs, and operating supplies (MRO)........... (+/-/nc)

- Please circle if there has been an increase (+), decrease (-), or no change (nc) in the type of suppliers over the last three years in:

  a) Key/Preferred Suppliers .... (+/-/nc)

  b) General/Provisional Suppliers ....(+/-/nc)

- Does your firm have a supplier certification program? Yes/No

  Your supplier certification is based on ________ (circle all that apply).

  (a) Supplier self-certification (b) ISO 9000 quality standards

  (c) Your firm's own in-house certification program (d) Others

- Does your firm have a strategic alliance program with one or more suppliers? Yes / No

  There has been a(n) _________ {increase/decrease, or no change} in the number of your partnership or strategic alliance programs with your suppliers over the past three years

  d) Has your firm decreased its supply base over the past three years?

  Yes / No

e) Is your firm considered a key or preferred supplier to your customers?

Yes / No

- Is your firm considered a key/preferred supplier to your customers? Yes / No
- How important are the following factors when selecting a key/preferred supplier for your organization?

	High Low
a) Ethical standards	5 4 3 2 1
b) Technical expertise	5 4 3 2 1
c) Industry knowledge	5 4 3 2 1
d) Commitment to quality	5 4 3 2 1
e) References/reputation of supplier	5 4 3 2 1
f) Ability to meet delivery due dates	5 4 3 2 1
g) Price of materials, parts and services	5 4 3 2 1
h) Financial stability and staying power	5 4 3 2 1
i) Honest and frequent communication	5 4 3 2 1
j) Supplier has strategic importance to your firm	5 4 3 2 1
k) Reserve capacity or the ability to respond to unexpected demand	5 4 3 2 1

- How important are the following issues when evaluating your key/preferred suppliers' performance?

	High Low
a) Quality level	5 4 3 2 1
b) Service level	5 4 3 2 1
c) Correct quantity	5 4 3 2 1
d) On-time delivery	5 4 3 2 1

e) Price/cost of product 5 4 3 2 1

f) Use of Electronic Data Interchange (EDI) 5 4 3 2 1

g) Willingness to share sensitive information 5 4 3 2 1

h) Presence of certification or other documentation 5 4 3 2 1

i) The flexibility to respond to unexpected demand changes 5 4 3 2 1

j) Communication skills/systems (phone, fax, email, internet) 5 4 3 2 1

k) Quick response time in case of emergencies or special requests 5 4 3 2 1

l) Willingness to change products/services to meet your changing needs 5 4 3 2 1

m) Willingness to participate in new product/development/value analysis 5 4 3 2 1

How important are the following issues in assuring that suppliers' products and services conform to your specifications?

Suppliers need to: **High Low**

a) Maintain adequate records of all inspections and tests 5 4 3 2 1

b) Maintain procedures to control and verify the design of the product 5 4 3 2 1

c) Maintain adequate gauging and testing devices for inspection and testing 5 4 3 2 1

d) Ensure that crucial processes are carried out under controlled conditions 5 4 3 2 1

e) Ensure that the quality policy is understood, implemented and maintained 5 4 3 2 1

f) Ensure that purchased product and materials conform to their specifications 5 4 3 2 1

g) Establish and document their quality system 5 4 3 2 1

h) Comply with all requirements of your firm 5 4 3 2 1

i) Have a comprehensive internal quality audit system in place 5 4 3 2 1

j) Investigate causes of non-conformance and take corrective actions 5 4 3 2 1

k) Verify whether quality activities comply with planned quality system 5 4 3 2 1

l) Provide their personnel with written inspection and testing instructions 5 4 3 2 1

- How important are the following issues with respect to your firm's attempts to improve customer service and satisfaction?

	High Low
a) Your firm's ethical standards	5 4 3 2 1
b) Your firm's financial stability	5 4 3 2 1
c) Your firm's ability to meet delivery due dates	5 4 3 2 1
d) Your firm's effort in striving for continuous cost reduction	5 4 3 2 1
e) Your firm's commitment to continuous improvement in products & services	5 4 3 2 1
f) Quality of your products and services	5 4 3 2 1
g) Successful resolution of customer complaints	5 4 3 2 1
h) Determination of future customer expectations	5 4 3 2 1
i) Making it easier for customers to seek assistance	5 4 3 2 1
j) Being flexible to your customers' changing needs	5 4 3 2 1
k) Determination of key factors for improving customer satisfaction	5 4 3 2 1
l) Understanding how your customers use your products and services	5 4 3 2 1

3

Where are Service Chains?

Sandeep Kayastha

Production and delivery of services are increasingly being done by multiple firms, yet a concept similar to supply chains does not exist for services. A concept of service chains will help service firms to design and manage their service chains efficiently, just as the concept of supply chains has helped manufacturing and material handling firms. In this paper we argue that the concept of supply chains cannot be used to develop a concept of service chains. We advise the researchers to take a different approach for developing the concept of service chains.

A firm is a part of large economic system comprising its buyers, suppliers, competitors, governments[1] and other firms with which it does not transact business. It buys inputs, transforms them and sells the outputs to other firms. Buyers and sellers, who transact business with each other, become interdependent and affect each other's performance. Besides buyers and suppliers, a firm's performance can also be affected by those firms with which it does not transact (Lee and Padmanabhan, 1997).

1 Throughout this paper the terms firms, entities, parties and companies stand for legal persons. We have used these terms interchangeably.

Source: The Icfai Journal of Services Marketing, March 2004.

Management researchers extensively use "chains" to capture interdependencies between different activities of a firm or between different firms. The most popular chains in the management literature are supply chains and value chains. Other useful chains include rent chains (Baron, 1995), revenue chains (Cachon, 2001), service-profit chains (Heskett *et al.,* 1994), consumption chains (MacMillan and McGrath, 1997), demand chains (Korhonen, Huttunen and Eloranta, 1998) and green chains.

Supply chains, one of the two most popular chains, deal mainly with the production and flow of materials and physical goods. Suppliers, manufacturers, wholesalers and retailers of food, engineering, chemical and consumer goods industries use Supply Chain Management (SCM) in a big way. SCM, has helped them shorten their cycle times, lower inventories and improve product availability with fewer physical, manpower and financial resources. Entities of supply chains achieve such superior performances by collaborating with each other to increase the size of the pie, rather than by competing among themselves to grab the largest share. SCM exploits interdependencies that exist between the entities of supply chains.

Service sector is the largest contributor to the Gross Domestic Product (GDP) of most developed and developing countries. The service sector contributes more than 70% to the GDP of countries such as Canada and the US, and its share is rising. Yet, a concept similar to supply chains for services has not appeared in the academic literature. The largest and fastest growing sector of most economies has thus remained unexplored by the concept of chains. Interdependencies of firms providing entertainment, banking, insurance, education, telephone and healthcare services remain to be studied and exploited. Although a few authors and researchers have begun analyzing chains of services they generally deal with services involving physical goods or people (Hanna and Newman, 2002/2001 in healthcare, not Fitzsimmons). These authors invariably use the concept of supply chains for analyzing chains of services.

This paper advocates for the development of an exclusive chain for services and is divided into three sections. The aim of the first section is to show that production and delivery of many services can be considered as products of service chains. This section also presents three properties that any chain must have before it can be called a chain. In the second section, we show that service chains are becoming important as the production and delivery of many services is increasingly being done by chains. Major drivers that are responsible for the growth of service chains are also identified in this section. In the third section, we argue that the concept of supply chains cannot be used for service chains. The aspects in which service chains differ from supply chains are discussed in this section.

Do Service Chains Exist?

Production and delivery of services can be done by one firm or by multiple firms. Many services that customers buy are outputs of processes involving multiple firms.

Take the case of payments at retail stores. Until credit cards became popular, buyers paid for their purchases by cash. Payments through credit cards involve multiple entities. They undertake a series of transactions to transfer funds from customer to retailers. Credit card users make payments to their credit card issuing banks, and not to the retailers. The credit card issuing banks pay to acquirers, and the acquirers in turn pay to the retailers.

Until recently, only the state-owned Department of Telecommunications (DOT) was allowed to provide telephone services in India. A telephone call then involved three parties—the calling party, the DOT and the called party. Deregulation has ended the monopoly of DOT. Subscribers of telephone services are now split among the Bharat Sanchar Nigam Limited (BSNL), rechristened DOT, and numerous other telephone companies. Hence, a telephone call may now involve four parties—the calling party, the calling party's service provider, the called party's service provider and the called party. As of now, most of the private telephone companies operate in small regions and they do not have a nationwide network. When a call originates from the network of a private telephone company for another city, an additional telephone company provides connectivity between the networks of two private telephone companies.

A courier service too involves multiple firms. Since most courier companies do not own the entire infrastructure and resources, they buy services of other firms. A typical courier company sends its employees in leased vehicles to collect packets, does sorting in leased buildings and gives the packets to airlines for transporting them to other cities. After taking the delivery in another city, the company again sorts the packets in leased buildings and delivers the packets using leased or hired vans. If the company does not operate in the addressees' areas, it may engage the services of delivery agencies.

In all the three above-mentioned cases, services are provided through multiple entities, or chains of entities. Chains have three properties. Any chain of services must have these properties before it can be called a service chain. The first property of a chain is that it must comprise three or more entities. This property is satisfied in all the three cases. In the case of credit cards, the entities involved are customers, credit card issuing banks, acquirers and retailers. Entities involved in telephone service are calling parties, called parties and service providers of both parties. Whereas, in the courier service case, the entities involved are senders, courier companies, airlines, delivery agencies and addressees, who handle packets, and lessors of automobiles and buildings, who provide resources to handle the packets.

The second property of a chain is that it must have a common thread that binds all entities of the chain. Entities of a chain transform or handle something common. The common thread of supply chains is physical material since their entities deal with the same material. The common thread of service chains can be physical or non-physical. In courier services, physical packets constitute the common thread. The forms of common threads in telephone services and payments through credit cards are non-physical—voice signals in the former case and funds in the latter case.

The last property of a chain says that because the entities deal with the common thing, they must affect each other. A chain cannot produce or deliver the end output if any of its entities fails to perform its function satisfactorily. The three cases pass this test too. In the courier business, delivery times and delivery performances are collectively determined by all entities of the chain. In the case of credit cards, timely transfer of funds is determined by efficient processing by credit card issuing banks and acquirers. Similarly, in telephone services a call cannot materialize if any of the telephone companies fails to process the call.

Growth Drivers of Service Chains

Not long ago the operations of service firms were simple. They used to produce and deliver the service themselves. This form of production and delivery of services is now undergoing a change. Production and delivery of services by single firms are giving way to service chains. Service firms now engage other firms to perform parts of their production and delivery processes. Both internal and external factors are contributing to the growth of service chains.

The previous decade has seen many manufacturing and service firms curtailing their operations to a narrow range of core activities, and outsourcing the rest of the activities to other firms. Processes commonly outsourced by them include security, data entry, janitorial and payroll services. Often the outsourced processes are performed not by a single firm but by multiple firms, each firm performing only a few activities of the outsourced process. For example, outsourcing of processes like billings and collection of payments by state electricity boards involves multiple firms. Each of the firms involved in a process performs only a few activities of the process.

Deregulation of public utilities and commercial services such as telephones, banking, insurance and air transport has also contributed to the growth of service chains. Private firms which provide these services do not perform all processes themselves. They get some of the processes or activities done by other firms.

Information technology (IT) is another major growth driver of service chains. Earlier, firms performed entire service processes from beginning to the end under one roof. IT has made it possible and economical to split information processes into numerous discrete activities that can be easily outsourced to firms situated far away. The outsourcing of call centers and medical transcription services to developing countries has happened largely due to such applications of IT.

Need for an Exclusive Service Chain

Manufacturers, wholesalers, retailers and other firms that deal with the same materials and physical goods are realizing that they all are interdependent on one another in complex ways. SCM enables managers to exploit the interdependencies. SCM initiatives such as redesign of supply chains, and integration and coordination among the entities of supply chains have improved performance of numerous firms. Operationally, SCM improves fill rates, delivery performances and resource utilization and reduces inventories, cycle times and resource requirements.

A concept similar to supply chains is also required for services. It should help service firms in the same way supply chains have benefited manufacturers and others who deal with materials and physical goods. The concept of service chains will enable service firms to capture interdependencies on other entities of their service chains. They can then exploit the interdependencies to design and manage service chains.

Service chains resemble supply chains in basic aspects—both comprise three or more entities, both have common threads, and entities of both are dependent on other entities of their chains. Service chains, in fact, differ from supply chains in many important aspects. Operational concerns in managing service chains and supply chains are also at variance. The concept of supply chains, therefore, is unlikely to be useful for managing all kinds of service chains. Instead of stretching the concept of supply chains to accommodate special characteristics of service chains, it would be better to develop an exclusive concept of service chains. The important differences between service chains and supply chains, and their impact on managing service chains are discussed below because a new concept for service chains will gain acceptance only if it can accommodate such differences and concerns.

Common Thread in Service Chains

Existence of a common thread is essential for any chain. Identifying the common thread, however, is not always easy, especially when its form is non-physical. Take the case of transfer of money by a customer to the seller through the banking system. The customer deposits cash in a bank and directs the bank to transfer the money to the seller's bank account. Note that the transfer of money does not involve transfer of "same" currency notes. The common thread in this case is funds, which are non-physical, and not the physical currency notes.

Identification of the common thread is also difficult in those service chains in which risks are exchanged. Sellers who sell goods and services on credit face risks of non-payment of money by buyers. Sellers can reduce their risks by asking the buyers to give bank guarantees. In a bank guarantee, buyer's bank guarantees the payment in case the buyer fails to pay to the seller. The bank does not pay anything to the seller if he is paid by the buyer. In the latter case, it may appear "nothing" flows from the bank to the seller. But the common thread in this service chain is the "flow" of risk.

Flow of Resources in Service Chains

Supply chains deal only with the flow of materials and not with the resources that are required to transform or handle materials. In contrast, certain kinds of service chains deal only with the flow of resources. Subleasing, for example, involves a chain of this kind. A sublease involves owner of the property, a tenant and a subtenant. The owner leases his property to a tenant who in turn subleases the property to a subtenant, without involving the owner (McCarty and Bagby, 1993).

Service chains of the above kind differ from supply chains in two ways. First, materials and physical goods in supply chains flow only in one direction, except for refills, repairs and returns. Reverse flows, however, are always present in a subleasing. After the sublease agreement expires, the subtenant returns the property to the tenant, and when the tenant's lease agreement with the owner expires, he returns the property to the owner.

Second, supply chain entities hold materials and physical goods with them for short durations, generally not exceeding a few weeks. They quickly move the transformed material to the next entity after performing operations on the material. However, the duration of subleases are very long. Subtenants and tenants often hold motor vehicles, machinery, land and buildings with them for many years. In other words, entities of such service chains do not wish to minimize inventories.

Customers and Suppliers in Service Chains

Suppliers and customers in supply chains are distinct entities. The "suppliers are suppliers and customers are customers with generally no overlap between two groups" (Sampson, 2000). The manner in which customers and suppliers exist in service chains can differ from that in supply chains.

Customers in supply chain entities are found in the same direction as the flow of materials and suppliers are found in the reverse direction. In service chains, customers and suppliers are rarely located in this way. Take the case of a courier service business in which the courier company picks up packets from senders, uses airlines to transport packets to another city, and hires delivery agencies for making deliveries. Using the traditional approach of considering customers as ones who pay, senders are customers of the courier company, because they pay to the company, and the courier company is the customer of airlines and delivery agencies, because it pays to both of them. Note that customers in this case are in the direction opposite to the flow of packets.

An entity of a service chain can have customers (or suppliers) on both sides of the stream (Zsidisin, Jun and Adams, 2000). In telephone services, calling parties are customers of their service providers and called parties are customers of their own service providers. The called parties' service providers, in addition, have calling parties' service providers as their customers because they (called parties' service providers) provide connectivity for the calling parties' service providers. Note that both upstream and downstream entities are customers of the called parties' service providers.

In fact, an entity of a service chain can be a supplier as well a customer of another entity of the chain. This happens in repair services. Entities that supply inputs (broken televisions, for example) to repair shops and the ones who take their outputs (repaired televisions) are the same. Such situations in which an entity acts both as a customer and as a supplier has been referred to as customer-supplier duality (Sampson, 2000).

Simultaneous Operations in Service Chains

Downstream entities of supply chains perform operations on the material only after upstream entities have finished their own. A delay generally occurs between the completion of the operation by upstream entities and beginning of the operation by downstream entities. During this period of delay, the material waits as inventory. Inventories help entities of supply chains to decouple their operations, thus reducing the need to closely coordinate the production and shipment schedules. Inventories can also reduce the capacity requirements of manufacturing firms close to the average demand.

In contrast, entities of certain service chains may have to perform their tasks simultaneously. In telephone services, for example, all companies have to process voice signals simultaneously. Hence, telephone companies cannot schedule their operations independent of one another. Since customers of telephone companies do not want to wait and because telephone calls are not inventoried before delivery to the next entity, telephone companies require large capacities to meet the peak demand. The need for coordination and the need to have large capacities are prevalent in such service chains than in supply chains.

Operational Objectives of Service Chains

The operational objectives of supply chains include reduction in cycle times, inventories, transportation costs and stockouts. Many of these objectives are irrelevant for managing certain kinds of service chains. For example, reducing the inventories does not make any sense in service chains in which materials and physical goods are not transformed or handled. Reducing the transportation time and costs in such service chains may also be unimportant. Also, location of facilities including co-location, which is so important in supply chains, may not be of concern in many service chains. Not surprisingly, call centers and medical transcription centers that have come up in developing countries are located thousands of miles away from their clients.

Summary

Supply chains deal mainly with the flow of materials and physical goods. Now that the manufacturing sector contributes to less than a third of most developed and developing economies, supply chains cater to a small part of their economies. Even though services are growing in importance, a concept of service chain is yet to appear in the academic literature. A concept of service chain can dramatically transform the performances of service firms in the same way supply chains have done for manufacturing and material-handling firms.

Supply chains differ from service chains in many important aspects. Instead of stretching the concept of supply chains for service chains, researchers need to take a different approach for developing the concept of service chains.

(Sandeep Kayastha is an Associate Dean, Icfai Business School, Hyderabad. He can be reached at kayastha@ibsindia.org).

References

1. Lee, Hau L and Padmanabhan V (1997), "The Bullwhip Effect in Supply Chains". *Sloan Management Review.*, Vol. 38, No 3.
2. Baron, David P (1995), "The Non-market Strategy System." *Sloan Management Review.*, Vol. 37, No. 1.
3. Cachon, Gerard P (2001), "Turning the Supply Chain into a Revenue Chain." *Harvard Business Review,* Vol. 79, No. 3.

4. MacMillan, Ian C and McGrath, Rita Gunther (1997), "Discovering New Points of Differentiation." *Harvard Business Review,* Vol . 75, No 4.

5. Heskett, James L, Jones, Thomas O, Loveman, Gary W, Sasser W E and Schlesinger, Leonard A (1994), "Putting the Service Profit Chain to Work." *Harvard Business Review.* Vol. 72, No 2.

6. Korhonen, Pertti, Huttunen, Kati and Eloranta, Eero (1998), "Demand Chain Management in a Global Enterprise-Information Management View." *Production Planning & Control.* Vol. 9, No. 6.

7. Hanna, Mark D and Newman, W Rocky (2002), *Integrated Operations Management,* Prentice-Hall of India. New Delhi. 2002.

8. McCarty, F William and Bagby, John W (1993), "The Legal Environment of Business" Irwin: Burr Ridge.

9. Zsidisin, George A, Jun, Minjoon and Adams, Laural L (2000), "The Relationship Between Information Technology and Service Quality in the Dual-Direction Supply Chain." *International Journal of Service Industry,* Vol. 11. No. 4.

10. Sampson, Scott E (2000) "Customer-Supplier Duality and Bi-directional Supply Chains in Service Organizations." *International Journal of Service Industry,* Vol. 11. No. 4.

4

BOOK REVIEW

Extending the Supply Chain
How Cutting-Edge Companies Bridge the Critical Last Mile into Customers' Homes

P Sashikala

This book examines some of the most high-profile practitioners of telephone and Internet-based order processing and fulfillment. The authors explain the detailed working of companies which use various supply chain models. The book also depicts various examples and various practical tools that assist in maintaining a customer-focused fulfillment operation.

There was a time when the milkman would drop in the milk packet, dry cleaner would pick up clothes and everything was at door service, the same continues today too, only the pattern has changed. As the lifestyle of the people is continuously changing, customers do not have time to go to shops to buy things. This case is of more money but less time so the concept of home delivery

Source: The Icfai Journal of Supply Chain Management, March 2006. This is a review of the book "Extending the Supply Chain – How Cutting-Edge Companies Bridge the Critical Last Mile into Customers". The book is written by Kenneth Karel Boyer, Markham T Frohlich and G Tomas M Hult and published by AMACON Books.

has been popularly increasing. Various companies are using the Internet to efficiently link their premises with the consumer's homes. The continuous improvement of supply chain would always decrease the cost to the retailer.

The evolution of supply chain management started with Ford's highly integrated River Rouge plant in the early 20th century. The term 'extended supply chain' creates opportunities to establish bonds with consumers. The key advantages of extended supply chain are: Convenience, customization, quality and experience. However, the four strategies that are required to deliver products to customers are semi-extended, decoupled, fully extended and centralized extended strategies. The key decisions associated with the extended supply chain are order fulfillment and direct delivery to the end consumer.

Decoupled Extended Supply Chains

Over the years outsourcing and Internet have become important forces. Outsourcing the non-core activities made businesses grow most effectively and to forge closer links with strategic partners and customers in the supply chain and co-ordinate the flow of information and products. Many global companies like Amazon and Dell are following the famous supply chain strategy "Decoupled extended supply chain". The main thing about this is that the products are delivered by specialized third party logistics partners. The basic decoupled extended supply chain model consists of six basic information flows that must all be carefully designed and managed in order for a successful chain.

The first information flow is the ordering and payment system, followed by order tracking. The third information flow is flow from retailer to distributor and this done through Internet or EDI. The fourth information flow is only visible to customers and finally the last two are for returns. The term "mass customization" is a strategy that involves products that are made in customized ways to individual customers. The internet is the answer for mass customization. Decoupled Extended supply chain model is widely used in Groceries, Fashion and Apparel businesses.

The term Third Party Logistics (3PL) plays an important role in the supply chain. It acts has as direct link to end customers and plays a huge role in overall decoupled retailing process. The fundamental issue in the decoupled supply chain is to see how products get into the hands of the customers and how 3PL is playing an important role in getting new solutions in achieving this. An example of United Parcel Service's (UPS) is explained in this book which is taking steps to achieve decoupled supply chain.

Semi-Extended Supply Chains

This is a kind of strategy based on store-based order fulfillment with indirect delivery. This is a low cost fixed investment since the retailers primarily utilize existing assets with minimal specialized investment. The authors have also explained the various advantages, challenges and drawbacks of semi-extended supply chains. The main advantage is that it is very economical. The primary drawback is that this model is less efficient in picking up orders since the existing retail stores are designed with different objectives. The example that is provided to explain this model is Best Buy, which stocks its CDs along with players so that the customers who buys players may also browse the CDs and buy them too.

The major challenge with this strategy involves managing inventory. To explore more about this strategy the authors have also explained a case which explains semi-extended supply chain model in detail. One of the cases is of *David vs. Goliath.* In this the company, Lowes Foods has started an online customer services which has grown immensely popular. This case also discusses the differences between the direct shopping and online shopping and the problems related to the online shopping.

To be successful, companies must carefully make several design decisions on how to coordinate their channels. Some of the key concerns are Balancing Convenience and Fulfillment Cost, Cross-Selling, Information Accuracy and Ease. Multiple channels of selling usually lead to increased sales, but without careful integration they can create customer backlash. Following this supply chain method the companies have been able to increase the customer loyalty, increase incremental sales and capture customers from their competitors.

Fully Extended Supply Chains

The concept of famous home delivery approach is known as fully extended supply chain. Many companies have started adopting this supply chain method. In this, the retailer's supply chain is continuously linked from the supply side all the way to the customer's front door. The first generation model of grocery business is most expensive one, so thus came the Piggly Wiggly's revolutionary second generation model where one comes to stores to pick up the items. There are two types of customers—one group who are ready to pay for extra service like home delivery and other, who are not ready to pay. There are, of course, people who are willing to pay as they are hard pressed for time. The authors in this book present analysis of people who are really interested in home delivery process. An example of UK grocer, Tesco, which uses fully extended supply chain model, is provided. The dot-com era retailers have refined and perfected this model. There are variety of lessons concerning this method. Going back the most important thing to minimize in home delivery is substitutions.

Centralized Extended Supply Chains

This strategy has three major advantages over strategies utilizing store-based order fulfillment. First, it eliminates a link in the supply by removing stores. Secondly, it sets apart decoupled extended strategy and finally, working from a distribution center rather than a store allows aggregated inventory, making it possible to hold less inventory while having a wide range of products and more stock. The companies, which are illustrated in the book, that use this method are Office Depot, which is one of the largest retailers and Ocado, a groceries company. There are several success levers that can be applied to centralized supply chains and they are Convenience, Relationships, Availability and Freshness. In grocery industry, delivering products to customers directly from distributor should be fresh and quick.

Meshing Operational and Marketing Goals

The relationship between an organization operation and its marketing activities has always been a critical element to achieve desired success. The authors give examples which explain the meshing that is to be needed between operational and marketing strategies to succeed in the online grocery industry.

Groceries are typically viewed as the most universal commodity in the market place. The use of Bar Coding and UPC Codings has led to greater integration and coordination between marketing research and sales. Internet is used as a technological tool to improve the value-added benefits offered to customers in the entire grocery supply chain. The companies like Web van and other online grocers have had some problems using internet. With a few notable exceptions, what all internet grocers have overlooked is that the marketing strategy of low prices needs to be matched with an operational strategy that is of low cost. The companies that have achieved this are Tesco, Sainsbury's and Albertson's.

Meshing operations and marketing is a Hexagon and it has been an important one. It has customer orientation, competitor orientation, value chain coordination, logistics management, supply chain management and operations management. The combination of all these will help a proper meshing operations and marketing.

Marketing – Tapping Customer's Latent Desires

For decades companies have struggled to design their strategies and structures to be market oriented." What customers want and What are their needs" these words have become an important slogan in marketing strategy. Delivery on the needs and wants of customers have taken on a much broader forms.

Four key concepts are of critical, strategic importance in the new era of business, fast cycle times, globalization and spanning the last mile to customer. These are: Expressed customer need, latent customer need, responsive market orientation and finally proactive market orientation. The market-oriented firm's attempts to find and satisfy customer's expressed needs via response active and market also attempts to satisfy customer's latent needs via proactive actions. This can be done only by total market-orientation where responsive and proactive actions are taken in coordinated sequences.

Being a proactive and driving markets come with major risk as well as potential rewards. Authors in this chapter have explained the concept of "driving market" which requires changes in the market structure rather than a change in the organization. Three generic approaches have been identified that would allow an organization to drive the structure of the market in which it is operating. They are Deconstruction, Construction and Functional modification. They have also given the examples of Deconstruction—Dell, Computer Corporate and Intel Corporation. The examples of constructive approach are Apple computers, CDNOW and *Omanhasteaks.com.*

For shaping customers behavior, two basic approaches has been explained. They are Direct and Indirect approaches. Always going after explicit need often requires the organization to be proactive in its market-orientation behavior. This requires the organization to have a total market response and with proactive actions in a coordinated sequences.

Supply Chain Design – How to Bridge the Last Mile

Bridging the last mile to deliver goods directly to customers is the strategy that has been around for a century or more. New technologies such as the internet, integrated supply chain systems, automated sorting hardware and new management techniques offer the potential to significantly improve the efficiency, speed and accuracy with which home deliveries can be made.

The three fundamental activities of last-mile supply chain are Ordering, Fulfillment and Delivery. The ordering process is focused on physically managing the supply chain. The fulfillment process has substantial challenges and opportunities with regard to productivity, accuracy, quality and substitutions. The delivery process is one of the most challenging aspects of the supply chain because there is a fundamental trade-off between efficiency and customer convenience. To explain the delivery process, the authors have explained the relative efficiency of eight direct business. They are: US postal services, dairy, parcel shipper which is B2B (FedEX, UPS, Airborne), parcel shipper which is B2C (FedEx, UPS, Airborne), office supplies, grocery home delivery, grocery home delivery from store and finally grocery home delivery from DC.

The most efficient delivery method is to not to offer any choice when their delivery occurs. The new technologies such as Enterprise Resource Planning (ERP), Flexible Manufacturing Systems (FMS), Bar Coding, Automated Storage and Retrieval Systems (AS/RS) rely heavily on computerization and information systems. Technology is often a driver for supply chain change, particularly within last-mile supply chain.

Information Technology: Facilitating Learning and Streamlining Transactions

The objective of this chapter is to examine the role of information technology in extended supply chains. This chapter also focuses on three main key concepts. They are: to examine the key approaches for designing website that must be simple for the customers to use, to streamline transactions so that customers gain comfort and efficiency as they make repeat purchases and finally, to examine the critical importance of integrating the order tracking system.

The main principles that are required to have an effective website are content, structure and navigation, visual design, functionally, interactive and finally, an overall experience. One of the most important things for e-commerce is to streamline transactions for repeat purchases. The example is Amazon which tried so hard to patent its one-click order process. There are two types of orders; they are First-time order and Follow-up order. The more a website simplifies and streamlines both the initial and the repeat ordering process, the more likely customers are to return. Too many websites can be described as what is commonly known as "brochure ware"—pretty-looking sites that do not link to any actual inventory or fulfillment systems. This chapter also tells that how customers have to be self-source that is to place their own orders. It also explains how to connect IT systems as much as possible to the customers as they get an accurate read on whether their order is in stock or not.

The Future of the Extended Supply Chain

The last-mile supply chain offers tantalizing prospects as well as challenges. Changes in life and business are constant. Much as we acknowledge that fact, it also scares us. We tend to restore it. However last-mile supply chain present an opportunity to take advantage of change. There are numerous companies experimenting with last-mile solutions. Many of early efforts to bridge the last mile resulted in spectacular failures. Last-mile supply chain are quite similar—some have failed, some have succeeded but we can all learn lessons from studying both the failures and the success. The book encourages the readers, who may be customers or retailers, to master the last-mile supply chain.

(Kenneth Karel Boyer is an Associate Professor of Operations Management at Michigan State University; Markham T Frohlich is on the Operations and Technology Management Faculty at Boston University, and was previously at London Business School; and G Tomas M Hult is an Associate Professor of Marketing and Director of the Center for International Business Education and Research at Michigan State University.)

(P Sashikala is a Faculty Member at the Icfai Business School, Hyderabad. She can be reached at sashikala@mail2.ibsindia.org).

5

BOOK REVIEW

Living Supply Chains
How to Mobilize the Enterprise Around Delivering What Your Customers Want

J Venkataraman

The book brings out the point that supply chain management can be a competitive advantage in the present day environment. Supply chains are omnipresent. Managing supply chains actually involves understanding the interaction between human behavior, information technology and infrastructure. The author has pioneered the idea of "dynamic alignment" which is to treat the supply chain as a living being. An interesting analysis of country cultures with supply chain models has been made by the author.

Some companies seem to get their products to their customers with glorious ease. Several other companies, meanwhile, get caught up in squeezing the costs out of their supply chains so that customers end up walking out of the doors. Or just as bad, they woo customers by providing premium service, only to find that the cost is unsustainable.

Source: Best Books, November 2006. This is a review of the book "Living Supply Chains: How to Mobilize the Enterprise Around Delivering What Your Customers Want", written by John Gattorna and published by Prentice Hall.

The author has set out to find an answer to the above phenomenon among companies and has come up with this book *Living Supply Chains,* a new model for understanding one's customers and practically allocate resources to the customers effectively. The author dwells upon the concept *"dynamic alignment"* in detail, which according to the author is a principle of matching changing customer needs and desires with different supply chain strategies. It is dynamic because it more accurately tracks the ebb and flow of people's energy. It is as alive as the people who buy your goods and services.

Through the dynamic alignment model, the book provides a structured way of linking customer expectations to the operations side of the enterprise and systematically modifying fulfillment processes as customers change their buying preferences.

The author quotes the examples of Dell, Nokia, Zara, Li & Fung as some companies with outstanding supply chain management systems. They can deliver products and services to their customers with breakneck speed and in a way that makes it look easy.

"Dynamic alignment treats the supply chain as a living being. The liberal view on supply chain is any combination of processes, functions, activities, relationships and pathways along which products, services, information and financial transactions move in and between enterprises." The author proposes the integrating elements of dynamic alignment framework in Table 1.

Table 1: Integrating Elements of Dynamic Alignment Framework

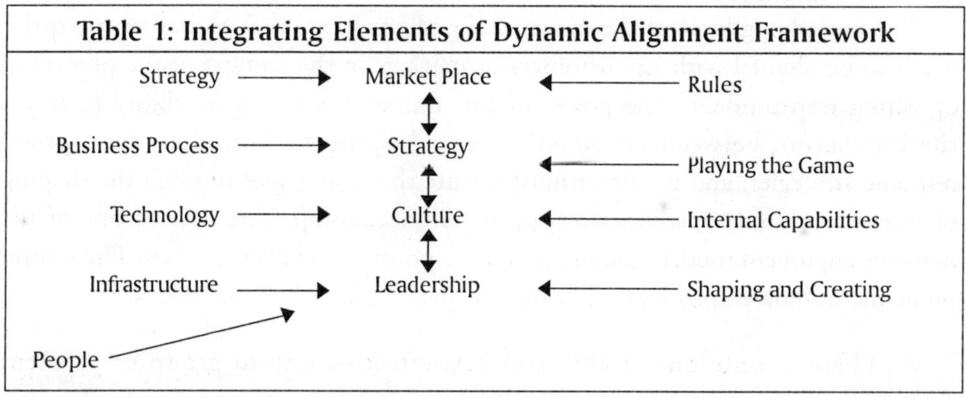

Watch the Customer and Not the Competitor

The firm should focus more internally especially on their resources than having a myopic focus on competitors and external environment. The author brings out the behavioral forces at work in supply chains using the P - A - D - I management styles, encompassing Producer – Administrator – Developer – Integrator.

- Producer – P: Force for action, results, speed and focus
- Administrator – A: The opposing force to D, and represents stability, control, reliability, measurement, logic and efficiency
- Developer – D: The force for creativity, change, innovation and flexibility.
- Integrator - I – The opposing force to P, and represents cooperation, cohesion, participation and harmony.

The author also describes the four levels of "Dynamic alignment" as:

- *Level 1: Marketplace Logic Framework* – **Certainty/Uncertainty, Low competitive intensity/High competitive intensity**
- *Level 2: Strategy Logic Framework* – **Reactive posture/Proactive posture, High risk/Low risk**
- *Level 3: Culture Logic Framework* – **Direct control/Indirect control, Internal focus / External focus**
- *Level 4: Leadership Logic Framework* – **Thinking preference/Doing preference, Individual orientation/Consensus orientation.**

The underlying logic of the dynamic alignment framework is that an enterprise needs to be aligned with its customers or markets in the context of the prevailing operating environment. The power of this framework lies in its ability to reveal the interaction between customer's needs, helping to formulate appropriate response strategies, and to successfully execute those strategies through the shaping of internal cultural capabilities by appropriate leadership. The bottom line of the dynamic alignment model is building more responsive overall enterprises. The second point the author emphasizes on is that all pathways lead to customers.

A. There is only one "right" and cost-effective way to group or segment customers depending on their dominant buying preferences and behaviors.

B. Supply chain configurations that lack a dynamic capability to "flex" between different delivery service propositions will invariably lead to service failures and reduced operational and financial performance.

C. For the best outcome, link behavioral segment at the customer end and suppliers at the source end, with a network optimization model that allows a clear line of sight on the best pathway through an otherwise complex network.

The author argues that genuine flexibility can only be achieved through multiple alignments. The organization must be "hard-wired" to a limited number of customer segments via a hybrid organizational structure and a unique combination of processes and corresponding technology applications. Then if customers change their buying behaviors under pressure of new operating conditions in their respective markets, it simply means, they move to another of the previously identified dominant buying behaviors for that product or service category. They are thereafter serviced in the predefined way for the segment. The author is convincing when he points out that alignment of the appropriate value propositions with customer's true needs and expectations significantly improves the operating and financial performance for (i) Better Service, (ii) Improved Margins, (iii) Facilitates Functional Excellence and (iv) Allows Development of New Service Offerings.

The author has done extensive research on the taxonomy of supply chains. He analyzes in depth the work done by Marshall L Fisher on exploring the idea of multiple supply chains. The author also covers the development done by Hau Lee, the well known Stanford University professor. Bill Gilmour, IBM's global consumer product industry leader, argues that FMCG manufacturers need two supply chains to service their retail customers. This has also been commented upon by the author. The proposals of Booz Allen Hamilton and Jonathan Byrnes of MIT have also been critically examined by the author.

The demand chain strategy proposed by Godsel has also been quoted by the author. This sets demand chain strategies, drives market strategy, sets up the supply chain process strategy, and also sets up process enablers. The author in his model adds the missing behavioral dimension to supply chain.

As the author rightly puts it, supply chains are not inanimate mechanical structures. Products and services only move from raw materials and production sources to consuming markets because of human intervention. This can come from either outside the enterprise (customers) or inside (company personnel).

The author from his enormous consulting experience around the globe, over two decades, points out the two behavioral dimensions to supply chains:

A. Customers always exhibit a small but finite number of dominant buying behaviors for any given product or service category, usually no more than three, but four at the most.

B. The preferred dominant buying behaviors of customers can change temporarily under the pressure of changing conditions, such as lifestyle circumstances or the product life cycle. Behaviors usually return to the preferred position when conditioning return to normalcy.

Culture and Dynamic Alignment

The author also analyzes the country cultures with the supply chain models available. He uses the Hofstede's model on country cultures and analyzes how the differences in country cultures modify the way individuals and organizations behave in certain situations. The country cultures exhibiting different combinations of the above dimensions will have a pervasive influence on the way business is done in general and on how supply chains operate in particular, across all source and consumption markets. Given that many of the world's major companies are now global in reach, this is a factor that requires more understanding and sensitivity as the search for ever higher performance continues.

The author also discusses the leadership styles and dynamic alignment in the supply chain process. According to the author, effective leaders will be able to shape the subcultures and implement the strategy needed in a complex supply chain environment.

The author again uses the P-A-D-I model to broadly classify the leaders based on their style of functioning:

1. Traditionalist – A
2. Coach – I
3. Company Baron – P
4. Visionary – D

Essentially, leadership in and of organizations must be multi-dimensional and contain "biases" that truly reflect those in customer buying behaviors. As the author puts it, quite simply, great business leaders intuitively understand their marketplace and the internal cultural environment of their organizations, and have an uncanny knack of getting them to align.

The author deals with the four types of supply chains he has identified and brings out their characteristics in detail.

A. Continuous Replenishment Supply Chains

- One should know one's truly collaborative customers and suppliers.
- Lots of efforts required on building relationships.
- In this model relationships matter most.

B. Lean Supply Chains

- Focus on efficiency and lowest cost-to-serve.
- Lean concepts from manufacturing can be applied, but not so easily because of unpredictable supply chain operating environments.
- The author has given the example of Dabbawaallahs of Mumbai and Domino's Pizza, Australia.

C. Agile Supply Chains

- Focus on forecasting the capacity at different points along supply chain.
- Almost always one need to add "redundant capacity" in the form of inventory/labor/factory space.
- Responsive subculture is a must to participate successfully in a fast unpredictable market.

D. **Fully Flexible Supply Chains**

- Key to success is speed, innovation and passion.
- Strong decisive thinking skills are a must.
- Ability to give "most appropriate" responses is a major requirement.

The author also touches upon the new business models for new supply chains. Business should go well beyond simple "operational excellence". The author insists on looking at supply chain integration and collaboration. It is going to be supply chain versus supply chain in the near future according the author. He also envisages virtual supply chains with networking of businesses and adaptive new business models.

Key characteristics of new business models:

- Hybrid organization formed from a number of different entities
- Typically established as a joint venture separate legal entity owned and operated by at least two primary client(s) and their partner(s)
- Alignment of goals of partners and clients through profit sharing
- Responsible for management and operation of entire supply chain
- Continual flow of information between partners and 4PL (Fourth party logistics) organizations.

Author's prescription of nine principles for next generation supply chain business models:

i. Ensure that the new service company is co-owned and co-managed

ii. Facilitate rapid realization of benefits

iii. De-risk the implementation of new systems technology and other operational processes

iv. Take advantage of any state-of-the-art assets that are readily available from other specialist players

v. Reduce upfront implementation costs through financial engineering practices

vi. Infuse a subculture of innovation and continuous improvement

vii. Embed predetermined key performance indicators and corresponding incentives

viii. Recognize all the risks involved in the new model and confront them head-on

ix. Out-cycle your competitor's supply chains, in speed of decision-making and action as well.

The result of above according to the author is a completely new type of execution model that will deliver scale at speed, and paradoxically, at lower risk than traditional change initiatives. Why? It is the people factor that will ultimately decide the success or failure of a major transformation, and everything else fades into insignificance.

The author has identified several global critical strategic issues that will be faced by supply chains of the future. These include:

- Sustainability,
- Impact of oil prices on cost to serve,
- Future practice and forms of outsourcing,
- Adoption of supply chain "principles" by service organizations,
- Vulnerability of supply chains,
- Rise of genuine collaboration in supply chains,
- Challenges in tapping talent,
- Multiple organization formats,
- Spread of supply chain network,
- Adoption of the whole-of-enterprise mindset in managing supply chain operations,
- Collaborating with the enemy,

- Innovation, product design and product life cycles, and
- Managing inherent complexity in supply chains.

Conclusion

The book predicts coming of genuine collaboration in supply chains including among the competitors. This could be the order of the day in the years to come since collaborating with the enemy could be the only way to achieve the scale to compete on a level footing with major international players that have more natural scale at their disposal.

Overall, the book makes a very interesting reading and will be very informative and thought-provoking for all professionals who are interested in having an insight into the things to come in future, in supply chain management concepts and models.

(Dr. John Gattorna is currently Co-Director of the Center for Supply Chain Research and Professional Fellow in Supply Chain Management at the University of Wollongong, (UoW) Australia, incorporating the UoW Graduate School of Business, Sydney Business School and Dubai campuses. He is also a visiting Professor of Supply Chain Management at Cranfield School of Management, UK. He also teaches in the University of Thailand. He conducts programs in Supply chain management in France and throughout Asia Pacific. Dr. John is widely sought-after as a consultant to multinational companies and as a speaker on the international conference circuit and in-company workshops and briefings for senior executives across the globe, on supply chain management.

J Venkataraman is a Faculty Member at the Icfai Business School, Bangalore. He can be reached at jvenkataraman@ibsindia.org).

Managing Customer Relations: An Indispensable Link in the SCM Process

– N M Shanthi

Retaining valuable customers for long-run sustainability has been one of the major thrust areas for managers today. Hypercompetition has resulted in a plethora of products and services, which in turn has lead to crowning the customer as the king. His/her pre-purchase decision making and post-purchase evaluation ability have had a direct impact on the survival status of companies. Undoubtedly, this ability is nurtured by the abundance of information. What with the seething price-wars and near-saturation scenario, efficient cost-management through a perfectly channelled Supply Chain Management (SCM) process and customization of services by adopting the best Customer Relationship Management (CRM) practice are imperative for the long-run sustainability of a company. When companies operate on similar costs and prices, only those who link the other operational areas with the supply chain process in a highly efficient manner to cut costs, enjoy a competitive advantage over others. This competitive differentiation effected by cost-driven strategies is the need of the hour for realizing long-run profitability, and for enjoying the leadership position on a constant basis.

A well-defined set of SCM solutions have been in practice for over two decades now, and companies have understood that cost-management efficiency would lead to higher returns. Managing costs in SCM means managing the inventory based on real-time demand. While demand forecasts were conventionally made using pre-determined statistical processes, it had become rather a regular on-line duty for operations managers to fine-tune the demand-based inventory system. With companies claiming to be experiencing improved efficiency in operations through systematic implementation of SCM processes, the competitive scenario is demanding a re-look at the processes to refine them to suit the new-scene requirements. The changing market scenario requires remodeling of the conventional theories and processes.

When demand becomes highly vulnerable to unpredictable forces, forecasting becomes a tough task. Wrong forecasts mislead the SCM efforts, resulting in increasing costs and decreasing profits. Intense competition and resultant price-wars are driving companies towards saturation; hence competitive differentiation is looked-upon as a saviour to protect a company's earning interests. In hypercompetitive environments, where markets are witnessing price-wars, competitive differentiation can be achieved only through efficient cost management practices, since companies operating on lesser costs earn higher profits. Cost leadership is the buoyancy that determines the float of market leadership.

Strategists see customer retention as cost saving, especially when the processes are focused on retaining the most valued customers. As a result, companies calculate the Customer Lifetime Value (CLV) to segment the most valued customers and cater to their demands. The 80:20 definition in CRM says it all. The most valued customers are those who contribute to a major portion of revenues for a company. It could be 20% of the customers contributing to 80% of revenues as is given in the definition, or any proportion with the basic concept that less number of customers contribute to higher revenues. Looking at the rising costs of customer acquisition that companies today are experiencing, it is important to understand customer retention imperatives on the Supply Chain Process, for competitive positioning and profitability.

Customer Insight

SCM has been synonymously used with Demand Based Management (DBM) by practitioners, since it is felt that demand generates supply. Today's market system goes against the traditional Say's law of market that stated "Supply creates its own demand". The reality is, supply doesn't create its own demand. It rather creates stagnation and deflation. Demand is driven by consumer needs. To extend it to present day trends, it is driven by expectations. In the competitive environment, where there is minimal price differentiation, consumers buy products not just to satisfy their needs, but also their expectations. While needs could be as basic as desires or wants, expectations

Contd...

Contd...

are outlined based on a definite set of perceptions. The one who meets these wins. When much attention is paid at creating demand, which is an expensive business, sustaining the created demand is that which needs to be worked out for survival.

CRM strategies focus on customer retention, with a well-laid process that begins from identifying the needs of the customers, segmenting the customers based on their needs, and satisfying the needs with customized product and service deliveries. An important vertical of the strategic process that determines the supply chain flow is customer feedback. The plan of action that a company is required to make in the production and operational area to satisfy its customers is derived from these feedbacks. These feedbacks give an insight into customer expectations, and enable the strategists to forecast demand and design supply strategies accordingly.

Linking CRM and SCM

It looks very simple when we say demand generates supply, and that CRM is linked with SCM when the understood demand is fulfilled. But there are several interlinked processes between CRM and SCM, which make CRM an indispensable link in the SCM process. At the very basic level, it aims at keeping the inventory low, because a well-determined demand forecast means a definite output obtained from a defined combination of inputs. But today, there is a more sophisticated level, which aims at incorporating the various marketing and service staff into the SCM process through electronic links. The transaction data is shared between the various departments in the organization through an effective ERP implementation. The canalization of data in the SCM process is done in the following manner described.

Flow of Data in the SCM Process

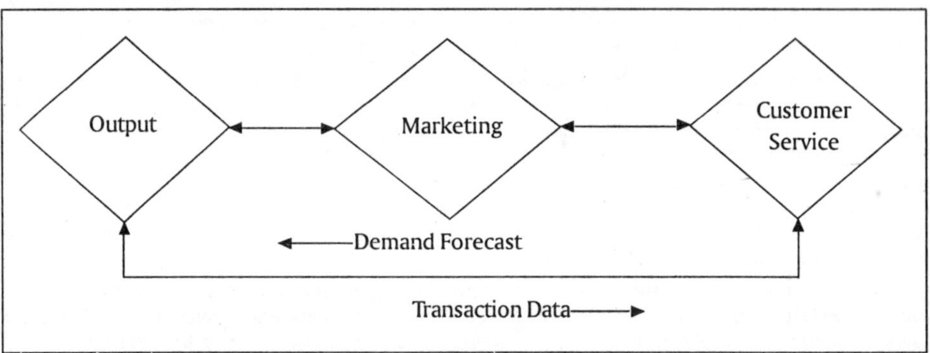

The output is determined by demand, and demand is determined by forecasts. The customer service department plays an important role as a provider of insight into customer expectations to the strategists, from the customer feedback generation system, which is updated on a regular basis. Once the output is determined, the inventory decision making takes place, and the production process begins. The demand fulfillment activity starts effectively from the marketing link, which gets information on the output, based on which strategies are framed to target the market for which the supply is generated. The flow of promotional strategies that follow, makes the job focused, and the department sees to it that it properly reaches the target segment. The next and the most important link is customer service, which is gaining importance today owing to an inbound need to retain customers. The department is the closest to the customer, and needs to know what happens in the other links. For example, when a query is placed as regards availability of a product, the support staff should be aware of the supply status and give information

Contd...

Contd...

accordingly. Any misleading information is bound to affect business. So, the transaction data needs to go to the customer support cell for profitability to increase. This department also gives alarm, when there is supply-demand mismatch, arising out of dumping and negative demands, from the customer-defection figures. This helps to keep supply under control, until corrective measures are taken.

The customer service departments of today are considered the nervous systems of business. The technology era and electronic revolution, coupled with tailor-made training programs to improve real-time support skills, are improving the efficiency of the support staff. The distance barriers are being broken, and customers are being easily reached through cables and satellites. Besides regular services like billing and complaint redressal, the customer support staff also renders value-added services based on the customer's specific requirements. The expectations of customers are channelled to modify outputs, and output information reaches the support staff to enable understanding of the expectation-satisfaction gaps. CRM, thus, becomes an indispensable link in the SCM process, linking profitability and costs to customer retention.

(N M Shanthi is Former Faculty Member at Icfai Research Center, Chennai. She can be reached at shan_venky@yahoo.com)

Source: Marketing Mastermind, January 2005.

6

Innovating the Service Chain
(Beyond Repair and Replace)

Steven Titch

Warranty management functions can be spread out among different systems from different vendors, beginning with enterprise resource planning (ERP) systems and customer relationship management (CRM) systems and extending to more specialized warranty systems. The article emphasizes that manufacturers should focus their efforts on innovating the warranty management process into three phases such as overhaul of transactional processing, supply chain integration and reengineering model.

John Kerr wants to eliminate the service call.

The general manager for global quality systems at $14 billion appliance manufacturing giant Whirlpool Corp. (Benton Harbor, MI), Kerr is in charge of the company's sweeping effort to organize the data contained in thousands of warranty reports, field service repair notes, and dealer and retailer feedback forms in a database that can be mined and analyzed.

The knowledge gained from such systems, Whirlpool believes, can then be used to pinpoint component problems, identify patterns in quality problems, and set off early warnings of possible product failure. And that can allow Whirlpool and Kerr to reduce—if not eliminate—service calls.

Automated warranty management and analytic systems like the one Kerr is working on can condense the time between identifying a problem and fixing it in the supply chain. In the past, that process could take six months or longer, Kerr says. The introduction of better tools that can gather and analyze post-sales data means cutting this lag time significantly, to the point where a design change or component replacement can be made before thousands of potentially defective appliances are shipped.

And avoiding that kind of mistake can save big money. Just ask Dell Computer, which, analysts say, is spending upwards of $400 million to replace 4.1 million defective laptop batteries.

Warranty management has become the latest area of innovation for appliance manufacturers such as Whirlpool, which uses a warranty management solution from SAS Institute Inc. (Cary, NC), as well as for manufacturers of automobiles, heavy trucks, and consumer electronics.

In the automotive industry, these initiatives were sparked by the Transportation Recall, Enhancement, Accountability, and Documentation (TREAD) Act, a legislative response in 2000 to a string of fatal tire failures on Ford Motor Co. sports utility vehicles. The law requires auto manufacturers to record and track all data received from warranty reports, dealers, and repair shops, with the aim of identifying and fixing potential manufacturing defects before they become widespread in the market.

TREAD was followed in 2004 by the Sarbanes-Oxley Act, which, in addition to forcing companies to document financial controls, required manufacturers to break out the cost of things like warranties and post-sales service.

Combined, the two laws have opened manufacturers' eyes to the true cost of warranty management. For example, GM and Ford together spent $8.7 billion on 2005 warranty claims, up from $8.3 billion in 2004 and $8 billion in 2003, according to a study by *Warranty Week*, an industry newsletter, which looked at data reported to the Securities and Exchange Commission. The top 50 US-based warranty providers together reported $22.2 billion in warranty claims last year, up from $20.4 billion in 2004 and $19.2 billion in 2003, according to the same report.

Such numbers have forced managers to revisit their service strategies and explore opportunities for change. Warranty management "is one of the biggest areas of controllable expense," says Thomas Wright, industry principal for automotive at SAP Americas (Newton Square, PA).

"Coin-Operated Process"

Warranties are akin to insurance policies. Offered free or for an additional charge, the policy covers the cost of repair should something go wrong with a product. Since repair is either free or discounted to the consumer, when something needs to be fixed, the manufacturer reimburses the repair shop.

As with any other claim, the repair shop must document the problem on a form. Generally this is done through coding for example, 0435 might mean "defective belt." In addition, there might be a space on the form for comments, where the repair technician might write, "Belt was worn due to friction."

But, historically, there have been problems with the data generated by such processes. For one thing, warranty and repair data tends to be unreliable, says John Thomann, a private consultant in the areas of field service, service parts logistics, and warranty management.

"Data tends to be scurrilous," he says. "The repair man wants to be reimbursed, so he will code a report in such a way that he will [be]. It's a coin-operated process." Legacy warranty management systems didn't always provide incentive for accurate or complete reporting by service providers, who often feared payment would be held up or denied. The process also lent itself to error. Oftentimes, manufacturers would demand that repair shops deal with hundred of codes. "No one can possibly know all of them, or have the time to look through the whole list to find the precise code," Thomann says.

Finally, information hasn't been regularly shared between manufacturers and their suppliers, mostly out of fear of finger pointing, which trumped improving quality control, Thomann says.

Now, armed with a better understanding of the cost of quality, manufacturers are realizing they can use IT systems to mount a double-sided attack on the cost of warranty management and post-sales service. First, they can build more accurate databases that lower the cost of warranty fulfillment by verifying that reported problems are eligible for coverage and identifying and eliminating fraud. Second, they can use analytics to track post-sales service complaints and nip product problems in the bud.

The warranty management systems at the heart of these efforts manage, transmit, and store documents and create the historical record. Warranty management functions can be spread out among different systems from different vendors, beginning with enterprise resource planning (ERP) systems and customer relationship management (CRM) systems and extending to more specialized warranty systems.

SAP, Oracle Corp. (along with recently acquired Siebel Systems), and Infor Global are among the providers of ERP and CRM platforms that support warranty management, claims processing, information gathering, and storage.

Manufacturers like Whirlpool are attempting to take all the data collected by warranty management systems and create analytics that can reduce the time needed to take corrective action. Such analytics mine the record created by warranty management systems, looking for patterns and trends that can be used to identify defects, forecast life cycles, reduce risk, and improve design.

SAS Institute Inc., Cognos Inc. (Ottawa, ON), Business Objects SA (San Jose, CA, and Paris), and Oracle are some of the vendors that provide business intelligence software that uses data from CRM and warranty management systems to identify and analyze problems, support decision-making, and help spot trends.

Attensity Corp. (Palo Alto, CA)—another Whirlpool vendor—as well as SPSS Inc. (Chicago) and ServiceBench Inc. (Fairfax, VA) provide analytic tools that specifically look at unstructured data contained in notes, reports, memos, and other warranty-related documents.

Three Phases

So where should manufacturers focus their efforts to innovate the warranty management process? SAP's Wright divides the reengineering process into three phases. The first is an overhaul of transactional processing – the mechanism by which manufacturers deal with their service networks. This means streamlining codes and standardizing the reporting process so that manufacturers get more accurate information and dealers and service shops get paid more promptly.

The second phase is supply chain integration. This pushes some of the cost of quality back to suppliers. This, Wright says, is where trend analysis enters the picture. "It's here where I ask: What component is failing? Is it single source or not? Is it a product flaw or spec flaw?"

The automotive industry is in the middle of a big transition to this type of analysis. Fifty percent of the systems in an automobile are electronic, Wright says. With them come all sorts of operational parameters and failure profiles. An otherwise sound component, for example, may fail under a certain combination of conditions—internal engine temperature, outdoor humidity, state of battery charge, amount of vehicle vibration.

Warranty analytics can correlate variables from widespread sources and extract patterns that would have gone unseen in the past. The most potent example was the Ford-Firestone tire failures in the late 1990s. In those cases it was a combination of air temperature and vehicle speed that was causing tire blowouts. Over the course of several years, incidents were reported from Arizona to Saudi Arabia, but the underlying cause remained elusive. Today's analytics, say executives such as Michelle de Haaff, vice president of products and marketing at Attensity, might have pegged the problem sooner.

Attensity is part of the third phase of Wright's reengineering model—analysis of unstructured data, including the written comments, emails, and repair notes that account for 85% of all post-sales reports. An SAS partner in the Whirlpool implementation, Attensity offers a text analytics tool that captures unstructured data and uses it to build matrices that can be easily searched and mined for predictive information. "Manufacturers get early insight. A response in 200 days is cut to 100 days," according to de Haaff.

All Your Parts

Predictive analysis may be the high-tech side of warranty and post-sales management, but that still leaves many nuts-and-bolts issues, literally. Parts supply is another aspect of post-sales support, and warranty management systems can be used to create the supply models for warehouses, depots, and distribution centers, says Bob Salvucci, president and CEO of MCA Solutions Inc. (Philadelphia), a supplier of service planning and optimization software.

A key question for any company, Salvucci says, is where it should place inventory in the supply chain in order to satisfy service contracts. Boeing, an MCA customer, has 250,000 active parts in more than 1,000 locations, Salvucci says, all designed to be delivered within 24 hours.

When parts inventory management systems like those from MCA are tied to post-sales data, manufacturers are in a much better position to set up distribution channels that allow parts and services to reach customers more quickly.

And post-sales service support can be just as important to today's virtual manufacturers such as MCA customer Cisco Systems as it is to Boeing and Whirlpool.

With manufacturing increasingly outsourced, post-sales service becomes a chief element of brand equity, Salvucci says. For instance, when it comes to its routers, all Cisco owns is the intellectual property. A serious defect in any area of the supply chain could cause serious problems that would ultimately reflect on the brand. The key, then, is to innovate and stay as informed as possible and be able to act quickly on information. "Cisco doesn't do manufacturing, it doesn't do field service, it doesn't do repair," Salvucci says. "It's a virtual company. The brand is invested in the customer relationship. And that relationship is managed with warranty and service contracts."

A New Paradigm in After-Sales Maintenance Services

– D Thiyagarajan

After-sales service is a compulsory strategy to increase the speed and effectiveness of after-sales maintenance and repair services. Despite the fact that services are not the core business of manufacturing, distribution and engineering companies, services are increasing in importance. As the products in the International market become more and more related, and margins decrease, supply chain management and services are becoming key differentiators between companies. High-quality service has become a necessity to retain customers for future sales. Previously, service departments in such companies have been run as cost centers only, often isolated from other departments. Today, most of them are professional profit centers, integrated with all parts of the company. After-sales service organizations have either field service or depot service as their core business[1].

Some of the companies use different types of service supply chain network designs to support the differential levels of service offered across the Enterprise and non-Enterprise segments. Recent transportation method infrastructure permits attainment of non-Enterprise service Standards without positioning parts inventory at locations that are very close to customers. This leads to fewer echelons and more centralization of inventory. Enterprise service standards are more demanding, however, and thus require multi-level networks and forward positioning of parts inventory[2].

Managing After-Sales Service

Managing the after sales supply chain spans operational areas, and requires redefining customer service and inventory management processes. There are three steps that enable an after sales supply chain transformation:

- Move returns validation and "avoidance" upstream.
- Automate reverse-logistics processes with technology.
- Measure and report on performance to drive improvements[3].

Principles to Perform the After-Sales Service

Quality

The company should always do best for the highest level of excellence in dealing with their consumers and in delivering a superior degree of service.

Simple Access

The company must give simple, clear directions and procedures to distributors, service centers and consumers for obtaining better-quality and efficient service.

Fairness and Earnestness

After-Sales Services must provide support that is fair and practical with regard to price, repair lead-times and professional answers to all service problems.

In order to achieve these goals the company should start by introducing and explaining some terms and definitions to ensure a clear understanding of these service policies

(D Thiyagarajan is a Research Associate at Icfai Business School Research Center, Chennai. He can be reached at thiyagu_d@rediffmail.com).

[1] *http://www.ifsworld.com/solutions2/service_management/after_sales_service/default.asp*

[2] After-Sales Service Supply Chains: A Benchmark Update of The North...

[3] *http://www.mbtmag.com/current_issues/2007/feb/views8.asp*

7

Issues in Modeling Service Chains

Sandeep Kayastha

A concept similar to supply chains for services is yet to appear in the academic literature. The absence of transformation of physical materials and goods in service chains make the service chains different from supply chains on several dimensions. This paper argues that models of supply chains cannot accommodate unique features of service chains. We advise researchers to take a fresh approach to model service chains.

Introduction

Manufacturers are revisiting their logistics strategies in diverse industries like steel and agricultural products, automobiles and furniture, petrochemicals and computers. No longer do their plans endeavor to improve only internal logistics operations. The renewed interest in logistics focuses on integrating own operations with firms outside the organizational boundaries.

Inter-organizational integration happens at two levels. At the first level, the firm integrates its operations with its transacting firms. This level of integration aims to eliminate operations repeated by transacting firms, like inspection of components by suppliers before shipping and again by buyers after receiving

Source: The Icfai Journal of Service Marketing, September 2005.

them; joint planning of production and shipments; and joint investment decisions, like co-location of facilities. The Efficient Customer Response (ECR), Vendor Managed Inventory (VMI) and such other innovations are results of collaborations between manufacturers and their buyers and suppliers.

The second level of inter-organizational integration involves integration of the firm's operations with those firms with which it does not transact business. Manufacturers achieve this level of integration by managing the flow of materials much before it reaches their suppliers and much after their buyers sell the goods to own buyers. Such manufacturers monitor production plans and inventories of mines and steel mills even though they buy components from suppliers. On the distribution side they track sales, inventories, movement of goods and promotion plans of retailers, although they sell goods only to wholesalers. Managing the flow of materials and physical goods beyond one's buyers and suppliers is called Supply Chain Management (Mentzer *et al, 2001*). SCM is helping firms to drastically cut down costs and improve response times and availability of goods.

Just as production and delivery of physical materials and goods is done by multiple firms, production and delivery of courier, broadcasting, telephone and a host of other services too are done by multiple entities. Payments by customers to retailers through credit cards, for example, involve merchant banks, credit card issuing banks and network companies like VISA and MasterCard. Production and delivery of electricity to customers similarly involves multiple entities like power generating companies, transmission companies and distribution companies. Just as the processes in which multiple entities produce and deliver physical goods are called supply chains, the processes in which multiple entities produce and deliver services can be called services chains. A supply/service chain entity performs only a few activities of the process. If it fails to perform its activity, performance of the chain gets adversely affected.

The contribution of service sectors to the GDP of a majority of developed and developing countries far exceeds the combined contribution of their manufacturing, agricultural and mining sectors. Yet, a concept of service chain management on the lines of supply chain management has so far not appeared in the academic literature (Kayastha, *2004*). Concerns of banking, insurance, education, hospitality, healthcare, consulting, transportation and other service firms thus remain to be tackled.

The structure and dynamics of service chains that do not process or handle physical goods is different from that of supply chains. The issues involved in managing service chains and supply chains also differ. Some of the issues that researchers will have to consider for modeling service chains are discussed below.

Material Balance Equations

Supply chains deal with physical materials and goods. The quantity of material that enters a supply chain equals to the material that leaves it. However, inflow and outflow quantities in service chains that do not transform or handle physical materials and goods may not match. For example, in TV broadcasting service chains involving TV companies, cable operators and customers, the *quantity* of signals distributed by cable operators to customers far exceeds the *quantity* of signals they receive from TV companies. In such service chains, material balance equations—which appear in every supply chain model—will be absent.

Performance Drivers and Metrics

A vast majority of supply chain models are built to improve operational performances of the supply chains. According to Chopra and Meindl (2003) there are four drivers of supply chain performances. These drivers are the location and capacity of facilities, inventory, transportation and information. Some of the commonly used metrics to measure operational performances of supply chains are fill rates, stock-out rates, service levels, inventory turns, delivery and response time.

The four drivers and the metrics used to measure performances of supply chains are not relevant for all kinds of service chains. Inventory, for example, is not relevant for TV broadcasting and consulting service chains, since they do not deal with physical materials and goods. Similarly, the location of facilities of credit card transactions processing entities does not affect the speed of transferring funds. No matter where their facilities are located, credit card transactions are processed in the real time.

Service chains have their own drivers of performances. To build models of service chains researchers will have to identify relevant drivers and metrics of service chain performances. According to Stemmler (2003), drivers of finance-related logistics costs are the time, risk and processes. Transaction risk—a risk that transacting entities face from each other—appears to be an important driver of performances of service chains.

Transactions between service chains entities are riskier than those between supply chains entities. Downstream entities of supply chains get ownership and possession of physical goods after making payments to upstream entities. Service chain entities may not get possession of any tangible and valuable goods when they provide the service. In the credit card service chain, credit card issuing companies guarantee payments to merchant banks, although payments to them by credit card holders are not guaranteed. Loans extended by them to credit card holders are unsecured loans. In the telephone service chain too, payments to the telephone company by its post-paid subscribers are not guaranteed, although it guarantees payments to other telephone companies for carrying calls originating from its network.

The Bullwhip Effect

Physical materials and goods in supply chains flow in a linear fashion—goods move from the first entity to second to third and so on, but supply chain entities are interdependent in complex ways. The impact of actions of an entity on other entities of its chain hence is not obvious. For example, a small rise in the sales experienced by the retailer can have an amplified effect on the inventories and production of wholesalers, manufacturers, suppliers and other upstream entities of its supply chain. This phenomenon, which is called the Bullwhip effect (Lee *et al, 1997),* is the backbone of supply chain management. The Bullwhip effect results from independent actions of supply chain entities to maximize own profits, together with delays in producing and moving goods and delays in sharing information among themselves.

Do service chains also exhibit the Bullwhip effect? If so, does the Bullwhip effect in service chains differs from that in supply chains? Anderson and Morrice (2000) found the Bullwhip effect in a Mortgage Service Game played by their students. Akkermans and Bert (2003) also observed the amplification effect in their study of selling, provisioning, installing and billings processes of a telecom company. Delays were present in both cases.

There are virtually no delivery delays in service chains such as broadcasting, electricity and telephone service chains. Entities of their chains at same time handle same signals. Service chains in which delays are absent, the Bullwhip effect in them would result only from independent actions of their entities to maximize own profits. The nature of "Bullwhip" effect in such service chains, therefore, can be different from that observed in supply chains. For example, promotions by a telephone company to get more traffic during the New Year's Day and festivals can choke its telephone network. Its subscribers send millions of greetings SMS messages to their friends in a very short period. Traffic during such periods far exceeds the capacities of telephone networks. Consequently, many SMS messages are lost or their delivery is delayed. Promotional schemes during festive seasons not only clog the network of the company running the promotion, but they also choke the networks of carriers and other telephone companies on whose networks its SMS messages terminate. Subscribers who do not send SMS messages also suffer during such periods: They can neither receive nor make the calls.

Collapse of power grids can also be attributed to the Bullwhip effect. Power grids fail because power generating and transmission companies withdraw additional power when voltage in the grid begins to fall. While each one tries to maintain voltages of own lines, the collective impact of their actions breaks down the entire system in no time. Those who do not withdraw additional power also get affected by the collapse of the grid.

Service chains in which delays are absent the amplification effect in them is difficult to observe. The system reacts so fast that the whole system collapses instantaneously. Models to replicate the Bullwhip effect in service chains thus will have to explicitly consider absence of delays in them.

Pricing and Revenue Sharing

Supply chain entities sell goods to their downstream entities: suppliers sell goods to manufacturers, manufacturers to wholesalers, wholesalers to retailers and retailers to customers. Revenues of supply chain entities are a function of quantities of goods they sell to their buyers.

Agreements between transacting entities of many service chains are not sale agreements. They prefer revenue sharing agreements. In the credit card service chain, revenues of merchant banks and network companies depend on the revenues of credit card issuing banks. The latter share their revenues with the former. Agreements between TV broadcasting companies and cable operators are also revenue sharing agreements. Cable operators share their revenues with TV broadcasting companies. In the telephone service chain too, telephone companies carry each others' calls on revenue sharing basis.

Revenue models for supply chain entities aim to determine optimal combinations of price and quantity of sale to their buyers. Models for entities of service chains in which revenue sharing is prevalent will have to maximize revenues of their transacting entities. Only then entities of service chains can maximize own revenues.

Customers on Either Side

Supply chains entities buy goods from upstream entities, transform them and sell the transformed goods to downstream entities. Their upstream entities are suppliers and downstream entities are customers.

In many service chains, both the upstream and downstream entities of an entity of the chain are its customers. In the telephone service chain consisting of a caller party, a telephone company and a called party, until the calling party alone pays became vogue, both the caller and the called party were customers of the telephone company. The calling paid for making the call and the called party paid for receiving the call. Similarly, both buyers and sellers of foreign currencies are customers of banks. Banks charge commission from the buyers as well as sellers of foreign currencies.

Supply chain models for improving availability and fill rates are built to service downstream entities. Models of service chains in which entities on either side of an entity are its customers will have to consider servicing both the upstream and downstream entities.

Conclusion

Supply chains of steel, chemicals, automobiles, consumer goods, agricultural goods and other firms that transform and handle physical materials and goods continue to become shorter, faster, efficient and agile. Unfortunately, services have remained unaffected by the supply chain revolution.

Like physical goods, several services are also produced and delivered by multiple firms. But, a concept similar to supply chain management is yet to be developed for services. This paper shows that the dynamics and structures of service chains and supply chains differ on several dimensions. Models of supply chains cannot easily accommodate numerous unique characteristics of service chains and the concerns in managing service chains. Researchers, therefore, need to take a new and fresh approach to modeling in this rich and unexplored area.

(Sandeep Kayastha is Associate Dean, at Icfai Business School, Hyderabad. He can be reached at kayastha@ibsindia.org).

References

1. Akkermans, Henk and Vos, Bert (2003), "Amplification in Service Supply Chains: An Exploratory Case Study from the Telecom Industry", *The Journal of Production and Operations Management,* Vol. 12, No. 2.
2. Anderson, Edward G and Morrice, Douglas J (2000), "A Simulation Game for Service-Oriented Supply Chain Management: Does Information Sharing Help Managers with Service Capacity Decisions?" *The Journal of Production and Operations Management,* Vol. 9, No. 1.
3. Chopra, Sunil and Meindl, Peter (2003), *Supply Chain Management.* Delhi: Pearson Education.
4. Kayastha, Sandeep (2004), "Where are Service Chains?" *Services Marketing.* Vol. 1, No. 2.
5. Lee, Hua L, Padmanabhan, V and Whang, Seungjin (Spring 1997), "The Bullwhip Effect in Supply Chains", *Sloan Management Review.*
6. Mentzer, John T, DeWitt, William, Keebler, James S, Min, Soonhong, Nix, Nancy W, Smith, Carlo D and Zacharia, Zach G (2001), "Defining Supply Chain Management", *Journal of Business Logistics.* Vol. 22, No. 2.
7. Stemmler, Lars (2003), "Managing the Financial Supply Chain: Scope, Services and Problems", In Waters, Donald (Ed), *Global Logistics and Distribution Planning.* London: Kogan Page.

8

SOX (Sarbanes Oxley Act) and Its Impact on Retail Supply Chains

Kannan Natarajan and Satish Panchapakesan

The Sarbanes Oxley (SOX) Act calls for accuracy and speed in reporting of financial figures. It mandates control over the internal systems which are the origins of these figures. The act requires reporting and analysis of events which could have financial impact on the organization. Sarbanes Oxley Act demands considerable effort from retail supply chains which are characterized by multi-point inventories, high supplier base and fragmented information systems. SOX is just one of the several events which has the potential to severely affect the way the current supply chain processes work. This white paper analyzes the supply chain risk areas where the act can have significant impact. Supply chain risk points are identified and a framework is suggested to eliminate these risks. The paper proposes a supply chain which could adapt itself to regulatory demands like SOX and disruptions which occur with increasing frequency.

Introduction

The Sarbanes Oxley Act
The Sarbanes Oxley Act, also known as SOX or SOA, was part of a wave of new laws and regulations introduced in the United States to tighten corporate accountability in reaction to the corporate accounting debacles which destroyed investor confidence in financial statements and led companies to bankruptcy. It is designed to protect investors by improving the accuracy and reliability of corporate disclosures by requiring a broader standard than GAAP. SOX rules apply to all publicly registered companies under the jurisdiction of the Securities and Exchange Commission (SEC). The Securities and Exchange Commission (SEC) expects that a company's systems grow and evolve with its business and become capable of producing reports that are timely, accurate and reliable. Controls and procedures must be in place to gather, analyze and disclose all required information and companies must develop strong practices that demonstrate compliance.

Sections 302, 401, 404 and 409 of the Sarbanes Oxley Act provide specific direction for companies working to become compliant.

- *302 – Corporate Responsibility for Financial Audits:* Responsibility for accurate and effective internal controls is placed squarely on the CEO and CFO.
- *401 – Disclosures in Periodic Reports:* Financial reports to disclose all material off-balance sheet transactions and other relationships with unconsolidated entities that may have a material current or future effect on the financial condition of the company.
- *404 – Management Assessment of Internal Business Controls:* Annual reports must include an 'internal control report' certifying management's responsibility for creating and maintaining internal controls and processes for financial reporting, and should contain an assessment of the effectiveness of these internal controls and processes.
- *409 – Real Time Issuer Disclosures:* Companies should disclose information on material changes in their financial condition or operations on a rapid or current basis.

The deadlines for filing quarterly and annual reports have also been accelerated for domestic US companies fulfilling criteria of: a public float of at least $75 million, reporting to the SEC for at least 12 months, having previously filed an annual report and not eligible for small business special form. For example, annual reports on Form 10-K will have to be filed within 60 calendar days after the end of the fiscal year in 2004 and thereafter (from 90 days in 2002, 75 days in 2003).

Organizations need to be vigilant to respond to the requirements of SOX as the SEC will continue to issue guidelines on what will be required and when the rules will take effect. Companies must establish procedures for meeting their reporting obligations and find ways to seek transparency into financial figures and processes which produce these figures.

SOX and the Retail Supply Chain

Consider a major store promotion event which is forecasted to generate substantial revenue, and the key supplier is unable to deliver due to plant breakdown. The result is a sharp dip in the forecasted sale, fall in stocks price and grilling by investors over the inability to live up to earning predictions.

A study by the University of Western Ontario and the Georgia Institute of Technology concluded that supply-chain glitches could result in a 9 percent drop in stock price, and stock devaluation of up to 20 percent, within six months of the problem being publicly revealed.

Section 401 has significant implications for supply chain managers. All processes across the supply chain having direct or indirect bearing on financial figures, although not reported earlier, will now need to be tracked, evaluated and included in disclosure reports. This section requires companies to disclose off-balance sheet liabilities resulting from transactions and agreements that have material impact on future financial performance. Demand and supply misalignments directly impact agreements, thus making off-balance sheet transactions one the most challenging areas to evaluate in the entire supply chain process.

With concepts such as vendor managed inventory, collaborative forecasting and replenishment, efficient consumer response (ECR), the retail industry has been in the forefront for developing innovative solutions to business problems. While a strong business case drives such initiatives, the foremost concern, however, for any supply chain manager are the accompanying risks. Several characteristics of retailing such as distributed operations and inventory, innovative sourcing

Figure 1: Chief Challenges that Supply Managers Face while Striving to Conform to SOX Regulations

Source: Aberdeen Group.

strategies, manual processes, trade allowances, promotions and settlements involving holdbacks and deductions expose the industry to high risks.

Material spend constitutes the largest expenditures for any retailer. Hence materials management especially inventory control and purchasing occupy an important part in the compliance scenario for any retailer (Figure 2).

Some of the typical problem areas in the supply chain network are detailed below.

Global Supply Chain Operations

Global Sourcing

With opening up of global markets due to trade agreements, retailers will maximize global sourcing in a bid to lower their procurement costs. With suppliers across the globe, retailers risk losing visibility and hence control over their supply chain operations. Developing countries face infrastructure problems such as delays at

Figure 2: Supply Chain Problem Areas

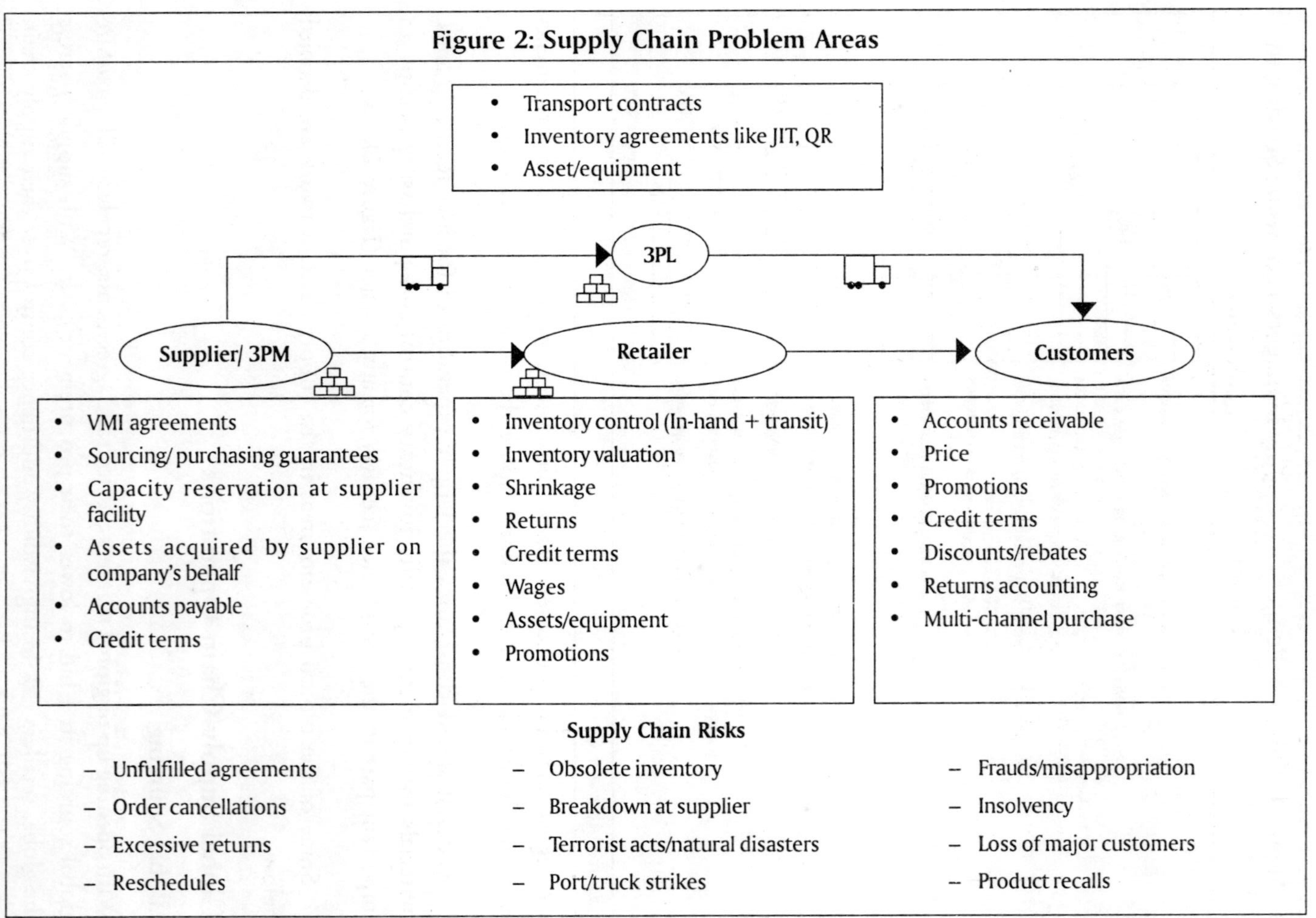

ports, poor roads & rail facilities, sub-optimal storage facilities, security issues, political turmoil etc. All these factors serve to increase the uncertainty faced at the retailer's end.

Visibility in the Supply Chain

In sectors like grocery, apparel and electronics inventory is often seen as a liability to be minimized due to short product lifecycles, seasonality and significant price erosion over time. These can create situations like huge returns or write-downs, customers turning to competitors, failure to reach projected sales or reduced margins. Large inventories represent a buffer that separates companies from actual product demand resulting in cases like Merck which took $700 million revenue hit in the fourth quarter of 2003 to reduce the amount of product inventory in its downstream supply chain and "moderate the fluctuations in sales currently caused by wholesaler investment buying."

Product Shrinkages and Obsolescence

Product shrinkages in form of obsolescence, expired dates, thefts, pilferages, damages are major causes of errors in reporting and accounting inventory. This is particularly severe for retailers who carry products with limited shelf lives or those requiring special storage conditions.

Product Returns

Liberal returns policies along with stringent environmental regulations have made product returns and its accounting a major challenge to retailers in the US and Europe. At high-risk industries regulated by strict regulatory and environmental rules such as US FDA (pharmaceutical industry in US) or WEEE (Electronics and Electrical industry), loss of visibility for these firms would mean massive write-offs of valuable items or stiff penalty from regulatory authorities. Issues like returning goods ownership and valuation for accounting purposes make the matter more susceptible to erroneous reporting.

Multiple Supply Chain Partners

Inventory Ownership

The retail sector faces the task of reporting of financial obligations created amongst supply chain trading partners. Each firm has its own financial objectives, and hence supply chain policies, that must be met to sustain their business profitability. Procurement commitments established between companies through new practices like scan-based trading, VMI, ECR and CPFR create a complex agreement liability with ownership and pricing being the most important factors.

Contracts with Global Partners

Entry of new sourcing destinations like Asia and Latin America has given rise to issues like local taxes and regulations which will have to be taken care of in the contracts. For a big retailer having hundreds of suppliers, tracing and interpreting contracts in case of a trade dispute or problem can be quite a challenge. Disputes could prove to be time-consuming and likely to affect the supply chain in terms of profitability and potential liabilities.

Supplier Management

The consolidation in the supplier base has led to dependency on limited number of large suppliers. Loss of key suppliers due to financial collapse or disputes could result in the firm facing temporary loss of sales or higher procurement costs or lower service levels, leading to heavy impact on earnings. Retailers develop smaller suppliers, providing them with support through various financial mechanisms. In addition to reporting such agreements, retailers need to constantly monitor their progress to anticipate any potential liability. Suppliers need to be constantly reviewed for financial stability, processes and ability to deliver products with promised service level and prices.

Contractual Agreements and Risk Assessment

Procurement function aims at reducing costs through volumes commitments or volume-based pricing. Capacity could be reserved at a key supplier's factory for a certain period based on forecasting for a particular season. Usually such deals are usually not a part of any reporting document. Post-SOX, along with such agreements, the risks and actual implications of the contract over its life needs to be reported. Procurement function has to do a risk assessment of such contracts. For example, the effect on procurement costs and hence earnings if the promised volumes are not reached or financial implications of penalties paid due to non-use of reserved capacity at supplier. Thus, it is important to account for all these risk elements and arrive at the net true liability in each of these arrangements.

Some of the typical off-balance sheet liabilities and commitments (the financial outcomes of which have to be reflected in the reporting) which are present in a retail supply chain are:

Events	Potential Risk	Impact
Purchasing commitments	Higher procurement costs and/or penalties	High
Minimum volume guarantees to suppliers	Monetary penalty can be incurred which will be reflected in higher procurement costs	High
Safety stock commitments	Assets can become potential liability in form of obsolete and non-moving goods	High
VMI agreements	Establishing ownership of inventory and costs at the time of reporting. Wrong order or excess order or breakdown at vendors plant can cause problems at the retailers end with potential loss of sales	High
Assets acquired by supplier on company's behalf	Liability arising to be mentioned in disclosure statements	Medium
Capacity reservations at supplier facilities	Liabilities arising due to inability to use the capacity as per agreement could result in monetary penalties	Medium
Termination/reduction of business relationship with major supplier	Increase in purchase costs and lower service levels; lost sales	High
Support to any supply chain partner through financial mechanisms	Such agreements to be reported and liability arising to be mentioned in disclosure statements	High

Outsourcing of Services

Processes such as order fulfillment for 'e-tailers', IT infrastructure management, customer analysis and loyalty programs, claims processing etc. are being increasingly outsourced. Many of these functions have a significant financial bearing for the retailer. It is critical to have a thorough confidence on the service organizations control over processes and IT capabilities. A company is as responsible for the controls of its service providers as it is for its own internal controls.

Systems

Each supply chain partner will have his own database formats, communication standards, ERP systems, proprietary programs and applications resulting in a potential minefield. The Hackett Group estimates that the average $1 billion

AICPA's Statement on Auditing Standards (SAS) No. 70 (Service Organizations) is such framework which could provide an acceptable level of assurance about the internal controls of service providers. SAS 70 is the authoritative guidance that allows service organizations to disclose their control activities and processes to their customers and their customers' auditors in a uniform reporting format. A SAS 70 examination signifies that a service organization has had its control objectives and control activities examined by an independent accounting and auditing firm. Most certifications related to Sarbanes Oxley use a 'Type II' report, which describes the controls plus provides for detailed testing of them for at least six months.

company maintains 48 financial programs, along with nearly three enterprise resource planning (ERP) systems. Data is typically located in ERP systems, special purpose systems, in word-processing documents, emails and spreadsheets. Companies having disparate and legacy accounting and reporting systems, require more interfaces and reconciliation procedures. This leads to errors, problems in locating and rectifying them and extending the time required for financial closure. A 2002 survey of 265 senior financial executives by CFO Research Services and CGE&Y found that only 2% of the respondents had their ERP system fully integrated (to the extent that accurate financial statements could be produced) with other applications.

SOX Direction to Compliance

Though SOX is primarily viewed as a compliance initiative leading to better reliability and accuracy of financial reports, there are a whole host of secondary benefits which can be realized as a result of the compliance measures. Accurate inventory control can lead to lower safety stocks, reduced damaged goods, rejections, incorrect or excessive ordering. Accurate reporting of returns helps in controlling returns, improving product quality, reducing warranty costs. Consistent and accurate reconciliation of purchase orders, invoices, receipts, and contract terms reduces overpayments and disputes; all of which help towards attaining accurate and true financial results.

Financial figures have its roots in the various supply chain processes. The essence behind SOX is that the all processes across the supply chain should be clear, consistent and traceable without any scope of manipulation. Thus, all financial figures or transactions should be drillable down to their origins. To achieve this, the first step is to clear the haze around the supply chain. Unless a process itself is not very clear to its owners, no IT tool can possibly help solve the problem. Hence supply chain processes should be honed and well-controlled before launching IT initiatives to achieve SOX compliance.

The step-by-step framework towards achieving compliance in supply chain activities is as follows:

- Map all the supply chain processes. Key persons involved in the process should be roped in along with a cross-functional team in order to assess the impact of the process on the entire supply chain. Document all the internal controls i.e. the key process drivers, information and physical flows; identify owners etc.
- Identify the critical processes/elements of the chain which have significant financial impact.
- Conduct risk assessment for these processes and identify gaps/potential problem areas. Look out for design and operational deficiencies like multiple or no owners, owner having no authority, employee's job function and corresponding authority, missing procedures, excessive paperwork, fragmented data etc.
- Modify the process to eliminate/reduce risk. Examine existing infrastructure to see if there are controls in systems that can be used on or if there are systems in place that could be used to automate tasks that are currently manual. Install control mechanisms/business logic/analytics to anticipate, manage and report risk.
- Assign ownership to each process and controls, with clear responsibilities and reporting structure.
- Link each supply chain element across processes to relevant financial reporting metrics and set a benchmark value for reference.
- Continuously review the supply chain for risks and potential area for modification.

Broad directions for compliance can start from adoption of best practices, the SCOR framework for companies looking to reengineer their operations and the 5S approach for companies looking to optimize their existing systems.

5S Approach

Business process improvement has an analogy in the philosophy of 'Kaizen' and 'lean manufacturing'. The basic ideas of these philosophies: simplification, waste elimination, standardization, root cause analysis and continuous improvement is exactly what is required for an organization seeking SOX compliance. The '5S' philosophy is a 'low cost' and 'high employee involvement' starting point or guidance framework for improving supply chain visibility. This should be done using internal resources and a cross-functional team including the process owners.

Sort (Seiri)

Focuses on eliminating unnecessary items from the workplace. Unnecessary processes, activities or entities clutter and complicate the supply chain resulting in high processing times or obsolete inventories. Such activities should be weeded out by mapping the entire supply chain step-by-step. Existing and required processes should be simplified.

Set in Order (Seiton)

Focuses on efficient and effective storage methods. 'A place for everything and everything in its place.' Data is distributed all over the supply chain in different formats and systems. This leads to delay in processing transactions, locating agreements, rectifying errors all of which lead to delays in financial closures or settlement of disputes. Supply chain exception generation or variance tracking is often hampered by the lack or rather unavailability of proper data. Once data or processes are set in order, financial figures can be easily traced down to their origins. An efficient data-storage and retrieval system facilitates quick location, retrieval and analysis of required information.

Shine (Seiso)

Focuses on daily follow-up cleaning in order to sustain improvements. Seiso will help create ownership in the equipment. Processes should be well documented. Once the process is clear and transparent, it becomes easier to allocate ownership to it. Assign ownership to each process and controls, with clear responsibilities and reporting structure.

Standardize (Seiketsu)

Focuses on standardizing best practices in the work area. It allows employees to participate in development of standards. Standardization leads to consistent and predictable processes which make possible easy detection of variances. Link each supply chain element across processes to relevant financial reporting metrics and set a benchmark value for reference.

Sustain (Shitsuke)

This is the most difficult to implement and achieve. The tendency is to return to the status quo and the comfort zone of the "old way" of doing things. This can be achieved through constant reviews by the concerned managers with the CEO taking the lead role. Training of employees is a must. Ensure that the new system is being maintained for a sufficiently long time so as to enable the employees to adapt to it. At the same time continuously review the supply chain for risks and potential areas for modification.

Compliance Through Best Practices

Companies should look out for solutions which will increase visibility and reduce inventory through better forecasting or best practices, control or lower liabilities resulting from agreements with partners and strengthen the bonds with partners across the supply chain. SOX compliance should be a part of larger strategic and tactical initiatives. The ultimate aim should be to move towards an adaptive supply chain which would swiftly adapt itself to any new compliance requirements or major disruptions. This section discusses some of the best practices and IT based tools which will help to achieve this aim.

Adaptive Supply Chains

In the words of Charles Darwin,-"It is not the smartest or the strongest that survive but those most adaptive to change". Unpredictable supply chain disruptions (terrorist acts, port strikes) or ever evolving environmental and compliance laws (Bio Terrorism act, SOX, 24 hr manifest), fast changing customer preferences are trends which demand adaptability to swiftly transform the supply chain in order to the meet the changed conditions.

The three key enablers in building an adaptive supply chain network are 'information quality', 'information speed' and 'information depth'; which is also what SOX compliance is all about. In practice these enablers can be built into retail supply chains by real-time technologies like RFID (radio frequency identification), 2D bar-code, GPS (global positioning system). Collaborative initiatives such as CPFR (collaborative planning forecasting and replenishment), GDS (global data synchronization) or EPC assist in leveraging these technologies through standardization. Data Synchronization in particular will help in streamlining the entire supply chain, producing clean product data and hence better direct materials sourcing.

Information depth and quality can be achieved through data warehousing/mining tools and retail specific software such as demand forecasting, assortment planning, store replenishment and promotions management. The aim is to develop a system that provides total visibility of the order, automates order management, facilitates collaboration among partners, monitors consumer demand across the network, replenishing when necessary, without having any manual intervention, other than exceptions.

CPFR is defined as collaborative business practices that enable trading partners to have visibility into one another's critical demand, order forecasts and promotional forecasts through a systematic process of shared brand and category plans, exception identification and resolution.

CPFR is intended to allow retailers and suppliers to predict upcoming supply and demand, and to use that information to synchronize the retailer's merchandise plan with the supplier's sales plan. CPFR tools facilitate collaboration on forecasts, promotional activities, replenishment plans with key suppliers. CPFR tools help in analyzing variances, reporting exceptions and events, all of which are critical given the amount of data involved and the real time needs of various parties concerned.

CPFR program results in accurate forecasts and hence lower inventory levels. Increased visibility across the partners results in lower safety stock requirements and a check on the supplier's performance.

Two areas in the retail supply chain where compliance efforts should be focused are distribution and in-store management. The next section talks about solutions targeted at these two areas.

Supply Chain Execution

Efficient distribution is an important component of managing inventory turns and reducing supply chain expenses. Special care has to be taken when dealing with time-sensitive and perishable products. Products must be shipped to market with no sacrifice in freshness or before their expiry dates. Retailers can take a hit on their sales as well be saddled with unwanted and useless products if their systems are not geared to move such products swiftly through the distribution channel. Inventory write-offs, cost of disposing expired goods coupled with lost sales can cause a significant dent in the retailer's earnings.

US FDA laws require an accurate and up-to date inventory status of food and pharmaceutical products. Same is required by the SOX but for a purpose of financial reporting. As a result of these inventory visibility needs and multiple laws to be complied with, there have been efforts made at integrating warehouse management and transportation systems using wireless technologies like RFID in order to expedite and track the flow of goods throughout the supply chain. The need for real time visibility coupled with the increasing demands placed on the manufacturers by large, powerful retailers have given the impetus to the fast growth of warehouse management and transport management solutions. The extent of integration directly determines the degree of visibility that organizations have.

Trade Management

Merchandise Management

Traditional merchandising decisions relied on variables such as buyer experience, intuition, or a change in season to stock the 'right' mix. An improper mix of goods could lead to huge unsold stocks and stock-outs at the same time; leading to out of control inventory figures or dent in earnings. Merchandizing solutions help aid compliance by avoiding these events through better control over product mix and store inventory.

Merchandise management is defined as the analysis, planning, acquisition, promotion, and control of merchandise sold by a retailer. Merchandise management solutions can help maintain a profitable product mix, optimize inventory levels, and improve pricing strategies. It allows optimize profitability through careful analysis of supplier relationships thus anticipating any problems at the supplier's end.

Promotions Management

Promotions carried out on one channel can have a drastic effect on sales in other channels. Typical outcomes are cannibalization of sales of non-promotional items, brand switching, product switching, store switching, forward buying etc. Companies struggle to accurately predict the overall effectiveness of their promotional and trade fund spending. These events could cause havoc even with the best managed supply chains in form of piled up inventory, product returns, lost sales all leading to missed revenue targets, decreased margins and eventual loss of investor confidence.

Promotion management tools are being increasingly used to help optimize promotions and fund allocation by forecasting results of programs before a business commits any funds. These tools determine the effect of the marketing plan on decision and action points (sourcing, multi-echelon inventory etc.) throughout the supply chain planning process.

Vendor Funds Management

Consumer packaged goods companies spend around $250 bn annually in advertising, marketing and promotion to promote their products. In November, the *Wall Street Journal* reported that the US Foodservice Inc., a division of Ahold NV, disclosed that inflated trade rebates from suppliers necessitated a restatement of earnings by $880 million. In February, the federal government indicted two Kmart executives for booking up front a $40 million manufacturer's payment that should have been recognized overtime. Post SOX, such events have put pressure on retailers to account for their promotional funds.

Vendor fund management tools help retailers to efficiently plan, execute and track their promotional campaigns. Functionalities offered by these systems are:

- Create accurate and fast promotions once the funding is acquired and the products are selected

- Make a record of the promotions and advertisement it creates so that it can call that up a year later if needed
- Ensure that retailers get all of the promotion funds to which they are entitled based on meeting specified purchasing or sales incentives
- Analyze where promotional funds are spent and how effectively.

SOX Compliance Approach at HP

HP is using the Supply Chain Operations Reference (SCOR) Model, a framework with a structure that links business process, technology, metrics and best practices, as well as the Customer Chain Operations Reference (CCOR) and in-house-developed finance chain models to scope, plan, and execute its immediate and long-term SOX compliance work. These models kept the project team on a systematic and disciplined approach to hone in on high-risk areas in the supply chain.

The first step in the compliance activity was to spotlight the financial account and business processes that affect them (e.g. net revenue, cost of goods sold, inventory, direct and global sourcing, fixed assets, goodwill, operating expenses, tax, and treasury). These areas were analyzed to determine significant accounts; high-risk areas were then identified in terms of process and applications. This formed the basis of further compliance work.

SOX Compliance IT as a Panacea

After business process improvements and best practices, IT is the most potent tool in the entire SOX compliance process. The cost-effective way for most companies would be to leverage existing tools to fill any of the gaps required for process control. They can augment existing systems with focused tools for analysis and reporting to satisfy the act's reporting requirements.

Efficiency of audits is often challenged by factors such as process complexity especially in the retail industry with multiple product categories procured from hundreds of suppliers. IT point solutions used for process improvement and optimization can aid in increasing the efficiency of audits with decrease in audit costs. Retailers should ensure compliance through an optimum mix of audits and IT tools.

The software industry's innovative skills have resulted in a variety of vendors offering applications designed to help automate processes that will make Sarbanes Oxley reporting more efficient. Most solutions either combine multiple platforms and applications into a portal that provides a snapshot for compliance checking or focus on business processes, streamlining procedures across applications. Retailers should look out for solutions offering visibility/transparency, financial controls, risk management, records retention, communication and business intelligence. But before opting for any software, companies should identify any existing features and functions of supply management systems already in place that can aid in Sarbanes Oxley compliance.

IT solutions for SOX compliance can be roughly classified down into three key offerings: process mapping, document management and in-line analytics.

Process Mapping

Process mapping tools allow the user to document and analyze the business processes of a company. The drawing of process flows allows for a quicker and better identification of key players and activities. Using these tools also allows for changes to be applied to the process flows as they occur in the underlying business process.

Business Process Management (BPM)

Business processes are the defining characteristics of any organization which control and describe precisely how business is conducted internally and externally, in terms of data and information flow, and the interactions between individuals and the organization. But the logic of business process tends to get hard-wired into highly expensive IT systems. So, whenever the processes are required to be changed or modified as it is in case of new compliance laws or a supply chain disruption, these hard-wired processes become the biggest obstacles to change. BPM is a tool that enables organizations to build flexible, responsive systems with speedy integration into existing software infrastructure. Business process management (BPM) systems can make it easier for organizations to respond effectively to the new requirements which can be then evaluated and integrated into the new process. BPM tools can address process modeling and integration, enterprise application integration (EAI), workflow and business analytics.

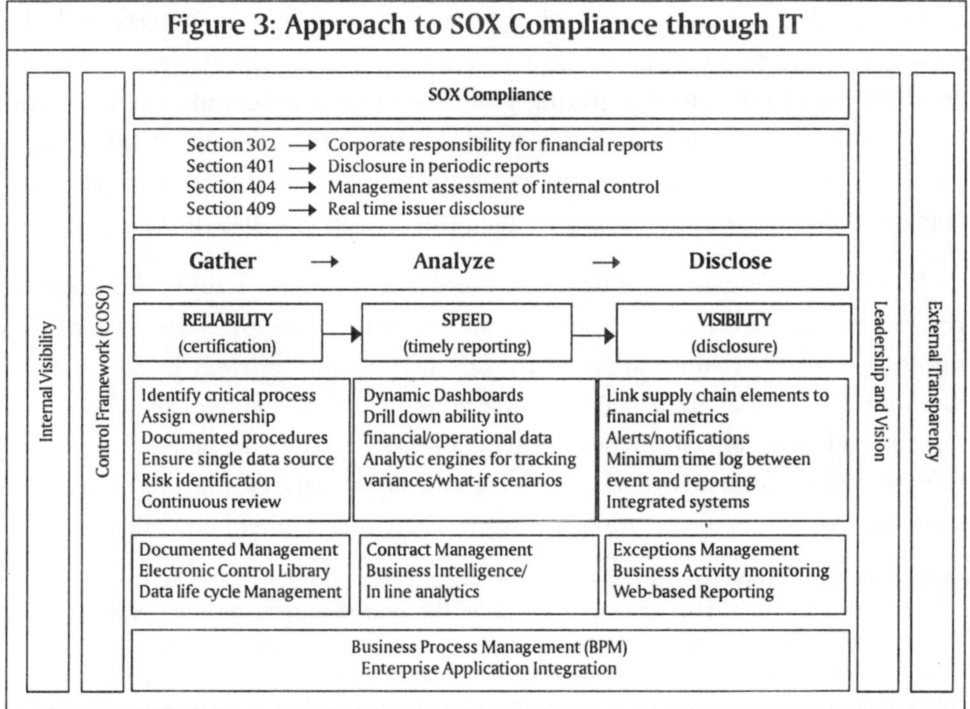

Document Management

Sarbanes Oxley requires existence of proper controls. So it is important to maintain controls information in such a way that it can be easily accessed and changed. Physical documents confirming the existence of controls and approved compliance are generally part of the Sarbanes Oxley initiative. Document management tools provide the necessary document repository. Use of a document management tool eases the burden of changes that will be made to the required documentation. It facilitates efficient audits and faster closing of accounts in addition to quickly solving disputes and issues of ownership and pricing through faster retrieval and interpretation of documents.

In-line Analytics/Business Intelligence

In-line analytics are used at business process checkpoints to check the pulse of the process. Analytic tools allow for automatic detection of material changes and reporting on these changes in real-time. Time-based analysis can be done to compare data with other data or models to determine trends or exceptions or root causes. Alerts can be issued to concerned users based on analytic engines. The triggers could be variances in actual versus budgets, or abnormal trends in revenue recognition or expenses. In addition to monitoring processes for anomalies, analytic tools also addresses the liabilities arising from a supply chain operation such as VMI, volume purchases etc. through codification and translation of the contractual terms and application of the same to project a time-phased picture of liabilities.

Business intelligence applications are decision support tools that enable, real-time, interactive access, analysis and manipulation of critical corporate information. Web enabled BI tools provide personalized browser based interface that functions as a centralized location for accessing existing enterprise information systems and external information sources. BI tools extend the value of corporate information through analytical processing and rapid delivery and presentation of accurate information to executives, managers, analysts and other knowledge workers.

A dashboard or scorecard presents visual, easily understood metrics and KPIs (Figure 4). Dashboards show critical metrics depending on the user requirement. Problem areas are highlighted for the user's immediate attention. The dashboard serves as a real-time barometer of business conditions and helps put the decision-maker in control. Dashboards aid in making proactive and predictive business management a reality. BI tools working in the background allows drilling through underlying data for analysis and comparisons.

Conclusion

Companies can use SOX as a catalyst to improve their supply chain performance. Companies that put together a supply chain risk management process with their partners will extract the biggest gain from their efforts. The key takeaways of SOX compliance for supply chain operations are:

Tighter operational controls through simplified and documented internal control

- Real-time visibility and transparency into supply chain transactions
- Adaptive supply chain networks.

Achieving compliance is easier than sustaining it. Efforts taken towards compliance should be built into the supply chain processes through internal reporting mechanisms, documentation, ownership and constant review. Internal

Figure 4: Sample Dashboard Showing Key Performance Metrics

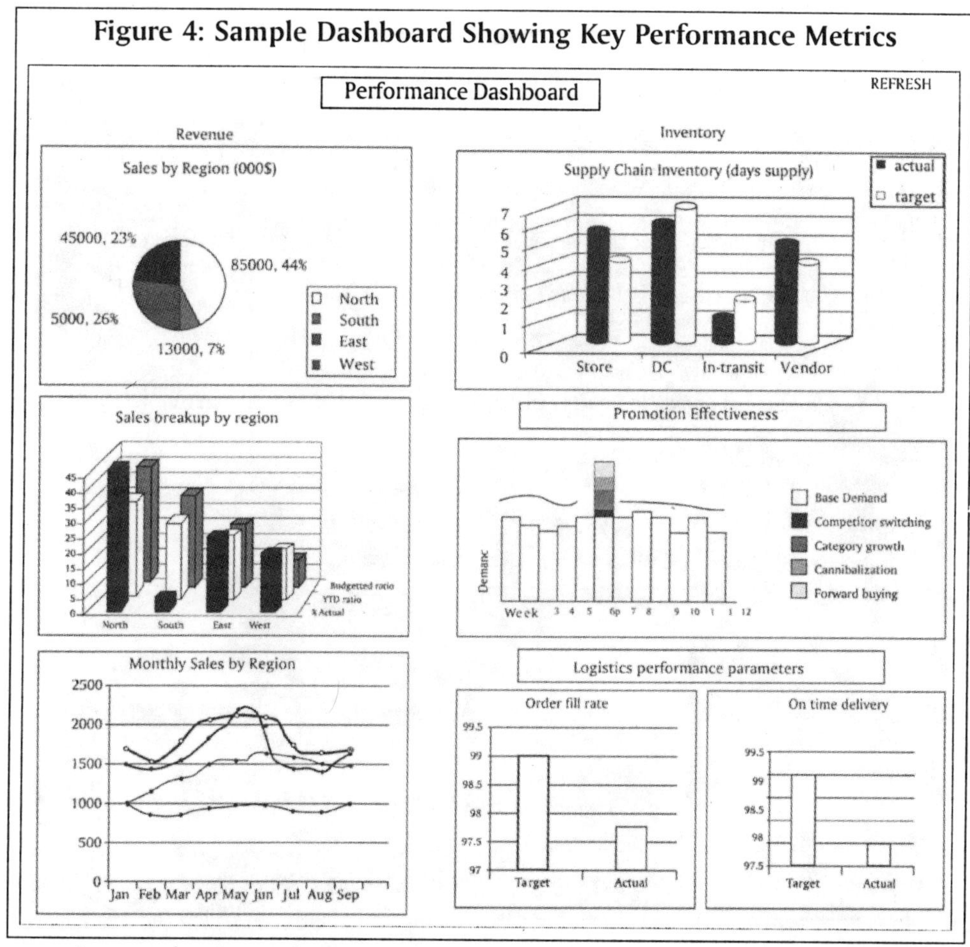

reporting mechanisms, documentation, ownership and constant review. Internal audit teams must be on the lookout for deviations. Third party certifications should be done at periodic intervals. Top management is the key driver for any large-scale initiatives such as SOX compliance. They should monitor the key metrics and keep people motivated to accept the changes and at the same time try to address the HR problems which are bound to arise during such an initiative. The company should develop the capability to anticipate or forecast impending disruptions on the horizon.

Supply management organizations are always under pressure to identify new avenues for cost and productivity improvements. SOX might be the answer.

Abbreviations

SOX – Sarbanes Oxley Act

GAAP – Generally Accepted Accounting Procedures

FDA – Food and Drug Administration (USA)

WEEE – Waste from Electric and Electronic Equipment (directive)

RFID – Radio Frequency Identification

GPS – Global Positioning System

CPFR – Collaborative Planning Forecasting and Replenishment

GDS – Global Data Synchronization

(Kannan Natarajan is a Supply Chain Practice Manager in the Retail, CPG and Distribution vertical of Wipro Technologies and Satish Panchapakesan is a Supply Chain Consultant in the Retail, CPG and Distribution vertical of Wipro Technologies.)

References

1. Levy & Weitz, *Retailing Management*, Tata McGraw-Hill.
2. Brealey & Myers, *Principles of Corporate Finance*, Irwin McGraw-Hill.
3. Sunil Chopra & Peter Meindl, *Supply Chain Management: Strategy, Planning and Operations*, Prentice Hall.
4. Hollander, Irwin, *Accounting Information Technology and Business Solutions*, McGraw-Hill.
5. H David Sherman and S David Young, "Accounting Minefields", *Harvard Business Review*, Jul-Aug, pp.129-135, 2001.
6. Zabihollah Rezaee, "The Six-Legged Stool", *Strategic Finance*, Feb, pp. 27-30, 2003.
7. *Andrew J Felo, Steven A Soliert, Strategic Finance*, "New Laws, New Challenges Implications of Sarbanes Oxley", Feb pp.31-34, 2003.
8. A Wayne Avellanet, 'Is what-you-see really what-you-got?: *Strategic Finance*, Sep, pp.24-28, 2003.
9. "Supply Managers Say SOX Only Part of a Compliance Strategy", *http:// www.aberdeen.com/ 2001/research/02040010.asp, Aberdeen Group*
10. *www.sap.com*
11. *www.cio.com*
12. *www.supply-chain.org*
13. *www.coso.org*
14. *www.sarbanes-oxley.com*

Section II

SCM Applications in Service Industry

9

Financial Supply Chain Management

A Lakshminarasimha and Jyothi G Rao

The article proposes the use of Financial Supply Chain Management (FSCM) solution to enable the Chief Financial Officers (CFOs) to effectively manage their receivables and payables; forecast their company's financial future; and reduce their working capital needs. The article introduces the basic concepts of supply chain management and proposes the benefits of optimization of FSCM; deals with the integration of Physical Supply Chain Management (PSCM) and the FSCM; and discusses the possible limitations of FSCM.

Introduction to Supply Chain Management

Supply Chain Management (SCM) has emerged as one of the most powerful business improvement tools available today. Suppliers, manufacturers, distributors, retailers, and a number of service organizations have discovered that they must transform their operations or be beaten at the market place by competition that have more creative and aggressive supply networks (Poirier, 1999).

Supply Chain Management (SCM) is a relatively new concept, which involves the integration of all value-adding components in the supply, manufacturing and distribution processes, from the raw material extraction stage right through

Source: The Icfai Journal of Supply Chain Management, Vol. III, No. 4, December 2006.

the various transformation value-adding processes, to the distribution and end-user consumption. The end objective is to maximize customer service, compress lead-time, and reduce inventory. Internet and Electronic Data Interchange (EDI) including using extended Enterprise Resource Planning solutions (ERP) facilitate quick communication of end-user demand and requirement in terms of specification, style or taste as the case may be, to the upstream stages of the supply chain network (Basnet *et al.,* 2003).

All these years, a company could achieve more profits by outperforming its competition or by outmaneuvering its suppliers or customers. Both the methods would produce similar results, therefore companies even in USA focused on adversarial bidding with suppliers and use of marketing techniques with customers. In this situation, cooperation between supply chain members was lost, as no one was recognizing the supply chain as a competitive unit (Lawrence, *et al.,* 2003).

The strategic importance of SCM is also emphasized by the recent observations of John Grossman, Vice President of Materials Management at Allied Signal, which pointed towards the premise that competition is no longer between company and company but is between supply chain and supply chain. (Elmuti Dean, 2002). This would imply that the strength of the supply chain is more important than the strength of the individual company.

Suppliers, and relationships with them, have traditionally been viewed solely through the lens of purchasing transactions and consequently as essentially adversarial, characterized by zero-sum power dynamics (Suppliers want to be paid more; customers want to pay less). Now, more and more companies are beginning to look at suppliers differently, not simply as cost centers but as true business partners. Senior management in supply management, often prompted by the desire to be viewed more strategically by, and add greater value to their internal business unit customers, is beginning to focus on the challenge of how to better identify, gain access to and leverage supplier assets, expertise and capabilities in order to support the strategic objectives of the enterprise (Jonathan Hughes, 2005).

The suppliers and distributors, who were once considered as adversaries, are now in the process of becoming partners as win-win situations are implemented in supply chains and this results in improvements for all the partners in the chain (Gryna, 2001). This is further collaborated by the finding that to be successful, companies will not seek to achieve cost reductions or profit improvements at the cost of their partners in the supply chain but will seek to make the entire supply chain more competitive (Elmuti Dean, 2002, Li and Chen, 2001).

The objective of Physical Supply Chain Management (PSCM) as explained above is to optimize the performance of the chain and thereby gain a unique competitive advantage. This is achieved through:

- Collaborative forecasting;
- Just-In-Time (JIT) inventory management throughout the chain;
- High quality customer service to achieve total customer satisfaction;
- Minimization of cost across the chain including costs incurred in logistics, distribution; and
- Maintaining a high level of flexibility in the operations in the chain so that the customer need in today's world can be met accurately and in time.

Financial Supply Chain

Financial Supply Chain Management (FSCM) relates to all the activities involved in the flow of cash, from the end buyer's initial order through final reconciliation of payments across the entire supply chain. FSCM includes:

- **Procurement and Risk Check**
  - Negotiation and purchase order placement.
  - Authentication, validation and credit check.
- **Fulfillment**
  - Insurance, financing.
  - Invoice and related documents.
- **Payment Decision and Cash Management**
  - Verification, discrepancy reconciliation.
  - Cash flow management.

The Goals of FSCM

Financial Supply Chain Management has similar goals to that of PSCM. While the overall objective is to attain customer satisfaction, FSCM also monitors the needs of the financial stakeholders of the organization. The goals of FSCM are:

- To accurately manage the sundry creditors across the supply chain;
- To accurately manage the sundry debtors across the supply chain;
- To reduce the working capital needs of the whole chain;
- To manage the financial rates for the whole chain through better negotiation with the financial institutions using the chain as an entity;
- To reduce the risk management costs through a better prediction of cash flows; and
- To install early warning systems for the benefit of the whole supply chain.

The supplementary benefits could include minimization of daily sales outstanding by ensuring quick cash flow across the supply chain. The financial supply chain, which deals with financial settlement, goes hand in hand with physical supply chain. Exporters want to know, when they will be paid. Importers would want to know when the goods would arrive, so that they can plan for inventory. Therefore, financial supply chain necessitates exchange of information between various companies forming the chain. The most important element in this financial supply chain is the sharing of information, which would aid companies to plan and initiate necessary actions.

Financial supply chain improves profitability by addressing twin challenges of managing cash flows and optimizing working capital, which are very important for successful financial performance in any company. How does financial supply chain help in cash flow management and working capital management?

FSCM links all parties' right from buyer's initial order right through payment to seller. This would enable a treasurer in a company to accurately forecast the flow of cash and goods, and consequently, plan for inventory and future cash requirements. A good FSCM would enable a finance manager to hold less cash and deploy cash to meaningful investment avenues. Idle cash held reduces returns to the company, and hence, the shareholders would suffer.

A typical financial supply chain for importers or exporters includes:

- Procurement—Purchase order.
- Risk Mitigation—Authentication, Validation, Payment Assurance, Credit Check.
- Fulfillment—Invoice/Documents, Proof of delivery, Insurance.
- Payment Decision—Data matching, Discrepancy Management.
- Cash Management—Money Movement, Foreign Exchange reconciliation.

Since a financial supply chain traces the cash flows, a finance manager can significantly reduce working capital needs by better inventory control. This also enables reduction of DSO (Days Sales Outstanding), which is an indicator of funds tied up in receivables, and increase cash flow predictability for sellers. While improving the bottom line, this enables lower financing rates on required working capital through more effective management of current assets.

FSCM reduces uncertainty regarding cash and goods flows and thereby enable inventory and receivables reduction. Reduction in inventory alone would reduce the cost of financing inventories significantly, which in turn enables improvement in bottom line.

According to Todd M Barnhart, "To put this in financial terms, the cost of financing the inventories of the Fortune 1000 companies in the early 90s is estimated at $150 bn. Big savings in Financing costs were available if inventories could be reduced—the US Department of Commerce estimated a reduction in the inventory/sales ratio from 4.8 turns to 5.4 turns over the period 1980-90".

Impact of FSCM

According to Barks (1989), performance of a business was earlier measured strictly in various formulae like costs over budget, damaged goods, stock-outs and the like. More than these formulae, effort needs to be made in containing these above variables not after the event has happened but early on – when the warning signs become evident. This can happen by optimizing the financial supply chains. Today, more and more companies are realizing that economic measures—not just internal measures but also external measures—are used to justify the importance of supply chain organization.

Considering all the benefits of FSCM delineated above, how can FSCM be implemented in an organization?

FSCM mandates that all paperwork be digitized. This would eliminate data entry operators who could be prone to errors. Besides, electronic invoices are almost error-free and easy to reconcile with purchase orders. Besides, it would aid internal management, while generating reports on total purchases/sales. Secondly, in order to implement FSCM, all payments and receipts must be made electronic. This would reduce float for a company besides enabling good internal control systems over receipts and payments. Finally, FSCM enables good working capital management. According to Todd Barnhart, "Once the processes are automated, contact with the supply chain financial departments is improved and most of the uncertainties are taken out of the payment chain, companies can begin to optimize their cash management. This may be purely internal process, managing cash against precise knowledge of daily payables and receivables, and improving credit decisions."

Financial Supply Chain and Risk Management

FSCM, apart from optimizing working capital requirement, also enables a company to mitigate various risks involved while dealing with customers.

FSCM, as pointed out earlier helps in information flow amongst all the members of the chain so that prompt actions are taken to avoid any kind of loss. Since various processes like validation of documentation, authentication and credit check are inbuilt into the FSCM, this would enable the company to know at any point in time how much credit is available for the purchaser/seller and what is the liquidity position of the borrower. His ability to pay is closely tied with the receivables position of the selling company. Hence, the selling company would know how much of funds are blocked in receivables.

The company's bank is also a part of the FSCM of the company. More so if the company deals with letters of credit or collections for international businesses. This would enable the bank to know about a company's position, and accordingly, its decision to give/increase credit facility to the company. The ability to estimate the impact of fluctuations in exchange or interest rates can greatly improve risk analysis.

Integration of Financial and Physical Supply Chains

Lack of integration between the two supply chains can spell disaster for the companies. Lack of sync between the two would unable the company to get information on time regarding the flow of goods and cash. This would hamper decision taking and further create excess working capital or nonproductive float. This lack of integration can cause various problems for both buyers and sellers. Buyers may end up with excess float and inability to take timely discounts and this would hinder optimize use of credit capacity. For sellers it may result in excess funds tied up in receivables and resulting in cash crunches, and which would seriously affect their responsiveness to their customers.

One of the significant advantages of FSCM, as pointed out earlier, is the flow of cash among the members of the supply chain. The benefits of financial supply chain percolates to all members of the chain, when the cash flow is smooth amongst the members. At no point in time should some members of the chain have surplus cash and cut off the flow to the remaining members of the chain, resulting in severe liquidity problems for those members. In other words, if the pivot company of the chain receives cash from its debtors, a good ERP system should be in place (which is a part of a good financial supply chain) which would immediately disburse cash to its suppliers. A good cash flow system within the chain would enable good working capital management among the members of the chain. This would further aid in strengthening the supply chain network. If proper financial supply chain does not exist, it would preclude all flow of financial information, and may affect cash flow among other members, which would hamper the physical supply chain.

Thus, it is imperative that a good financial supply chain is crucial for the existence of a good physical supply chain.

Limitations

As Warren H Hausman of Stanford University puts it "Quantitatively speaking, a company with $1 bn annual revenue could obtain an annual savings of nearly $10 mn, or almost 1% of revenues with improved financial flows". While it may be argued that FSCM is the main reason for improved bottom line, it is easier said than implemented. One of the chief reasons for effective supply financial supply chains is prompt information sharing between various partners of supply chains. In practice, companies may be reluctant to share financial information with each other. This would hamper the effectiveness of financial supply chain management.

Secondly, a technology solution would enable cash flow and help in the effective collaboration between the members of the chain. However, it must be realized, that all companies cannot afford technologies needed for effective FSCM.

Conclusion

The main theme of the paper focuses on the close interaction between FSCM and PSCM. An effective PSCM is not possible without a good FSCM. Technology is a very useful enabler in providing this interaction on a real time basis.

(A Lakshminarasimha is a Faculty Member at Icfai Business School, Bangalore. He can be reached at lnarshima@ibsindia.org

Jyothi G Rao is a Faculty Member at Icfai Business School, Bangalore. She can be reached at jyothir@mail2.ibsindia.org).

References

1. Basnet Chuda, Jim Corner, Joel Wisner and Keah Choon Tan (2003), "Bench Marking Supply Chain Management Practices in New Zealand", *Supply Chain Management an International Journal,* Vol. 8, No. 1, pp. 57-64.
2. Dean Elmuti (2002), "The Perceived Impact of Supply Chain Management on Organisation Effectiveness", *The Journal of Supply Chain Management* Vol. 38, No. 3, pp. 49-57.
3. Elmuti Dean (2002). "The Perceived Impact of Supply Chain Management on Organizational Effectiveness", *The Journal of Supply Chain Management: A Global Review of Purchasing and Supply,* August 2002. pp.49-56.

4. "Focus on Effective International Supply Chain Management", A Bank of America White Paper General References, ***http://corp.bankofamerica.com/public/products/pdf/treasury/International_Supply_Chain_Management.pdf.***

5. Gryna F (2001), *Supply Chain Management Quality Planning and Analysis,* McGraw Hill, pp. 403-432.

6. James S Keebler, "Financial Issues in Supply Chain Management", ***http://www.loc.gov/catdir/enhancements/fy0656/00010197-t.html***

7. Jonathan Hughes, (2005), *Inside Supply Management®,* Vol. 16, No. 10, page 14.

8. Lawrence F Barry, Daniel F Jennings, Brian E Reynolds (2003), *E-Distribution,* Thomson Learning.

9. Li S and F Chen (2001), "Measuring the Performance of Integrated Supply Chain Management", *Proceedings Midwest Business Adminstration Association,* March 2001.

10. Poirier C C (1999), *Advanced Supply Chain Management, How to Build a Sustained Competitive Advantage,* San Fransisco, Berret-Koehler Publishers, Inc. pp.1-22, 208-209.

11. Todd M Barnhart, "The Financial Supply Chain", *www.darwinmag.com*

12. Warren H Hausman, "Financial Flows and Supply Chain Efficiency", ***http://www.corporate. visa.com/md/dl/documents/downloads/supplychain.pdf?topic =gov***

13. White Paper on Financial Supply Chain Management, SAP Labs from the Web, ***http://whitepapers.zdnet.co.uk***

10

SCM in Banking Services

Y G Sivaram and Jangaiah Paladi

Supply Chain Management (SCM) as a concept has gained credence especially in the case of manufacturing industries. The versatility of this concept with regard to its application in the non-industrial sector is explored in this article. Considering that the service sector has gained prominence in the growth process of all the economies worldwide, we have attempted to present the relevance and acceptability of SCM in the banking system that forms part of the service sector.

Business organizations have started looking for techniques that give them market leadership, more so in the context of shortening product life cycles and faster imitation of technologies. It is in this context that Supply Chain Management (SCM), as a management concept, provides the framework for securing competitive advantage offering business organizations substantial cost reductions or better profitability, improvements in product development, quality, speed, and flexibility, leading to customer retention, and loyalty. Given this scenario, there has been an increasing interest in SCM among academics as well as practitioners of SCM.

Over the years, researchers have explored the concept of SCM and established its theoretical and operational bases, as are known today. To understand this

Source: Treasury Management, November 2004.

concept, we pick the definition of Prof. Panos Kouvelis, who defines SCM as, "A set of approaches used to efficiently integrate suppliers, manufacturers, warehouses, and retail stores so that merchandise is produced and distributed in the right quantities, to the right location, at the right time, and at optimal cost." Thus, SCM involves exchange of products, information and knowledge between firms, which are interlinked in the provision of an offering (a product or service) from its inception to the final consumption. It also requires the development and management of inter-firm relationships. SCM enables organizations to attain the following objectives:

- Synthesis of the businesses and resource networks
- Synergy between the actors of a supply network
- Synchronization of the activities and operations.

In this article, we attempt to apply the framework of SCM to the service industry in general, and show its relevance and importance to the banking industry in particular. In this process, we also try to integrate the role of IT as the most important instrument in delivering the services.

Scope of SCM in Service Sector

As a result of the requirements and possibilities mentioned above, physical supply chains have developed tremendously during the last decade. However, majority of the research during this time dealt with the management of the physical supply chains of manufacturing firms and the focus was mainly on logistics management. Consequently, business organizations have benefited strongly from reengineering production and delivery processes that reduced inventories. However, sourcing, procurement, financial transactions, and product delivery processes were still prone to errors and other problems, which resulted in losses. Making the entire supply chain more efficient holds the key to improving and maintaining competitiveness and providing solutions to the problems being faced by the organizations. Thus, SCM required something more than logistics management.

Economists say that when the economies develop, the share of service industries increase. Service industries assume a significant role in the economic development.

The services sectors' contribution is about two-third in the national products of developed countries. It is also stated that about half of the final value of a tangible product is made up of services component. Hence, there is a great need to apply the SCM concepts in service organizations, specifically the financial services industry.

While physical supply chains gained momentum and yielded results, the financial supply chains did not play their due role. The documents and payment processes that accompany a transaction lagged far behind their physical counterparts.

SCM Framework for Services Sector

Determination of the services exchange context is not simple as it is difficult to view the supply of services separately from the supply of goods. There are very few business transactions that involve either only services or only goods. In fact, each exchange of a product or service is a bundle of services and goods in different mixes. Moreover, services have some unique characteristics, which sets or defines the context in which a service exchange takes place and how it is different from products or goods. The characteristics that differentiate services from products are intangibility (i.e., the output of many services is not tangible), simultaneity, (i.e., the service is produced and consumed at the same time), perishability, (i.e., the services do not have shelf life nor can they be transported), and heterogeneity, (i.e., the required interaction between the service provider and the customer increases the possibility of providing diverse outputs from customer to customer).

There is a lot of diversity in the service sector, which uses products and services in production of the services. As such, making generalizations about management of the service organizations is not easy. This diversity provoked Silvestro *et al.*[1] to propose the following typology for service organizations:

Mass Services: These services are equipment-based. The contact time between the customer and the service provider is short, scope for customization and discretion is low, and the product-oriented service is produced in the back office. Public utility services, transportation services, news and confectionery retailing are some examples.

---

1 Silvestro R, Fitzerald L, Johnston R & Voss C (1992), "Towards a Classification of Service Processes", *International Journal of Service Industry Management*, 3, 2, pp.62-75.

In Service Shops: These services require both people and equipment. The contact time and the scope for customization are medium. Service is provided by the back and front offices. Retail banking, hotel and hospitality services are some examples.

Professional Services: These services are related to people and the front office. They require long contact time and have scope for high degree of customization and discretion. Management consultancies, corporate banking and legal services are some examples of this category.

Application of SCM Framework to Services Sector

The peculiar features of services make it difficult to apply the concept of SCM as it is. As, the supply chain of services tends to be different, there is a paucity of appropriate SCM tools in service exchanges, which warrant the development of an alternative model to spell out the concept of SCM in services.

As per the '3S' (Synthesis, Synergy, and Synchronization) Model propounded by Mihalis Giannakis and Simon R Croom, SCM in services involves:

- Corporate strategy decisions regarding the synthesis of the network of interconnected firms involved in the provision of a service to the final consumer.
- Business strategy decisions regarding the synergy of Inter-Organizational Relationships (IORs) between parties in the supply network.
- Operations strategy decisions regarding the synchronization of the supply and delivery operations of the service.

General framework for SCM in the service domain suggests that the level of intangibility of services has an effect on the anatomy of a supply network, the strength and behavior of the IORs between a service user and a service provider, and the activities involved in the provision of the service.

Now let us see how banks can use supply chain framework in providing their services. The supply chain of banking services comprises different activities and processes that together facilitate the provision of the required service to the customer. As part of the supply chain a number of banks, insurance firms, shipping organizations, communication companies and other financial institutions can be linked up. Typically, SCM talks about a customer being a supplier to another customer; this is more relevant in the banking scenario.

As we have seen above, the banking services fall into two categories: Professional and in-service shops. That is, providing some of their services require both people and equipment while other services are front-office oriented. However, the degree of supply chain integration depends on the size of the bank, the types of services provided, and the demand from customers for different services.

Banks come in varied sizes. The range of services they provide include personal banking, wealth management, and corporate cash/treasury management, to name a few. The mechanism of distributing the services could be direct—from the bank to the customer, or through some intermediaries, depending on the type of service/s that the customer requires. While many of the services provided are purely banking related, some are non-banking services such as selling insurance products, offering trade-related services etc.

The Key Elements of Supply Chain

In this context, we can identify the following as the key elements in the supply chain of banking services:

Products and Services

The basic decisions to be taken in the first stage of developing the supply chain are—types of products and how many products need to be retained and introduced in certain key areas such as types of deposits and types of loans and trade-related services. Another important point that has to be focused on, is the extent to which outsourcing can be done. For instance, we have a few private banks that have outsourced some of their services in the areas of deposits, loans and credit cards.

The focus of the strategic decisions regarding products and services should also be on resource availability, quality of assets and the need to meet customer demand and customer satisfaction. Consequently, operational decisions focus on scheduling work patterns and ensuring the availability of infrastructure for meeting the immediate demands of the customers.

Infrastructure and Resources

Banks must determine the economic and efficient capacity of the infrastructure and resources that are available with it. Many banks consider outsourcing an excellent alternative to be considered for those products and services that cannot be rendered effectively by banks' existing facilities. In the matter of choosing a franchise, the bank should focus on the franchise's ability in developing velocity, quality and flexibility at low-cost.

Liquidity

Strategic decisions in banks focus on liquidity. A delicate balance exists between too much liquidity and not enough liquidity. The decisions regarding liquidity positions to be maintained at the branch/bank levels revolve around the optimal levels of funds requirements. A level of liquidity is needed that ensures customer satisfaction even in a situation of fluctuating market demands. RBI's regulatory framework should also be taken into account for determining the correct levels of liquidity.

Location

The strategic location decisions focus on the location of branches, ATMs, off-site service centers, and distribution facilities. Long-term commitment must be made to locate service and delivery points close to the customer. Decisions concerning location should also take into consideration the cost factor and the readiness of competitors to spend resources on locating branches/ATMs to ensure that the bank is physically nearer to the customer. Simultaneously, Internet banking should be developed to benefit from a far wider customer reach.

Transportation

Strategic transportation decisions are related to decisions made on maintaining adequate cash levels at various delivery points such as branches/ATMs for meeting customer demands. Hence, using the correct transport mode at the appropriate time with adequate security considerations is a critical strategic decision. For the purpose of remitting excess cash, banks should also organize their transport facility to lift cash and deliver promptly at the currency chest of RBI. Holding excess cash only gives negative returns to the banks and adds to the costs.

Information

In the wake of increased use of interconnectivity in operations between the branches of a bank and also between different banks, effective supply chain management requires obtaining information from the point of end-use, and linking information resources throughout the chain for speed of exchange. Fostering innovation requires good organization of information. Linking computers through networks and the Internet, and streamlining the information flow consolidates knowledge and facilitates velocity of products. Account management software, enterprise resource planning systems, and global communications are key components of effective supply chain management strategy.

At this point, let us note that the SCM solutions coexist with, but are not the same as, Enterprise Resource Planning (ERP) software solutions. The primary purpose of an ERP system is to control the flow and execution of transactional information across the supply chain, whereas the SCM systems provide decision support. In essence, SCM system performs the planning required to allow ERP systems to execute the plan. The banks should plan their SCM systems in such a way that they easily integrate with the customers ERP systems.

Convergence of Physical and Financial Supply Chains

To make the total supply chain more efficient, banks can take over where the physical supply chain ends in a trade system. While suppliers want to receive payment quickly and certainly, buyers want to ensure when the goods will arrive, so that they can manage inventory levels and cash positions effectively. For treasurers or finance managers, managing cash flows will be certainly a great help in optimizing the investment in working capital and reducing the duration of the cash cycle.

Banks can implement supply chain solutions without substantial investment, or interruption of existing processes, simply by using new trading techniques, Internet-based technologies and with the cooperation of all parties concerned in the supply chain. The banking sector has an important part to play. It can offer new services including insurance and logistics in partnership with the insurance and logistics sectors to integrate and use common data to attain greater efficiencies for its customers. They can also reduce trade risk through closer interaction with the customers, and by offering greater transparency and visibility. The delivery of these services can be made over the Internet also.

Today, a majority of suppliers are SMEs. The ability to reach a new market segment is vital as the markets become global and the demand for financial services that support trade and industry increases globally. Banks have to use modern techniques to remain competitive in a global market.

More and more organizations, including banks, have already invested money to improve the efficiency of their value chain processes through Intranets. The advent of the Internet and the availability of secure communication outside the Intranets made it imperative to use technology for cost saving and other benefits. Some banks that are already evolving as specialist trade banks, are working towards improving their trade processes. They see themselves as trade facilitators between their customers and the customers of their customers, and their trading partners in between.

Together, these efforts have brought the physical and financial supply chains along with a convergence between the cash cycle and the trade cycle, thereby helping corporates to improve their working capital efficiency. In this scenario, the financial managers and treasurers are calling for comprehensive solutions that integrate cash management, trade settlement and finance, and logistics management.

Constraints and Solutions

What the corporates want is a simple solution that could solve the data exchange and communications issues and offer value-added features. For this purpose, banks must use a reliable and secure system that could integrate the key functions in the supply chain process, including sourcing, procurement, compliance, logistics, payment and settlement. The system must enable data inheritance across the whole supply chain process so that the data from a document in one function could be mapped and inherited into other documents in a different function. They can automate processes from the RFI to the PO, and the PO confirmation to banking for the LC application, and payment to logistics for the customs compliance, and the shipping instruction etc. All this can be performed with little or no manual input.

In this exercise, Web-based solutions hold the key to managing information across physical and financial supply chains. Sensing the need in financial supply chains, a number of online services have evolved that can simplify and automate trade finance documentation. Organizations such as *Bolero.net*, DC-Pro and CCEWeb offer services that simplify or automate the business processes and data that accompany the goods movement. Some online service providers such as TradeCard offer comprehensive solutions. TradeCard has moved the traditional paper-based process online as it automates the entire trade documentation process, allowing buyers and sellers to initiate, conduct and settle trade transactions online.

JP Morgan Chase Bank[2] is a case in point, in the context of corporate banking. It is the most active and visible financial institution working in partnership with a third-party logistics management company to provide a comprehensive, holistic approach across both the chains. JP Morgan has already defined trade services as the sphere, wherein merchandise can be bought and sold. It is able to differentiate itself from its competitors by bringing together related services such as trade, cash management, payments and treasury services under one umbrella. The bank's vision has led to substantial modifications to its business model, operations, and technology architecture. JP Morgan's solution enables its customers to manage information across the physical and financial supply chains for overall improvement in the transaction cycle. The banks' offerings go beyond the classical trade instruments and open-account financing options. Import services include Harmonized Tarriff System (HTS) classification, import and supplier data management, entry management and document creation, duty minimization, and post-entry reconciliation as also purchase order management. Its export services include Export Control Classification Number (ECCN) classification, order screening, license control and management, shipment and payment documentation preparation, Bolero and TradeCard services, and export finance.

However, the major issue for the banks in the Indian context is that they are highly regulated in terms of what they can and cannot offer by way of services. Some of the offerings mentioned here may be seen by the regulator as "non-banking" services, and hence are prohibited. If the regulators in India allow

---

2 Madhavi Reddy (2003), "Targeting Supply Chain Inefficiencies of Financial Markets—An Overview of JP Morgan's Trade Initiatives", IBS Trade Services Research Brief-Issue 1.1.

the extension of a bank's banking services into the supply chain activities of its customers, it will be complementary or ancillary to its income, and will aid in facilitating trade.

(Dr. Y G Sivaram, Faculty Member, Academic Wing, The Icfai University. He can be reached at ygsivaram@icfai.org

Prof. Jangaiah Paladi, Faculty Member, Academic Wing, The Icfai University. He can be reached jpaladi@icfai.org).

11

Supply Chain Finance – A Win-Win Situation

Sameer Sawhney

Supply Chain Finance (SCF) solutions are designed to adapt to today's rapidly changing environment. The SCF product umbrella offered by the banks covers the entire supply chain cycle from supplier finance to buyer finance—all on an open account basis. SCF can put the foot into the door for a relationship between a bank and a large corporate by providing a product which offers a predominantly off-balance sheet solution. The article emphasizes that SCF solutions create a multitude of benefits and a win-win situation for companies and their trading partners.

"Amidst growing international trade, companies are looking to their bankers to provide alternative financing solutions that will align with the way they manage their supply chain."

– Sameer Sawhney,
Regional Head, Transactional Banking,
India & South Asia, Standard Chartered Bank.

Source: Chartered Financial Analyst, October 2006.

The rapid expansion in domestic and international trade, increased competition among organizations, etc., have led companies to seek innovative ways to expedite and streamline their supply chains.

With profit margins getting thinner, coupled with the need to increase both the efficiency and efficacy of the distribution/sales chain, there is an increasing trend to shift to open account terms. Companies are increasingly abandoning the intensive paperwork and expensive Letters of Credit (LC) and are turning to trading on open account.

Banks have responded by creating Supply Chain Finance (SCF) solutions designed to adapt to this rapidly changing environment. The SCF product umbrella offered by the banks covers the entire supply chain cycle from supplier finance to buyer finance—all on open account basis. The buyer finance product provides a receivables management solution to the customer for the receivables arising out of its distribution network. The supplier finance product provides a solution on the procurements made by the company from its dedicated suppliers. Thus, these products cater to end-to-end financing requirements of a company's supply chain.

The SCF models are also extremely flexible, designed to align with seasonal peaks and changing country risk profiles and seamlessly fit in with companies' existing trading relationships. As a result, suppliers and buyers in the supply chain can enjoy transaction-backed financing with competitive interest rates and terms that align with their business cycle.

Buyer Finance

The bank specifies certain qualifying criteria for the dealers and distributors (buyers) of large corporates. Coupled with certain additional financial and credit assessments, the bank is then able to structure attractive working capital financing options for these buyers of large corporates towards their purchases made from the large corporate, either on a nil or partial recourse basis to the large corporate.

The parameters of selection broadly cover the following: The length of association with the buyer, the extent of business dependence on the large corporate, payment track record with the large corporate and the extent of control that the large corporate could exert on the buyer should one default to the bank. The key aspect of the credit evaluation relates to understanding the ecosystem of the large corporate and the strategic relationship with its buyers, which allows the bank to assess buyer risk in context of the large corporate's "halo effect" on its supply chain rather than on a stand-alone financials-based assessment.

As part of its due diligence, the bank analyzes both the individual financial strength of the buyer and the "stickiness" of the large corporate-buyer relationship. Thus, buyer finance structure, leverages on the strength of the bank's existing relationship with the large corporate and the large corporate's relationship with its strategic buyers. The combined strength of these two elements allows the bank to structure more competitive financing solutions for the buyers across pricing, structures and tenors.

Further, in a normal seller-buyer relationship, in the event of buyer payment default, the large corporate, after exploring various alternatives to enforce payment from the buyer, will "stop supply" to the buyer, in order to avoid further bad debts on this buyer. The inherent strength of buyer finance solutions is the buy-in of the large corporate to "stop supply" to the buyer should the buyer fail to honor one's loan obligations to the bank under pre-agreed situations between the bank and the large corporate. The strength of the "stop supply" coupled with the degree of dependence of the buyer on the large corporate for continuous supply of products acts as a very strong deterrent to the buyer to dishonor one's payment obligations both to the large corporate and the financing bank.

What is the Bank's Value Proposition to the Buyers?

The bank is able to add value to large corporate's recommended buyers around the following:

- Fund them with the additional working capital required for which the large corporate is unable/unwilling to extend its credit period in line with the receivables turnover period of the buyer.
- Provide financing to buyers to buy above the internal credit limit set by the large corporate on its individual buyers. The key factor behind this is that the bank, being in the business of risk assessment, would not be as conservative in extending credit limit to the buyer.

- Provide financing to buyers on a relatively unsecured basis, thus, relieving the need for the buyers to secure their lines with collateral.
- Provide financing at competitive rates to the buyers as the buyer-risk assessment is not being done solely on a stand-alone basis.

Benefits to the Large Corporate

- The large corporate is freed up from the administrative hassles of receivables management.
- The large corporate is able to offer an attractive financing option to its buyers and, thus, capture "channel loyalty".
- If the large corporate is an MNC, it is no longer constrained by its global credit policies. The large corporate is able to pursue its aggressive sales plan.
- The large corporate is able to save on the cash discounts which it offers to the buyers for early realization of the receivables.

Supplier Finance Program

Supplier finance is a bilateral supply chain financing program under which the bank offers packaged pre- and post-shipment finance facilities to the suppliers of its existing/targeted large corporate clients. This finance is provided for those parts of the suppliers' transactions, which have a direct linkage to the large corporate, and is based largely on the strength of the underlying buyer-supplier relationship.

Under this product offering, the bank specifies certain qualifying criteria for the suppliers of large corporate. Coupled with certain additional financial and credit assessments, the bank is then able to structure attractive working capital financing options in the form of bill discounting, invoice and Purchase Order (PO) discounting to these suppliers, either on a nil or partial recourse basis to the large corporate. The large coporate undertakes to route all payments against the financing done by the bank.

As in buyer finance, the key aspect of the credit evaluation relates to understanding the ecosystem of the large corporate and the strategic relationship with its suppliers, which allows the bank to assess supplier risk in the context of the large corporate's "halo effect" on its supply chain rather than on a standalone financials-based assessment.

The large corporate raises a PO on the supplier, who sends the same to the bank for availing pre-shipment facility against the PO. The bank typically pays up to 70% of the PO value to the supplier as a pre-shipment advance. The supplier processes the goods and ships the same to the large corporate, and also sends the post shipment documents to the bank to avail the balance payment against the PO as the post-shipment proceeds. On the due date, the large corporate funds the bank to liquidate the advance.

What is the Bank's Value Proposition to the Suppliers?

The bank is able to add value to large corporate's recommended suppliers around the following:

- Fund them for the additional working capital required for which the large corporate is unable/unwilling to extend advance, thus, squeezing the receivables turnover period for the supplier.
- Provide financing to suppliers on a relatively unsecured basis, thus, relieving the need for the suppliers to secure their lines with collateral.
- Provide financing at competitive rates to the suppliers as the suppliers risk assessment is not being done solely on a stand-alone basis.

Benefits to the Large Corporate

- The large corporate is freed from the cost arising out of the requirement of placing advance with the supplier and can ask for better pricing from the supplier on account of the finance made available through the bank.
- The large corporate is able to offer an attractive financing option to its suppliers and, thus, capture "channel loyalty".
- The large corporate's payables cycle is increased.
- The large corporate may be able to avail cash discounts which is offered by its suppliers.

Benefits to the Bank from SCF Products

SCF can put the foot into the door for a relationship between the bank and the large corporate by providing a product which offers predominantly off-balance sheet solution. This relationship can be further explored for cross-selling other products like traditional trade finance, deposits and cash management.

Additionally, through the SCF products, the bank can grow its middle market/ SME base in a relatively tough credit environment, which would not have been possible on a bilateral basis.

Over a period of time, the bank closely monitors the distribution and procurement channel of the large corporate and can become a strategic advisor to the large corporate in its strategy implementation.

Key Success Factors of the Product

- Choosing the right customer is essential to run an SCF program.
- Understanding the customer business is the key to structuring a financing program appropriate to that market/industry/product segment.
- High level of large corporate support significantly enhances the underlying credit comfort in the transaction especially in a difficult credit market.

A Win-win Solution

In short, SCF solutions create a multitude of benefits and a win-win situation for companies and their trading partners. Well-structured SCF solutions provide them with access to more capital on favorable terms allowing for higher inventory levels, more competitive pricing, and the ability to react to rapidly changing market demand.

(Sameer Sawhney is a Regional Head Transactional Banking, India & South Asia, Standard Chartered Bank.)

Supply Chain Finance – A New Kid on the Block

– Amit Singh Sisodiya and Akhil Thandulwadikar

Banks have provided Working Capital Finance (WCF) services to companies for a long time now. However, while providing finance for its day-to-day activities to an organization, banks usually looked at the particular entity (supplier or an original equipment manufacturer) in isolation, which provided a very narrow view of the company's credit-worthiness. But a new innovation in the field of WCF is all set to change this scenario. Supply Chain Financing (SCF), an advanced version of WCF has become very popular with both banks as well as customers because of the convenience it offers to a major manufacturer as well as its suppliers and distributors and also the banks themselves. In SCF, banks finance the suppliers and distributors of major Original Equipment Manufacturers (OEMs), i.e., the value chain starting from the supplier to an OEM and ending with the distributor, thus, ensuring a smooth flow of material in the value chain. Shyamji Mehrotra, Deputy General Manager, Allahabad Bank agrees, "SCF is an innovative finance mechanism by which bank meet the various funds requirements of suppliers/distributors, thus helping their seamless cash flow meet their working capital needs. It is a more advanced and sophisticated version of the age-old working capital financing. It covers the entire gamut of financing both the suppliers and vendors side."

The benefits of SCF, however, are limited to those suppliers/distributors that are associated with major OEMs and only those banks with a high level of IT integration can afford to provide this service. This means that smaller banks still have a long way to go before they too begin financing the value chain. Nevertheless, the concept seems to have a bright future.

How SCF Works

In case of financing the supplier, the banks open a line of credit to the suppliers after consultation with the OEM. The line of credit is specific to the product that the vendor supplies to the OEM. The OEM gives a guarantee to its supplier for a specified offtake of raw material over the year. The vendor approaches the banks on the basis of a recommendation given by the OEM and obtains better financing services for its working capital. The vendor then has to make sure that he supplies the material on time so as to be able to pay the bank. The payment from the OEM could be routed through an escrow account which ensures that the payment by the OEM is not diverted by the vendor to some other party.

Financing suppliers is considered very safe for the bank as there is little risk involved. First, because they approach only decent sized OEMs and second because the OEMs back the credit risk as they provide a guarantee to the supplier. The OEM benefits as it gets smooth supplies from the vendor and its working capital burden is also reduced. The supplier benefits because he gets cheap finance for its working capital needs.

This way all the three parties are benefitted; the banks save a lot of processing work, the OEM gets assured payments as compared to the system of supplying against Post Dated Cheques (PDCs) and the distributor finances his working capital at a low interest rate. However, banks consider supplier finance a safer option as compared to distributor finance which is considered to entail a higher risk.

Tech-savvy banks are usually better equipped to handle the financing of distributors as it involves handling of large amounts of data related to the customer. This also helps them provide data provision services to the customers. Whenever an OEM wants to have a look at the data related to a particular distributor he can get it from the banks. This way they save a lot of Management Information System (MIS)-related work at their offices.

Contd...

Contd...

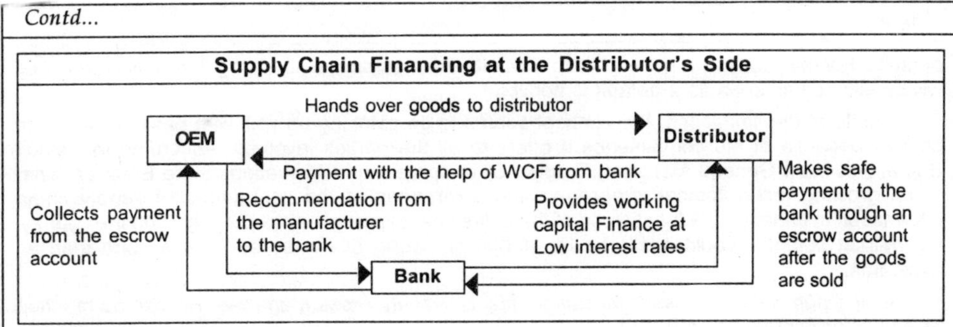

Challenges

In spite of the convenience it offers to a bank, and the value chain around an OEM there are certain challenges a bank has to over come before it decides to provide SCF. Some of these challenges are:

Information Technology

IT plays a major role in the functioning of SCF. SCF being a data-intensive activity relies heavily on the IT network of the value chain. If a value chain lacks proper connectivity then it is difficult for the banks to access all the data about the suppliers/distributors/OEMs. Without a proper information network, the monitoring of the performance of the borrowers also becomes a tedious task for the banks hence they may face a high default risk.

Geographical Reach

IT has removed the geographical barriers in most of the areas it finds application. But in SCF geographical reach plays a major role. The value chain of a particular industry maybe spread across the globe which makes it important for a bank to have presence in a particular area in order to be able to finance a supplier/distributor.

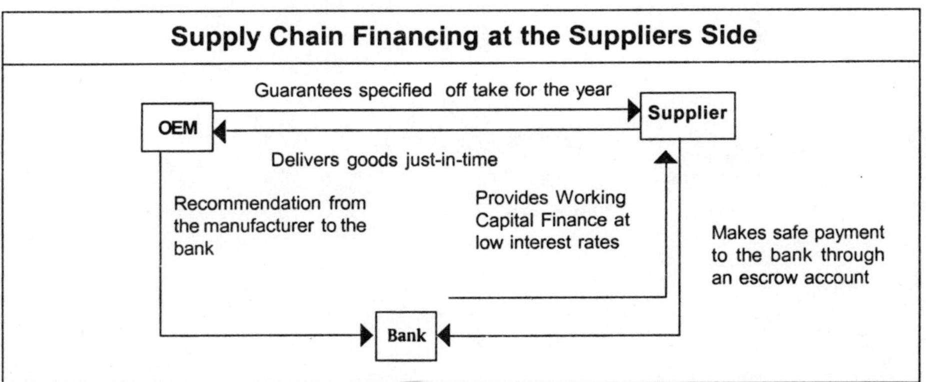

Identifying Bad Borrowers

Bad borrowers present yet another challenge for a bank. Because a bank depends on its OEM customers for identifying a prospective borrower, it needs to have in place a system which enables them to weed out bad borrowers at the slightest hints of a default. Shyamji Mehrotra says, "Since selection of beneficiaries is dependent on the quality of customers/suppliers of the corporate, a major challenge before the bank is weeding out bad borrowers on the slightest of

Contd...

Contd...

defaults. For this, banks will have to keep a monitoring mechanism so strong that redial measures will be initiated as soon as a default is noticed."

In spite of the limitations, the concept seems to be catching up well with banks around the country because of the convenience it offers to all the parties involved. According to Rajeev Sathe, Assistant General Manager, Product Development and Marketing, State Bank of India, "With growing technological integration and awareness of the usefulness of supply chain information to enhance the functioning of the entire chain among major OEMs around the country, the market potential could easily be Rs.30,000 cr." Soon SCF may become a norm than an exception.

(Amit Singh Sisodiya, Assistant Editor, Icfai University Press Magazine. He can be reached at amitsingh@icfaipress.org and

Akhil Thandulwadikar, Research Associate, Icfai University Press Magazine. He can be reached at akhil@icfaipress.org).

Source: Chartered Financial Analyst, September 2005.

12

RFID in Postal and Courier Services

Libor Švadlenka

Today, postal operations have implemented RFID in various closed-loop systems to measure, monitor, and improve operations. For example, RFID is being used to monitor international mail service between major hubs. The article explains that RFID (Radio Frequency Identification) can help postal and courier services by Tracking and tracing, Workload and transportation planning, and Asset management and security. RFID (Radio Frequency Identification)-tracked mailbags, which provide delivery status, have already been created for priority mail services. Tagged mailbags are automatically read at specific points in the network to provide this automated track-and-trace capability.

1. Introduction

Radio frequency identification (RFID) is an increasingly mainstream technology, whose mechanics are fairly simple: at various points along the supply chain, objects such as pallets, cases, carts and packages are detected by RFID readers. Mounted at a warehouse bay or truck entrance, or integrated with a portable handheld device, these readers detect an RFID tag mounted on the object and access the electronic product code (EPC) that has been programmed into the tag. In the

Source: Pošta, Telekomunikácie a Elektronický obchod, 2006.

future, this information will then be stored on an EPC global Network and accessed by eligible trading partners for use in supply chain management and other business applications. In this way, any object or container becomes intelligent and interactive, without the need for line-of-sight relationships, such as those required by bar codes.

The potential market for RFID in the postal and courier service is second only to that for the retail supply chain as shown in Figure 1.

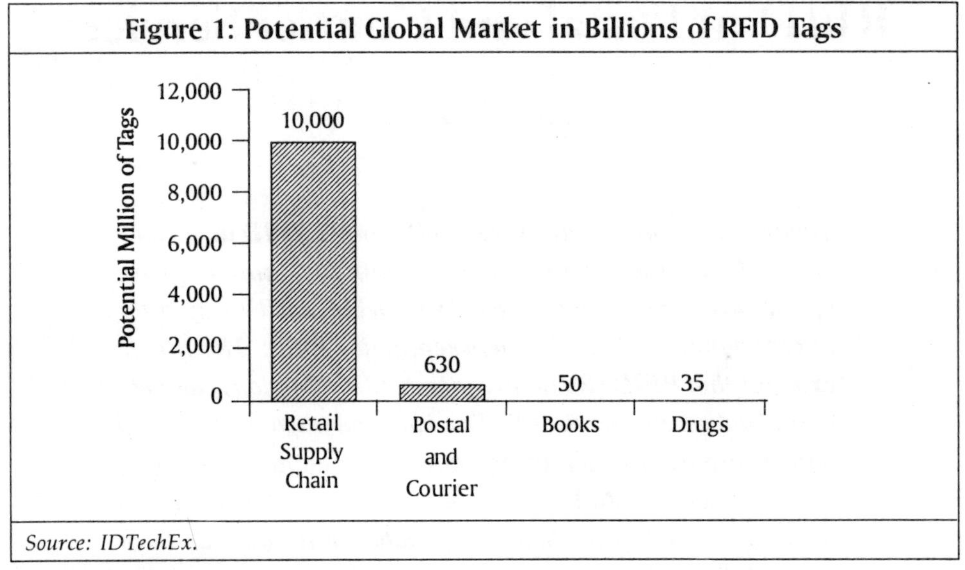

Figure 1: Potential Global Market in Billions of RFID Tags

Source: IDTechEx.

2. Brief History and Future

The earliest development of an RFID-like technology was in the 1940s for aircraft recognition systems. Later, in the 1960s and 1970s, RFID was evolved for use in nuclear weapon and railroad car tracking systems. These areas had needs for tracking critical or expensive items that could tolerate the high costs of tags and readers available at the time. The first large-scale applications came in the 1980s for cattle identification, where tags were actually imbedded under the animals' skin. Therefore, RFID is not a new technology; tagging has been around for more than half a century.

It is very likely that RFID will experience explosive growth in the next few years. This will be driven by adoption among prominent consumer products manufacturers and retailers as the next evolution beyond bar codes. For example the world's largest retailer – Wal-Mart, the world's fifth largest retailer – Metro, the largest retailer in the UK – Tesco, and the US Department of Defense already announced they will require vendors to adopt RFID for some applications. These organizations will adopt a form of the EPC for their purposes although using different flavors of the EPC standard. For global development of this technology is evidently necessary to harmonize their various standards into one global standard, however this will take some time due to the origins of each organization.

However, the ultimate consequence of such a dramatic increase in RFID usage will be price reductions, and improvements in quality and features of tags. Other organizations can look forward to a much easier time with RFID as the groundswell builds around these early adopters.

3. RFID Opportunities

The first opportunity from RFID is *lowering the cost of information.* Today, business information is often conveyed by a combination of bar codes and electronic data interchange (EDI) between computers. However, there are significant shortcomings:

- bar codes need to be physically oriented to be seen by a reader and must be read sequentially,
- bar codes cannot be changed once printed and are susceptible to dirt or scuffing,
- though the information connected with a bar code can be dynamic, transferring it to the point-of-need (typically the scan location) quickly and efficiently is highly uncertain.

In contrast, RFID tags do not need to be seen to be read, they can be read at a distance, even through or around many materials. Tags can electronically store large amounts of information, which can be changed and updated. And, since information is, by definition, attached to the thing itself, it's always available right at the point of use, without being separately transmitted. These features lower the labor needed.

The second opportunity from RFID is *increasing information accuracy.* By allowing information to be captured and stored instantly, wherever it is most convenient, RFID helps ensure the information is correct. In fact, because RFID increases the instances in which humans can be taken out of the loop altogether, it can help raise accuracy levels to near perfection.

Finally, RFID tags can *capture and convey new kinds of information* that are difficult or impossible to get using traditional methods. Tags can be made unique and they can easily carry encrypted authentication information. RFID tags can also be combined with sensors on a chip, making it possible to have tags actually collect data about conditions they experience.

4. RFID Threats

While RFID offers undeniable benefits, there are several dangers for organizations that apply it. Perhaps the greatest concerns involve *privacy.* The idea that things might be uniquely identifiable and tracked by an invisible sea of radio waves makes many people nervous. Several recent efforts to apply RFID commercially on a large scale have been delayed until privacy concerns are addressed.

Standards are lacking for commercial applications. There are starting points for important applications, like the electronic product code (EPC) – analogous to the common universal product code – for marking consumer products. However, few standards exist for many important applications. Initial efforts by the Universal Postal Union have created standards for RFID information encoding.

RFID usage can put *large demands on back-end computer systems.* When an item is being read automatically over and over and generating hoards of data (compared to bar codes) each time, transaction volumes on supporting systems can grow enormously.

Early adopters will need to balance many complex trade-offs when choosing which RFID technologies to use. Radio-frequency bands, tag formats, data encoding schemes, reader technologies, the items to be tagged and the environments where they will be used all need to be considered during system design. The options are complex and subtle, meaning that expert advice is all but essential to arriving at the best solution.

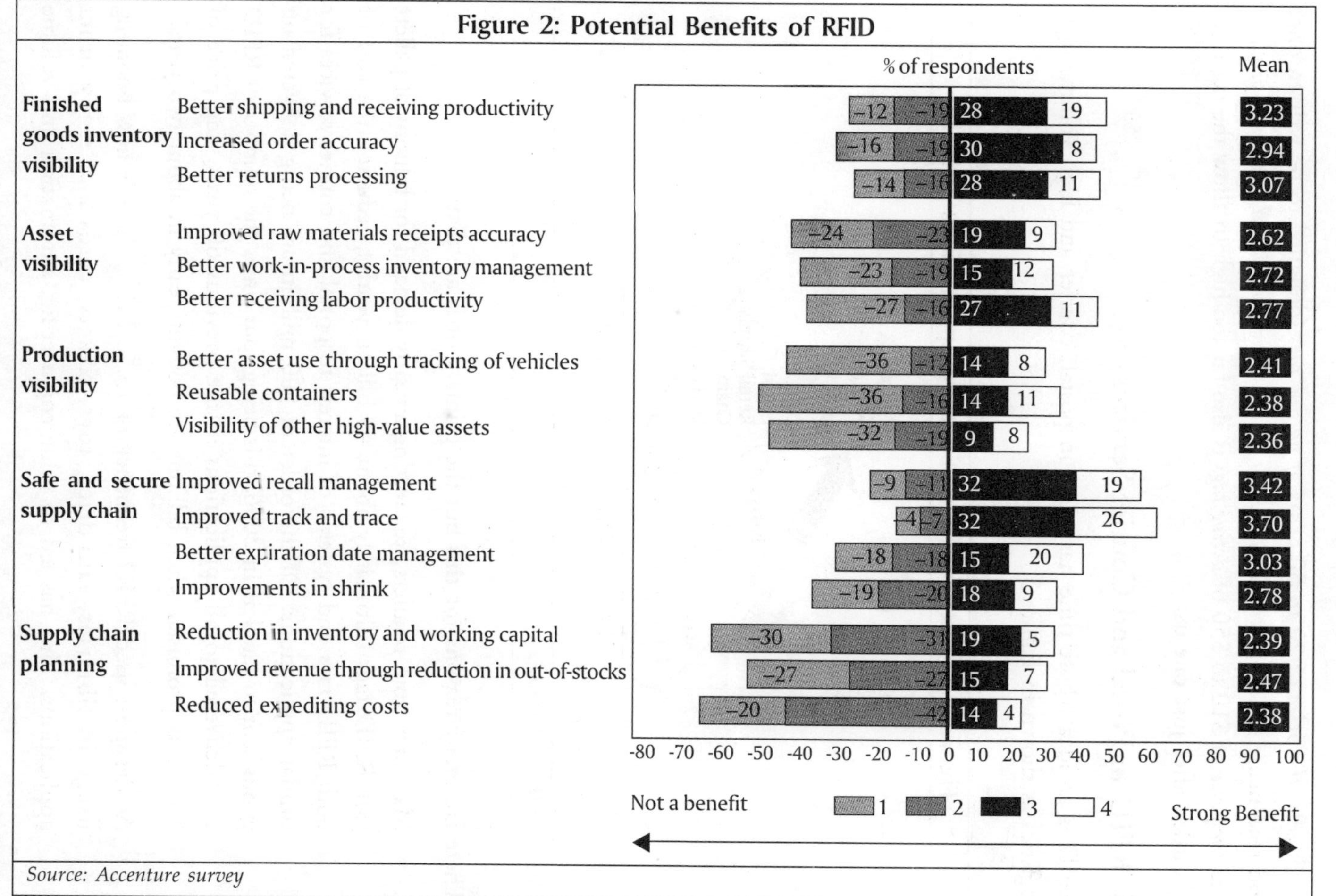

Figure 2: Potential Benefits of RFID

Source: Accenture survey

Finally, *the price* of 20 to 50 cents *of passive tags* (designed to be written once and read many times) is *still far too high for marking individual consumer products* and *the price* of \$10 to \$50 of *active tags* is also far too high to allow the tag to be discarded after just one use.

5. RFID in Postal and Courier Services

RFID is an idea whose time has come in postal, courier and high volume light logistics as shown in Figure 3.

Figure 3: Evolution of Cost-Effective Applications of RFID

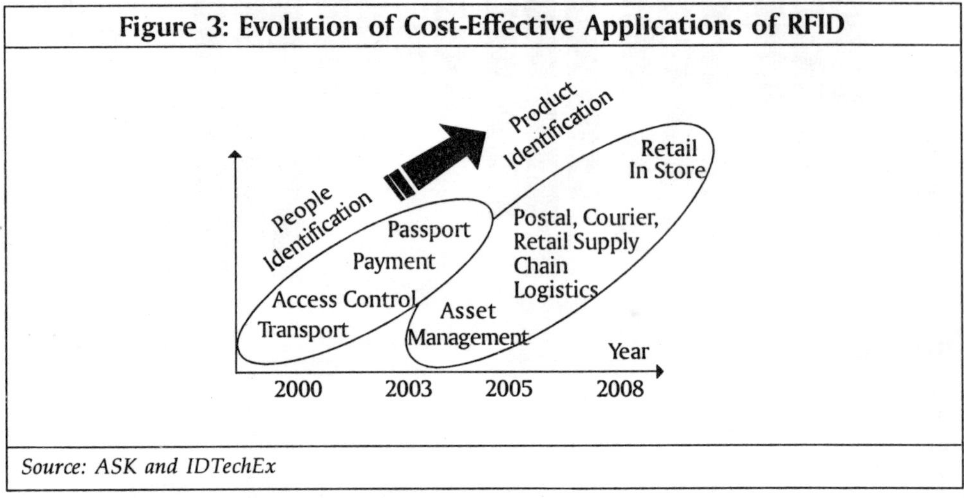

Source: ASK and IDTechEx

There are many reasons for this but the primary ones are that:

- Mandates from retailers are creating a yearly demand for billions of pallet/ case RFID tags (ultimately about 40 billion yearly), reducing the cost of both RFID tags and systems of interest to postal and courier services for similar applications. Of the order of 500 million are being delivered on goods sent to retailers in 2006, this being four times the number of RFID tags delivered to all applications in the previous 60 years. Tag price of 5 cents is promised when billions are bought yearly in about two years.
- At the most used RFID frequency of 13.56 MHz, there is now booming usage in libraries, laundries, toys, tickets, cards and many other applications. This has led to value engineering, automation and volume

production with prices of RFID tags and systems tumbling down and one billion RFID labels delivered in 60 years but the next billion RFID labels will be delivered under two years. Tag price reductions are in prospect here too. Indeed, this frequency is low enough for printed transistor circuits to be an option in 2007 and in mass use as labels by 2015. These replace the silicon chip, promising one cent price or less for complete RFID labels and eventually (after 2016?) direct printing onto items, just like barcodes today.

- Several companies (for example DAG Systems, SUBTROPIC) now offer or facilitate passive tags and systems that work at two to ten meters range and are usually more tolerant of water and metal than the old one. Using its new HF system based on new Schreiner RFID labels, it even reads metal cases at up to one meter when obscured by other metal cases. Only one year ago, those teaching RFID would say that HF tags, while being by far the most popular type, with over 55% of the market by value, could never work above one meter range and they only achieve one meter in a relatively unimpeded environment.
- For longer ranges (10 meters to two kilometers), tags with batteries are needed and here there is an advance from large devices with large batteries to ones with coin batteries and even many with printed batteries where the RFID tag takes the form of a label that may even act as a recorder of temperature, humidity etc at low cost. There are also new ways of locating things using beams with these active tags and ways of incorporating WiFi, ZigBee, Bluetooth, GPS or GSM for location and communication.
- Postal sorting machinery, fork lifts and other equipment is now increasingly available in RFID enabled form.

Today, postal operations have implemented RFID in various closed-loop systems to measure, monitor, and improve operations. For example, RFID is being used to monitor international mail service between major hubs. By randomly "seeding" tagged letters into trays, elapsed delivery time can be measured. This allows service issues to be identified and addressed in a reliable and cost-effective manner.

Other postal operations have piloted tracking mail containers to measure trailer utilization and to track container locations. Manual container tracking systems tend to break down when volumes are high and there's a deadline to meet departure times. By allowing information to be captured automatically, RFID makes sure it is done, even under stressful conditions. Postal managers can rely on the information to make decisions that improve transportation costs and to relocate containers when needed.

RFID-tracked mailbags, which provide delivery status, have already been created for priority mail services. Tagged mailbags are automatically read at specific points in the network to provide this automated track-and-trace capability.

Four additional areas can benefit from the cheap, accurate, and pervasive information obtained using RFID. Each of them has the prospect for returning substantial monetary benefits, as well as having the potential to significantly upgrade postal service capabilities, an ever more important consideration in the competitive delivery market.

5.1 Track and Trace

Most postal services provide at least a limited form of track and trace, particularly for premium delivery services. Today, tracking uses bar codes. Switching to RFID tags can lower tracking labor by eliminating the need for most manual piece handling. It can also allow many more checkpoints to be conveniently captured within the postal network. Clearly such a pervasive use of tracking would increase the information volume handled by back-end systems.

5.2 Workload and Transportation Planning

Either in combination with pervasive mail piece tracking, or in conjunction with higher-level container tracking, it will be possible to capture much more reliable real-time information on workload volumes within the postal network. This kind of information is at the heart of efforts to make the mail sortation and transportation networks more dynamic. It will be much more practical to adjust routings to lower transport costs and speed mail efficiently through the network. The same information can also be used to bring about more efficient utilization of the postal labor force. By including both available and constrained capacities within the labor force, the flow of mail can be optimized.

5.3 Asset Management

RFID can also be used to track items other than mail: vehicles, trailers, rail cars, and various containers, for example. These are expensive assets representing an enormous capital investment within the network and their availability continually affects the capacity of the network. Pervasive, reliable tracking of these assets using RFID makes it practical to know where everything is and allows for better informed decisions to balance resources.

5.4 Security

The value of the previous opportunities varies with each operator's environment, but everyone shares the need to dramatically increase the security of mail movements. RFID can play a central role in helping provide higher levels of mail security. By enabling continuous monitoring of access and other factors, RFID can promote physical security, which is further enhanced using RFID's ability to provide authentication services for mail, and by capturing more refined information on mailers and recipients.

6. Practical Usage of RFID in Postal and Courier Services

6.1 Deutsche Post/DHL Europe

Deutsche Post (after DHL acquisition) ships about 27 billion items yearly, DHL being responsible for one billion yearly. DHL has carried out successful item level tagging using 13.56 MHz tags and wishes to tag everything in this way using EPC coding. In 2005 it has been assessing bids for a 1 billion requirement for HF tags and associated systems. Cost reduction and service improvement are the main objectives but crime reduction is also a possibility. Trevor Peirce from DHL, speaking at Smart Labels USA 2004, said they intend to roll-out using 13.56 MHz, which they are satisfied will be robust enough for their purposes.

6.2 UPS Trucks

UPS is a follower in RFID. The company began a series of pilot tests in 2004 on both its package delivery business and its supply chain solutions business, which serve many customers who must comply with upcoming RFID mandates. In one trial, passive RFID tags are replacing bar codes on reusable fibreboard tote boxes used to shuttle packages through UPS's automated facilities. The objective is to extend the life of the tote boxes and to reduce the read-failure rates of the barcodes, which tend to wear off over time. In another pilot, RFID tags have been attached to UPS trucks in an effort to monitor cost-effectively vehicle activity moving on and off the property at three different locations.

6.3 UPS Tote Boxes

Much of the work to date has involved tinkering with the details of specific applications to achieve the right costs and performance trade-offs. For example, UPS has tried to balance the longevity of the tote box with the life of the tag, or to balance distance from the reader with the speed of the truck. Another challenge has been reducing the high rate of reader failures. UPS sees many opportunities to expand its use of RFID, particularly by starting to tag sensitive items. The handling of hazardous materials and high-value items, which currently require more human involvement are a priority here.

6.4 Swedish Post

Swedish Post has a parcel that detects and records tampering using RFID and other innovations abound, including RFID cards controlling driver access to postal vehicles and RFID enabled postal sorting equipment.

6.5 Taiwan's Chunghwa Post and Microsoft's Interest

Very interesting is the fact that company as large as Microsoft has entered postal market due to RFID. The global potential is illustrated by its decision to offer its first postal systems in Taiwan and elsewhere in East Asia. Concretely in late 2005, Microsoft started marketing its new RFID system for postal and courier services at a stamp exhibition in Taiwan. It wishes to persuade the Taiwan government postal service with a device it claims can ensure the smooth, safe and recorded delivery of tagged packages and parcels. Taiwan's Chunghwa Post company, is now considering whether to use the Microsoft RFID package.

7. Conclusion

RFID is a technology that has achieved its time. It's real, it works, and it's making never-before processes possible. Organizations that find ways to explore RFID, and at the same time create benefits, will be in the best position to leap ahead of their competitors as the systems mature and costs drop even further.

As I already said there is a great potential for RFID in the postal and courier service market because there are several possibilities to use it starting with track and trace to postal RFID system that completely automates the whole process of mail delivery from accepting the package to classification and dispatching.

Big, especially international, postal companies fully realize the significance of this technology and may try to apply it into their operation.

Although there are some difficulties restraining the development of this technology (especially the price of passive or active tags), it stands to reason that this problem will also be solved and this technology will replace current standard of automatic identification – bar codes with regard to evident benefits of RFID compared to bar codes.

(Libor Švadlenka, Ph.D., University of Pardubice, The Jan Perner Transport Fakulty, Department of Transport Management, Marketing and Logistics, Studentská 95, 532 10 Pardubice, Czech Republic, tel.: +420466036375, fax: +420466036374, e-mail: Libor.Svadlenka@upce.cz).

References

[1] The role of RFID in supply chain planning. [online]. Accenture 2005. [cit. 2006-02-01]. available from WWW: *<http://www.accenture.com/Global/Services/By_Subject/Supply_Chain_Mgmt/default. htm>*.

[2] RFID Applications for Postal Operations. [online]. Accenture 2004. [cit. 2006-02-01]. available from WWW: *<http://www.postalproject.com/documents.asp?d_ID=2490>*.

[3] RFID in the Postal Service. [online]. MoreRFID 2005. [cit. 2006-06-02]. available from WWW: *<http://www.morerfid.com/details.php?subdetail=Report&action=details&report_id=825&display=RFID>*.

[4] FABUS, J, GALOVIÈ, M., KREMEÒOVÁ, I. RFID a ich pouzitic v rámci liberalizácie poštových trhov. In KREMEÒOVÁ, I. (ed.) POSTPOINT 2005 : 28. - 30. September 2005. FPEDAS University of Zilina. Zilina : University of Zilina, 2005. p. 83-87. ISBN 80-8070-454-6.

FedEx Plans Freighter Service Between India, China by September

– Tunia Cherian George

GLOBAL express cargo carrier FedEx Express plans to introduce five weekly freighter services between India and China by September. This service would make Federal Express the only company from India offering a next-day service to China.

According to the Chairman and Managing Director for the Indian Sub-continent, Mr. Jacques Creeten, the additional flights proposed to improve connectivity in Asia would be operated on the US-India-China-Japan route.

The service, which is being planned to tap the growing business opportunities in India and China, would also help FedEx double its volume, expand its network and add to its customers.

Making use of the hub-and-spoke operational network, the express carrier currently operates five weekly West-bound flights and a once-weekly East-bound flight from India.

While the West-bound flights are operated on the Philippines-India-Middle East-France-US route, the East-bound flight is operated on the US-France-India-Philippines sector.

Asked if FedEx was considering an entry into the domestic business, Mr Creeten said the express carrier was specialised in the international time-definite high-value cargo business. An entry into the domestic network would only make sense if the company saw synergies between its international and the domestic business.

"This synergy does not exist at the moment and we will need evidence before we make any decision on entering the domestic business," he said.

The proposed take over of Blue Dart by DHL, its competitor in the global markets, would not impact FedEx, which was driven by global networks. He pointed out that FedEx was the single largest global cargo carrier accounting for 10.64 per cent of the global cargo.

"At the moment, the way international business is growing all our immediate investments would continue to be in growing our global business," he said.

FedEx saw greater opportunity in the international business and the biggest investments by the company would continue to be in aircrafts and technology, he said.

The company's technology investments would go to furthering technology support for inventory management as well as to enhance customer knowledge, he said.

Source: The Hindu Businessline, Friday, January 14, 2005

13

SCM in Healthcare Industry

Sathish Kumar Nagarajan

Supply chain improves inventory management with accurate medical supply and equipment orders, tailored to the patient's needs, and delivered on-time. The article describes how SCM improves patient care through a centralized database that can be accessed from different locations with less time consumption. This article discusses ways to improve the procurement process by automating the complete procure-to-pay process and analyzing purchase transactions to further drive continuous processes improvement through SCM. Finally, the article emphasizes on improved efficiencies and streamlines operations to generate significant cost savings through SCM.

Healthcare Organizations – An Overview

Today's healthcare organizations (HCOs) are struggling under enormous pressure to streamline operations and to provide quality care to the patients. Most of them are forced to shut down due to increase in the cost of day-to-day operations, which does not become visible as healthcare organizations are characterized by multiple operating units or subsidiaries.

The healthcare industry is the sole largest industry in the United States of America. A recent congressional report released in USA states that the current healthcare industry in the United States of America comprises over 7,50,000 physicians, 5200 hospitals and approximately 3.8 million inpatients and 20 million outpatients. In terms of qualified labor force and subsidiary jobs within the healthcare industry, it is projected that one in every 11 US residents works in the healthcare industry. Due to heavy competition among the healthcare organizations, almost all the HCOs are turning towards business process reengineering. Driven by the anxiety to deliver quality care under the constraints of time and money, all the HCOs are turning to information technology (IT) to achieve a competitive advantage. The ultimate goal of the HCOs is to deliver quality care to the patients. For quality medical care, it is very important to share appropriate patient information such as medical records, diagnoses and health plans. Apart from this, HCOs need to reduce cost of operations and eliminate inadequacy in internal administrative systems. To achieve these strategies, the solution for HCOs is an IT infrastructure that would integrate existing incongruent sources of information, hook up different branches and offices and provide uncomplicated and consistent access through intranet, extranet or internet.

Need for SCM in HCOs

The present healthcare industry comprises numerous business administration processes. This affects widespread flow of information between the different participants involved in the healthcare system. The stream of information among the various participants of the healthcare system is very fragmented. To overcome this, hospitals should have better communication with each other and also with the doctors in private practice. The doctors should also communicate with each other and with pharmacies, external laboratories and the paying authorities. In HCOs administrative processes such as hospitalization, inpatient records, outpatient records, medical appointments, accounting, sick-leave certification, and issuing prescriptions and orders are utterly time-consuming. The exchange of information is often impaired, thereby taking even more time and incurring additional costs.

The IT industries have shifted their focus to healthcare organizations and they are tactically positioned to become an influential supporter to the healthcare industry as it strives to implement well-managed and cost-efficient strategies.

Emerging information technologies can offer HCOs uncomplicated administrative billing practices as well as improved clinical treatment services through expert information systems, computer-based patient records, and other advanced information technologies.

Even though the healthcare industry has been slower than other industry sectors in implementing SCM, e-business and other IT solutions, most of the leading HCOs are focused on implementing SCM and various IT solutions. Implementing SCM system in HCOs provides the following benefits:

- Reduced paper-based patients record
- Reduced error rate
- Improved delivery of healthcare services
- Ease fraud detection
- Order entry system
- Reduced spillover effects
- Financial and cost accounting information systems
- Qualitative improvements in patient care
- Patient flow system
- Administrative information system
- Pharmacy and materials management information systems
- Human resources management information system
- Patient relationship management system
- Laboratory information system
- Operation theatre system
- e-procurement system of medical supplies
- Telemedicine system
- e-learning system.

Figure 1: Different Actors in HCO Supply Chain

Service Receivers	Service Providers	Paying Authorities
• Patients	• Hospitals	• Private HI
	• Doctors, Dentists	• Statutory HI
	• Care Facilities	• Other Insurance
	• Pharmacies	• Patients
	• Pharmaceutical Industry	
	• Other Therapists	

Figure 1 illustrates the actors in a Healthcare Organization.

Challenges for Implementing SCM System in HCOs

Implementing SCM System in healthcare organizations is more challenging than implementing it in other industries. This is because it is more difficult to forecast anything with regard to HCOs since a healthcare provider should manage many different processes, each having unpredictable outcomes. Also, the treatment of each patient varies from another in terms of processes, staffing, reports and facilities used.

In HCOs the delivery processes are labor-intensive where the chief cost for healthcare organizations is labor, unlike manufacturing where the primary cost is raw materials. Therefore, HCOs need to have their primary focus on managing staff and care processes; hence their SCM system must be designed with these perspectives in consideration. The HCOs still face challenges in converting their existing system to an SCM system. Healthcare organizations rely upon a network of relationships between physicians, hospitals, laboratories, patients, insurance companies, government agencies, and employers/staff, and all of these relationships must be integrated in the SCM system. Also, a healthcare SCM system must integrate the activities of various service provider entities of the HCOs that may have significantly different resource requirements.

SCM in Healthcare Organizations

Implementing SCM system in HCOs reduces the complexity of the work process and improves the reliability and robustness of the data involved in the process. A core SCM system can integrate and assist the healthcare organizations in achieving their objectives in key areas such as:

- **Data Warehousing:** Storing of a large amount of clinical, financial, administrative and operational information in an integrated centralized decision support database that provides instantaneous uncomplicated access to healthcare practitioners. It provides reliability and security to the information through authentication capability.
- **Computer-based Patient Records:** A computer-based patient record is a computerized collection of all clinical and organizational/administrative information relating to the care of a single patient. These electronic records contain information such as patient information, lab reports, pharmaceutical receipts, and billing information. The computer-based patient record provides ability to have immediate access to information from the centralized database. It reduces 60% of the time consumed to retrieve the patient record manually. It provides accurate and up-to-date information to healthcare practitioners. Since a computer-based patient record contains the real-time information about a patient's medical history, it helps healthcare practitioners to provide better care to their patients. SCM system allows the computer-based patient records to link with the laboratory, nursing, pharmacy, administrative and clinical decision support systems which helps healthcare practitioners to deliver healthcare services effectively.
- **Document Imaging:** It is the process of scanning and storing images in an electronic format from the paper form. These electronic images can be shared and accessed by the clinicians and administrators in various geographic locations.
- **Expert Information Systems:** All HCOs have a set of rules that are involved in delivering care for that particular treatment. The Expert Information System applies these rules in order to assist physicians in the administration of healthcare services. Expert Information System plays the role of an effective decision-making system in HCOs.
- **Telemedicine:** It is the process by which HCOs can distribute medical services and information from one geographical location to another.
- **Materials Management:** Material management provides features like ordering, invoicing, logistics and payment for supplies and equipments from different vendors and service providers of HCO.

- **Prescription Ordering:** Prescription ordering is the process through which HCOs place an order with a pharmacy for the delivery of medication.
- **Test Ordering and Results Reporting:** These transactions include the ordering of lab tests by physicians and return reports generated by a lab specialist.
- **Coordinating Benefits:** It is a process used by HCOs to resolve which payer is financially responsible for the reimbursement of previously delivered healthcare services.
- **Referrals and Pre-authorizations:** This process involves sending the patient to another provider for the purpose of receiving treatment.
- **Provider Appointing and Scheduling:** This process provides the facility to schedule the hospital facilities and other resources of the HCO.

Figure 2 illustrates the integrated process in a Healthcare Organization.

Figure 2: Integrated Process in HCO

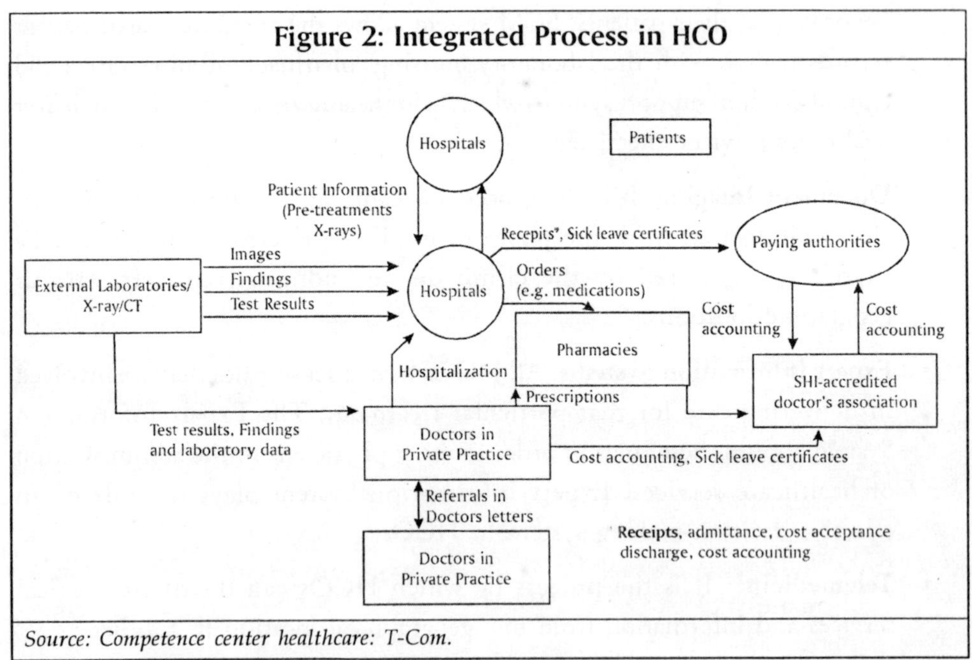

Source: Competence center healthcare: T-Com.

Medicine Supply Chain

Medicines play a vital role in healthcare organizations. They save lives and allow people to receive healthcare facilities which can provide preventive treatment. Medicines can also help in reducing the cost of healthcare. The important elements to be considered for medicine supply chain are as follows:

- Consolidation of drug/medicine procurement process
- Demand Planning
- Inventory Management.

Consolidation of the drug/medicine procurement process: A consolidated medicine procurement process can ensure benefits such as reducing cost and improving services. The leading healthcare organizations should have centralized purchases, simplifying processes and increasing transparency.

Demand Planning: It is very important for healthcare organizations to maintain the right drugs in stock. Healthcare facilities must accurately predict the medicines they need and manage the supplies they have. Most of the organizations face problems due to inconsistent methodologies and a lack of understanding the real demand for each hospital or health center. There are two popular methods to estimate demand for medicine:

i. Estimation, depending on the information available and historical data of medicine to predict the future needs.

ii. With limited historical data, the morbidity method forecasts demand for medicines based on the expected number of diseases and their treatments.

Inventory Management: Implementing a good inventory management system can enhance the level of service and reduce costs of the medicine supply chain. The two best methods are Pull System and Push System (See Figure 3).

i. In a Pull System, each level of the supply chain determines the medicines and quantity to be ordered by using the formula that considers demand patterns, distribution frequencies, costs and inventory levels.

ii. In a Push System, a higher level in the supply chain determines the medicines and the quantity required.

Figure 3: Inventory Management

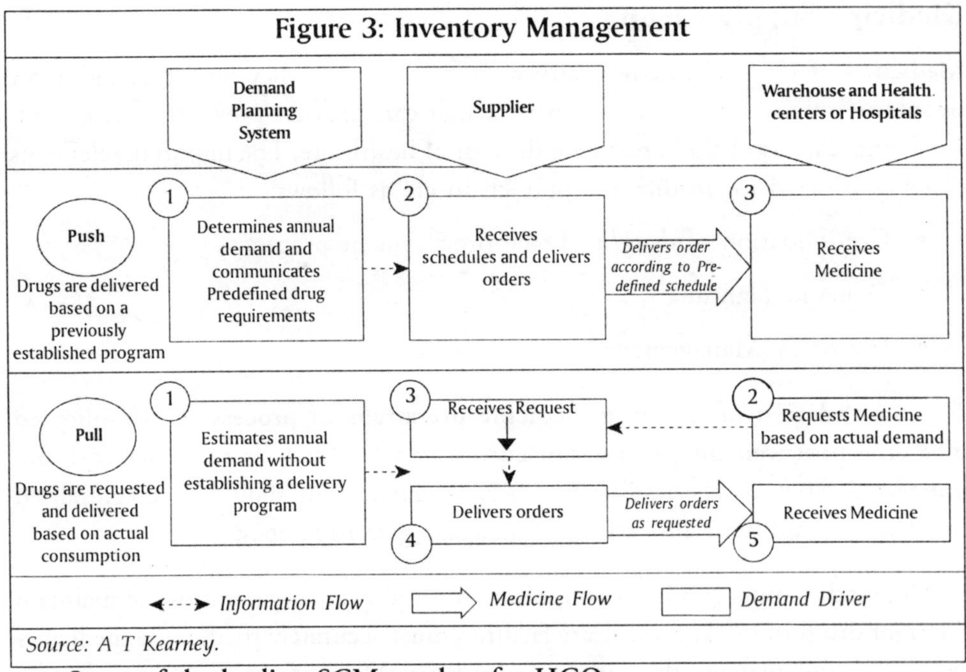

Source: A T Kearney.

Some of the leading SCM vendors for HCO:

- SAP
- IBM
- The Sage Group
- Oracle.

Table 1 illustrates the percentage of SCM implementations in the industry.

Table 1: SCM Implementation in Various Industries (in percent)

Industry Sector	Percentage
Logistics	57.2
Banking and Finance	52.9
Insurance	48.1
Retail Distribution	35.5
Process Manufacturing	34.9
Wholesale Distribution	33.3
Healthcare	21.8

Case Study: SAP for Healthcare Organization:

"SAP has given our hospital the opportunity to work with a state-of-the-art technology" .

– Jesus Diaz Garaygordobil,
Marketing and Information Technology Director, Hospital San Jose

SAP provides SCM solution called ***mySAP*** for healthcare organizations which integrates the latest medical technologies and adapts itself to evolving medical IT structures and clinical processes. SAP provides a set of solutions to streamline end-to-end operations from care planning, to patient care, to aftercare management and from materials procurement to sales and billing. SAP helps out the healthcare organizations in the following ways:

- Increases healthcare business relationship between clinical and administrative departments, physicians, healthcare providers and payers through a user-friendly portal which improves the sharing of information between the various departments and provides apparent system-wide information.
- Increases the quality of patient care through well-defined treatment plans and regulating quickly to patient demands.
- Improves process effectiveness in procurement processes, patient accounting, billing, and workforce deployment.
- Minimizes risk of system distraction and provides a reliable information system.

Hospital San José in Mexico is a non-profit, self-funding hospital committed to providing maximum level of care to its patients. Implementation of SAP helped them in achieving their goal and Hospital San José became the first organization in Central America to successfully implement SAP. Hospital San José comprises 1,200 employees/staffs, 400 physicians and medical professionals. It treats thousands of people affected by various diseases and used different medical technologies which made the clinical and administrative process more complex. To overcome these complexities Hospital San José implemented its first SCM solution by SAP. mySAP SCM was implemented in October 2002. Implementation of SAP made various departments in the hospital communicate with each other without any interruption and solved problems like billing, manual patient records, and information issues. mySAP's integration and visibility brought accurate and up-to-date information that was accessible to various hospital staff and facilitated communication between the patient information department, laboratory, operating room, billing department and other sections. This in turn decreased the liability of managing equipments and inventories. It also improved the process of calculating and managing purchase and procurement. Since Hospital San José is a non-profit and self-funding hospital it must have a clear understanding of what needs to be billed, where revenue comes from and which materials are purchased. SAP enables the hospital to handle complex insurance reimbursement and itemized billing requirements.

Conclusion

The healthcare industry has been a late adopter of supply chain. Today's healthcare organizations are characterized by multiple operating units or subsidiaries which do not become visible in the costs of operation. Even today most of HCOs are not automated and integrated and still rely on paper-based transactions. SCM provides complete integration of the procurement and managerial process in HCOs. Implementing a successful Supply Chain System in the healthcare organization simplifies workforce management, streamlines the human resource process, integrates supply chain management, takes control of finances and enhances the security of the data.

(Sathish Kumar Nagarajan is a General Manager, Ammfo Systems India Pvt. Ltd., Chennai. He can be reached at administration@ammfosystems.com).

Reference

1. *www.atkearney.dk*
2. Thompson T G and D J Brailer, "The Decade of Healthcare Information Technology", United States Department of Health and Human Services, 2004.
3. *www.sap.com*
4. *www.academayforhalthcare.com*
5. *www.ahima.org*

14

Supply Chain Management in the Entertainment Industry

R Santhana Krishnan and D Thiyagarajan

Effective supply chain management in Entertainment Industry could solve most of the problems it is facing today. More than 100 billion gigabytes of contents in combination of images, text, audio, video, graphics or a combination of these circulates our homes, offices, hotels and other user desired areas through the legal or the illegal channels. The entertainment industry itself is to blame for this sorry state of affairs and the illegal operators merely capitalize on a consumer demand that sadly remains unfulfilled by the industry. This article discusses the drawbacks in the supply chain management system in the areas of Procurement side management, Inventory management, and Selling side management in the entertainment industry, and suggests how best these can be overcome. This article explores different media of entertainment in relation to Supply Chain Management and the future challenges in the Supply Chain Management.

Today entertainment has become a part of our lives. A situation has been reached today where work related stress is an everyday reality and entertainment is the only source to relieve our stress and make us mentally fit for future work loads. In this thriving industry more than 100 billion gigabytes of contents in images, text, audio, video, graphics or a combination of these circulates our homes, offices, hotels and other user desired areas through the legal channel or the illegal channel. Unlike a product, these can be easily stolen and reproduced from a main source and then circulated to many users without paying the legitimate owner a pie. Supply chain management in this industry poses a daunting challenge.

In order to attain productivity, streamlined procurement processes, optimal inventory levels, speedy delivery mechanisms and robust business intelligence at the point of customer contact will help. Very often, the industry is itself to blame for this sorry state of affairs and the illegal operators merely capitalize on a consumer demand that sadly remains unfulfilled by the industry. Let us see how.

- *Haphazard procurement process* results in total confusion. Procurement process varies so widely that it would be a different process for new films, old films, English films, foreign films and for regional films. It is this divergence that creates price differences and supply credibility on which others capitalize and swiftly deliver results.
- *Lack of optimal inventory levels* in the chain is because inventory is demand-oriented and not policy-oriented. Thus, all needs of the customer are not met by the industry leading to denial of a demand and then the customers starts looking at a grey market as a supply source.
- *Speedy delivery mechanism* industry sources are known for their inefficiency in this regard and the grey markets forte is its speedy delivery mechanism, in a jiffy you have it. They draw consumers magnetically.
- *Robust business intelligence at the point of customer contact* is rather said than done. Despite laws, despite checks the illegal channel thrives. How? It is too difficult to maintain suveilance as the source can be anywhere at any point of time making it difficult to check.

Now having seen the drawbacks in the supply chain management system in the entertainment industry, how these can be tackled and set right is the matter of serious concern. An ideal course of action to solve the existing problems may be as follows:

A. Procurement Side Management

Content managers must bear the following facts in mind while procuring contents for distribution down the line.

Shelf life: Contents should be in tune with satisfying the customer's current demand. The shelf life of contents should automatically change to the demand patterns and change of customer interests.

Wide operability: Today customer is always on the move and likes to view the same contents on different devices and media. At home, he may prefer his TV and in his office, the PC and when traveling perhaps on his mobile phone. Thus, contents devices should be multi-device operable.

Vendor managed content: In this concept the vendor is allowed to manage the content rather than the manufacturer managing it. In this system content producers after producing content store them in their repositories and do not push it down the line. As and when a carrier smells a demand for any of the stored content with the producer he procures it and distributes it. This way carriers and retailers are not dumped with unwanted contents that don't move. Since there are a multiple number of producers supplying contents to carriers, the content inventory gets spread to suit the different tastes and preferences of buyers.

B. Inventory Management

A major area of logistical interest in the supply chain management is Inventory management and has become a critical activity for content managers. These involve the following:

- Converting contents into digital format and creating data.
- Search and indexing of the contents now stored as data.
- Treating each media asset as a separate inventory item.
- If possible to store them as componentized.
- Ascertaining the value of each inventory according to its productivity.

Classifying content-assets: Once the above tasks are done next the content-assets have to be classified according to the market dynamics. They can be classified as:

1. Content-assets in current demand, the ones having a ready acceptance in the market.
2. Content-assets not in current demand are the ones, which neither has a current or a future demand.
3. Content-assets that can be reused
4. Content-assets in componentized form, which can be reused.

A content manager has to exercise caution while deciding on assets as not having demand for a sudden event or a happening may suddenly create a demand for the same.

Categorizing the contents based on their shelf life: The next task under inventory management is estimating the shelf life of the contents stored according to their usefulness. They can be categorized as:

- Contents with present acceptability.
- Contents that may have a linkage to a future event and gain acceptability on the event occurring.
- Future trends and the relevance of the contents to it.

Content-Asset Valuation

Content managers have to arrive at the total value of the content-assets in their repository, which is also the present market value. It can be arrived by adding the present sale value of the contents stored plus the income earned through licensing opportunities plus potential income syndication opportunities plus value realizable from the contents componentized plus the net present value of future projected sales plus special values attributed to assets of strategic importance.

C. Selling Side Management

Unlike in a product chain where the products have to move down the channels, in the entertainment industry there is a complicated portion attached to it – Selling Right! The supply chain must ensure that despite this complication the product reaches the customer in the minimal of time. Another unique dimension of managing supply chains in entertainment industry arises from the fact that these goods are not tangible and it is absolutely essential the content managers know their customers. It isn't easy as they have to understand customer tastes and dislikes which can be varied and difficult to comprehend at times. A good system should have the following features to be effective.

- *A healthy subscriber management system:* focuses on customer needs to ensure customer satisfaction which can be achieved by
  - Offering better services so that the customer remains loyal and committed to the outlet.
  - Providing feedback on customer requirements so that such contents are adequately stocked.
  - Providing information on content shelf life.
  - Ensuring contacts with customers at sales point in order to understand his or her psychographic and demographic characteristics.
- *Availability of device specific content storage units:* It ensures whatever be the customer's playing device there is an appropriate content unit available for his use.
- *Content collaboration:* It is impossible to have stock of content units to suit the demands of all customers as their taste, language and culture varies. In such situations a content manager should have an effective network of other content suppliers, preferably with an online system, where contents availability can be searched, located, procured and sold.
- *Transforming global contents to suit local needs:* Nowadays global contents dubbed in local languages are in demand. Sometimes captioning or translation may be preferred. This means delivering the same content in different languages to different regions. Content sellers should effectively meet this challenge to net all kinds of customer needs and preferably have the information listed online.

A Focus on Different Media of Entertainment in Relation to Supply Chain Management

1. Digital Entertainment

With the development of next generation DVD players that can playback more than the MPEG2 DVD format, the competition has heated up. With CES Microsoft announcing that several leading DVD player manufacturers like Panasonic, Toshiba, Shinco and Apex constituting about 99% of the DVD player industry will be supporting Windows Media Audio on their DVD players, the demand for content devices in this area becomes enormous.

The demand could be even more in this sector because Windows Media attains increased compression efficiency with the result that a single DVD can hold up to four movies on a single DVD and still maintain a high quality playback resonance. Some film distributors have started selling single movie on a CD and have discovered that it is an inexpensive alternative.

Rights management on CDs and DVDs does operate in two ways. The rights are available with the CD itself or the device has to be popped into and right applied for on online.

2. Television and Cable Television Entertainment

This is one area, where supply chain management is very effectively managed and rights enforced effectively. Have you ever come across a TV serial on a media format available in the grey market? No, the reason is simple, all production content are stored and telecast by the respective television channels themselves with no scope for piracy in between. Moreover, since the customers are flooded with so many channels and so much entertainment, they do not have the time to see all the programs telecast on the different channels and therefore, the demand for these contents in portable formats almost is non-existent.

3. Movies

The production team at the time of commencing the movie itself identifies a producer who launches promotional activities and identifies a distributor who in turn identifies sub-distributors who enter into agreement with cinema to play the movie on certain dates. It is the responsibility of the distributor to transport the film to the cinema theaters as a part of wider co-ordination of print use across territories. It is during these occasions that piracy creeps in and the chances are more for piracy of a movie with great expectations despite the fact that any single print needs to be moved many times from the main prints warehouse, on to a van, to the cinema, onto an assembly bench through the projector then back to the process and then on to the next cinema.

Supply chain management with regard to films is quite tricky as it is replete with many challenges that wipe away profitability. It is also a time-pressured activity, as movie releases are supported with extensive campaigns across different media with a time commitment on the distributor to deliver the film on time. Some of the other challenges in the supply chain management are:

- *High Distribution Costs:* The cost of sending films to theaters across regions, country and around the world is quite expensive.
- *No Security:* Distributors have little or no control over a film after it leaves their premises. Nothing can be done if it reaches wrong hands or gets damaged during the delivery process.
- *Wear and Tear:* A movie print gets scratched/damaged with usage necessitating the need for a new print.

4. Personal Computers

With the widespread availability of broadband connectivity, the PC as an entertainment hub is now a reality. This new capability is posing a tremendous challenge to film distributors. Their focus is how best to exploit this enormous opportunity without losing control of the content in the process. Studies reveal that already as many as 5,00,000 digital movies are being exchanged illegally over the web. How can technology help to bridge the gap between the customer wants of finding, acquiring, playing-back and exchanging movies online with the film industry wants of securing contents and arriving at business models that work to give great consumer experience is a challenge.

5. Internet

It has come a long way with the first upsurge in 1994 first generation streaming online of rather poor quality audio to that of current level high quality streaming of good audio quality and acceptable video quality when played back on in a small window through the web.

The second generation digital media streaming introduced rights management that secured rights for contents that authorized its playback. The third generation of digital media on the internet where Microsoft is focusing relates to:

- Achieving *security* through better and effective rights management solutions.
- Providing *quality* experience to customers when watching movie on TV.
- Inventing business models that are *economical,* which can make digital rights management easier and distribute contents online cost effectively.

Piracy in the Entertainment Industry

A major challenge of the film industry is to prevent itself from losing Rs.1 billion every month due to piracy alone. Most film makers lament that 50% of their revenue is lost because of piracy. Modern technological developments have spurred the "piracy revolution" as it is easier than learning alphabets to copy a movie or songs from legitimate sources without paying their due and use it for one's own purpose. The next challenge is from ruthless opportunists who see a goldmine of an opportunity in pirating from legitimate sources and selling it to the needy.

Future Challenges in the Supply Chain Management in the Entertainment Industry

The answer seems to lie in "digital distribution and exhibition of contents" to overcome many of today's challenges. The supply chain can be more effectively managed with the implementation of the following:

1. **Streamlining the Distribution Process** – Films can be sent digitally over the IP network to the targeted theaters instead of transporting the bulky and expensive film reels to theaters.

2. **Developing an Integrated Digital Rights Management (DRM) System** – Digital theater contents will not leave the content owner's facility without securing its digital rights. The system will also ensure in tracking and offering licenses to the ones who need the content so that the content owners are clearly aware when and where and to whom the license was given.

3. **Digital Preservation** – Unlike films which deteriorate with usage, digital quality will remain the same even after its 1000th usage.

4. **Demographic Specific Advertising is Easy** – Ads in digital formats can be served from one location targeting specific theaters based on contents being screened in that theater to suit their particular demographic needs.

Conclusion

In supply chains relating to the entertainment industry collaboration, a popular buzzword in enterprises was easier said than done in the past. The relationship between retailers and suppliers had remained transactional or even adversarial with customers placing orders and waiting for deliveries without even a feedback. Even when communication materialized it was usually a haggling over prices or complaints about late shipments or poor quality of products.

Not so any more, planning, forecasting and fulfillment tools, has given both ends of the supply chain access to *"actionable information"*. Both suppliers and customers have access to updated data relating to inventory levels, price fluctuations and, production capabilities and shipping progressions.

In the words of Mickey North Rizza, research director at AMR Research, "Supply chains are evolving, the ideal supply chain encompasses the entire product life cycle, from product development through to promotions and customer support". In other words it is not possible to track a product's entire life cycle without hearing the voice of everyone along the supply chain, and therefore, collaboration is essential at all the stages of the chain.

(R Santhana Krishnan is a Consulting Editor at Icfai Business School Research Center, Chennai. He can be reached at santhana_krishnan2006@yahoo.com and

D Thiyagarajan is a Research Associate at Icfai Business School Research Center, Chennai. He can be reached at thiyagu_d@rediffmail.com).

References

1. Julian Richards, "Supply chain for digital media" April 2006.
2. "SCM for media and entertainment", IBM .
3. "Digital media Distribution Opportunities for the Film Industry", *Windows media,* 2002.
4. Ashish Chawla, "The Digital Content Supply Chain", Wipro Technologies, 2002.
5. David Sin, "Distribution: The Logistics of Distribution", *Screen online.*
6. Subhankar Bhattacharya and William Comerford, "DVD Supply Chain", Infosys, April 2006.
7. A V Balakrishna, "Piracy in the Indian Film Industry", *Advertising Express,* October 2006.
8. V Parthasarathy and A V Balakrishna, "Independent Film-making and Distribution", *Advertising Express,* October 2006.
9. Sanjit Kumar Roy, "Indian Cable TV Industry Changing Dynamics", *Effective Executive,* March 2006.

15

Measuring Food Supply Chains

Venkata Nimeesha Posa

Food supply chain networks are being formed and interconnected via forward and backward integrations of the supply chain and also through horizontal and vertical cooperation. For measuring food supply chain apart from traditional performance indicators like costs and quality of products other performance indicators like People, Planet and Profit are to be considered. In case of food industry, measurement is the new index of quality and the basis for trade in food products.

Like all other industries, food industry is also trying to compete and increase sales. All food firms are under tremendous pressure from the investors to increase the earnings. In this new era of globalization, corporate social responsibility and customer satisfaction are the main driving forces for the food supply chains. Measuring supply chain activities has become an important and a novel factor in food industry. Food consumers from all parts of the world are demanding important criterion of food products like prompt delivery, quality and safety. This trend is being supported by many market-pull factors like globally increased demand for food products, origination from diverse sources, increased food related

Source: Icfai University Press Professional Reference Book on Supply Chain Performance Measurement And Improvement, 2006.

health problems, increased concern over the hygienic factors of the food and changing food habits of the consumers. .To meet the expectations of consumer preferences like maintaining consistent food supply chain of top quality, hygienic and nutritious foods, gaining customer satisfaction by rebuilding the consumer confidence; measurement system has to be introduced to the food supply chains.

Since the last decade, research on performance measurement has started gaining significance. Especially, measurement in the food supply chains has increased significantly. This is because of the changing business scenario, increased investments in the food industry and the changing preferences of the customers. Western-European markets are demanding new attributes of food like guaranteed quality, diversity, associated services information, safety and integrity. The basic attributes like demand and supply are no more the major attributes to be fulfilled. Now they have crossed the borders of nations and became international processes. In this global business, food products are being imported and exported internationally. There has been an increased demand and concentration on food supply chains. Cross-border flows of livestock have increased enormously and the food products have created international forms of cooperation. However, the supply chains of food industry have become more complex because the Food Supply Chain Networks (FSCNs) are being formed and interconnected via forward and backward integrations of the supply chain, continuous innovations, alliances and also through horizontal and vertical cooperation. As a result, the Performance Measurement System (PMS) of the supply chains needs to be altered because adopting the traditional measurement systems may have the limitations for the optimized FSCN.

In FSCN, different companies strategically collaborate in one or more areas of the supply chain. When collaborating, they will conserve their identity and autonomy. Hence, in a food supply chain we find many supply chains and business processes. Owing to this, organizations keep changing their supply chain settings and further because the partner of one supply chain may be the competitor for the other. Van Der Vorst refers, "Chain actors may be involved in different supply chains in different FSCNs, participate in a variety of business processes that change over time and in which dynamically changing vertical and horizontal partnerships are required". (Van Der Vorst, 2006)

Understanding FSCN Framework

In understanding FSCN framework in line with the thoughts of Lambert and Cooper (2000), the following four major elements need to be explored:

Framework for Chain/Network Development

While developing a chain or a network, the most important and first step is to identify all the facets of the network, including the participants, the processes within, the resources, the products, and the relationships between each of these components. Jack GAJ Van Der Vorst (2006[1]) has identified four key elements for developing a Food Supply Chain Network (FSCN). These are:

a) *The Network Structure,* which identifies the boundaries of the network and the key elements in the network, their roles, and other configurations within the network. The main objective is to classify the elements, which contribute to the company's objectives and are critical enough to require managerial attention.

b) *Chain Business Processes* are activities, measured and structured to produce specified outputs. These can be marketing, finance, customer relationship management or new product development.

c) *Network and Chain Management* deals with coordination and management of the processes in the network structure. This involves managerial and behavioral components (Lambert and Cooper, 2000), which include "physical and technical components", and "managerial and behavioral components".

d) *Chain Resources,* also known as transforming resources, are used for the actual production and delivery of the product to the customer. These include men, machines, and the ICT (information, information systems and information infrastructures) components.

Refer Figure 1 for understanding the network development of FSCN.

An FSCN may contain more than one Chain Business Process, which uses the same business activities within the network. A precedence relationship may be said to exist among the business processes and activities in the FSCN. All of them nevertheless relate directly to the overall objectives of the FSCN.

Figure 1: Framework for Chain or Network Development (Adapted From Lambert and Cooper 2000)

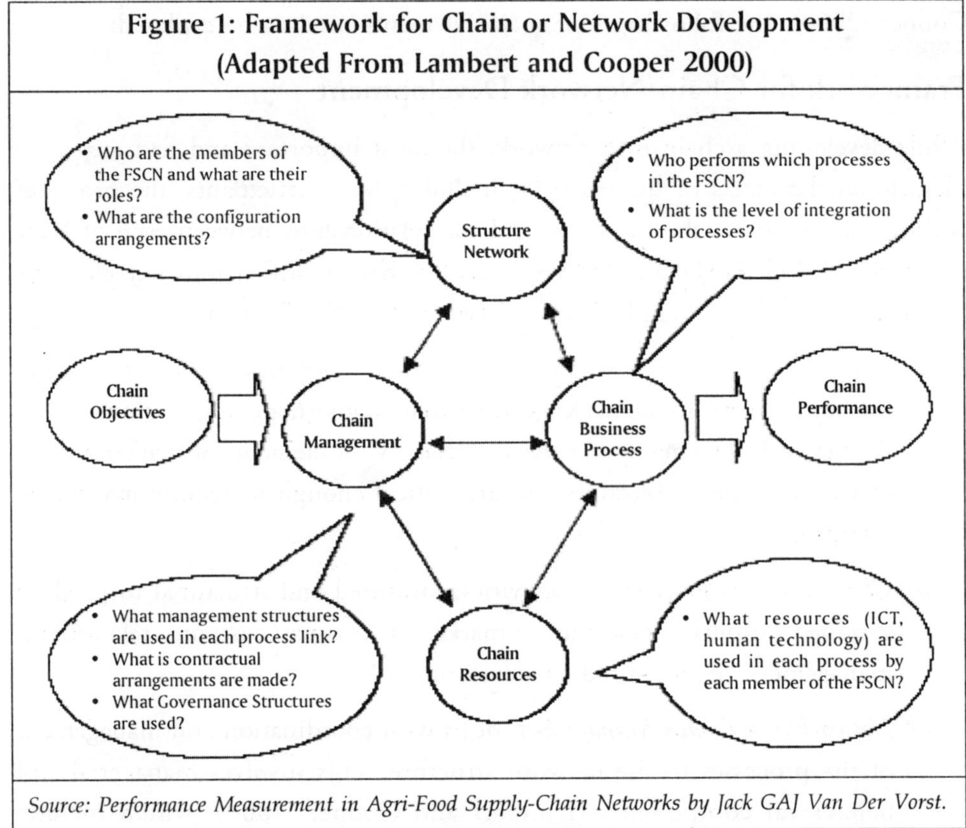

Source: Performance Measurement in Agri-Food Supply-Chain Networks by Jack GAJ Van Der Vorst.

Jack GAJ Van Der Vorst has also identified three Generic Value Propositions: network differentiation and market segmentation; integrated quality; and network optimization. These may be found existing together and even separately within the network.

Supply chain performance measurement is the process of determining the level of output in relation to the overall objectives of the FSCN, in conformance with the end-use customers' and stakeholders' expectations. Performance can be measured by comparing the actual performance with the pre-determined targets, using performance indicators or performance metrics. These key performance indicators are determined by the actual objectives of the supply chain network.

Hence, it is important to define the actual objectives of the FSCN and then determine the four key elements mentioned above, along with the other important external factors like the market, production characteristics, product and the competitive strategy.

Performance Measurement

Measuring performance of supply chains is the cornerstone of operational success. Performance measurement is defined as the process of quantifying the effectiveness and efficiency action (Neely *et al.* 1995). Effectiveness is measured in terms of the extent to which customer requirements are fulfilled. Efficiency is measured by considering how efficiently the company resources are used to achieve customer satisfaction. Performance measurement systems are defined as the overall set of metrics used to measure both the efficiency and effectiveness of actions. In case of measuring supply chains, many methods and metrics are proposed. But there are no standard metrics for supply chain. This is mainly because the networks of supply chain are highly complicated to measure. However, many researchers are making few attempts for systematic collation of the measures for measuring supply chain performance. Supply chain measures are categorized as follows:

- Qualitative or quantitative measures.
- The attributes they are going to reflect in the supply chain cost and non-cost (Gunasekaran, 2001; De Toni and Tonchia, 2001); resources, flexibility, outputs (Beamon, 1999); quality, flexibility, delivery and cost (Schonsleben, 2004); composite measures, input and output (Chan and Qi, 2003).
- The strategic, tactical and operational focus of the measures (Gunasekaran *et al. 2001).*

The process in the supply chain the measures are relating to traditional and basic supply chain metrics are based on costing and accounting systems. Measuring supply chain performance needs to balance the financial and non-financial measures at various levels and points of the supply chain. The best approach for maintaining this is the balanced scorecard approach. For measuring the food supply chain apart from traditional performance indicators like costs and quality of products other performance indicators like people, planet and profit (which are termed as 'Triple P') are to be considered. Few of the examples like environmental chain profile (Profile of animal-friendliness), guaranteed product quality and integrity, hygiene and safety parameters and objectives of supply chain are to be considered for selecting and defining the measures for supply chain. Refer to Table 1 for understanding the key performance indicators of the food-chain networks.

Table 1: Example of Logistic KPIs for Food-chain Networks on Three Hierarchical Levels (Van Der Vorst, 2000)

Level	Performance Indicator	Explanation
Supply-chain Network	Product availability on shelf	Presence of a large assortment and no stock-outs
	Product Quality	Remaining product shelf life
	Responsiveness	Order cycle time of the SC
	Delivery Reliability	Meeting guaranteed delivery times
	Total SC Cost	Sum of all organization costs in the supply-chain
Organization	Inventory Level	Number of products in store
	Throughput Time	Time needed to perform chain of business processes
	Responsiveness	Flexibility of the organization: lead time
	Delivery Reliability	% Orders delivered on time and in right quantity
	Total Organization's Cost	Sum of all process costs in the specific organization
Process	Responsiveness	Flexibility of the process
	Throughput Time	Time needed to perform the process
	Process Yield	Outcome of the process
	Process Cost	Cost made when executing the process

Source: Performance Measurement in Agri-Food Supply-Chain Networks by Jack GAJ Van Der Vorst.

In the measurement of food supply chain network, defining and measuring performance at each and every instantiation of the whole supply chain network and to the level of participating organizations and also executed processes is required. Hence, in addition to the above-defined key performance indicators mentioned in the Table 1, to construct a PMS of food supply chain, the following key aspects need to be addressed:

- Considering the performance metrics at multiple aggregation levels of supply chain, a balanced set of metrics need to be defined for measuring food chains. The following attributes are to be considered for maintaining the balance of metrics:
  - Indicators for the chain network structure like Return On Investment (ROI), total added value
  - Indicators for the output of the chain, like logistics metrics, such as responsiveness, lead-time, delivery, reliability, inventory levels, product quality and so on
  - Indicators at process level related to utilizing chain resources like utilization degree, process yield and so on.
- Metrics that could dynamically respond to the sudden changes, like change in customer requirements, resources and performance overtime, operating inputs etc.
- Measures that could measure the basic criteria, such as validity, usefulness, economy, robustness, inclusiveness and consistency.

Obstacles in Performance Measurement

- Lack of integrated communication and decentralized reporting between factories, decentralized centers, etc. Due to this, integrated analysis is hindered.
- Standard measurement methods, metrics and KPIs are not defined for measuring supply chains.
- As the development stages of each and every supply chain participant vary, defining standard metrics is very hard.
- Companies are not ready to disclose the problems of their supply chains, as other organizations may become the competitors.

Conclusion

The introduction of measurement in food supply chains is the result of continuous research and development in improving quality of food products and also in improving safety management. In many industries such as software, airline, telecommunications etc., security is the main aspect to be considered for measurement. In the case of food industry, measurement has became the new index of quality and the basis for trade in food products. The purpose of the food supply chain measurement is to keep track of the process right from farmhouse or farmer till food product reaches customer. This helps to identify the problem stages and take steps to resolve the problem and improve the quality and accuracy of delivering products to customer. Hence, measurement could be considered as a means for ensuring product quality and also as the tool for safety management. A well implemented measurement approach for food supply chains helps in tracing the problems and identify the stages that need to be improved by tracing back to the original producer as well as tracing forward to the individual customer. It could also be used for identification of products effectively and the management of recall when safety and quality standards are violated. When looked at from the customers' perspective, measuring food supply chain helps to build trust and increase confidence in the quality and the hygiene factor of the food. For producers and retailers, measurement helps in overall cost-effective quality management system, which assists in continuous improvement and reducing safety hazards through determining and isolating sources of hazards. Of late, technology is also supporting in implementing and maintaining effective food supply chain measurement system. Technological innovations are supporting customers to resonance food business practices, so that it would be easy to meet customer demands for accessible and reliable information about the source and life cycle of the food products.

By considering all these important benefits of measurement, an efficient measurement system has to be developed for evaluating food supply chains. Every supply chain has to implement appropriate measurement system. Approaches are to be selected in such a way that they have their value and impact on both the top and the bottom line of the supply chain.

(Venkata Nimeesha Posa, Research Associate, Icfai Books a division of The Icfai University Press. She can be reached at nimeesha_posa@yahoo.co.in.)

16

Poverty-Sensitive Value Chains in the Tourism Industry

Eugenio Yunis

The influence of the tourism supply chain could be felt on may activities related to Tourism Industry in several factors, ranging from the products selected by tour operators, to the selection of suppliers by tourism companies. The supply chain of tourism, and especially that of hotel companies, can be substantially improved in developing countries and LDCs in order to better contribute to poverty alleviation objectives and other Millennium Development Goals. A first step is to gain awareness and accept that local suppliers can offer goods (such as food and furniture), as well as services (guides, transport or laundry).

In spite of many difficulties that have affected tourism over the last few years, including natural disasters, health scares, oil price rises, exchange rate fluctuations, wars and terrorism, as well as other economic and political uncertainties international tourist arrivals worldwide have continued to grow steadily, beating all expectations last year to reach 808 million. The tourism receipts corresponding to these arrivals have reached 682 billion USD in 2005.

These figures demonstrate once again the resilience of tourist movements; they reflect the unstoppable desire of people to travel and devote part of their income to this purpose.

Tourism growth in recent years has been characterised by two main trends; firstly, by the consolidation of traditional tourism destinations, like those in Western Europe, North America including Mexico, and some Caribbean islands; and secondly, by a pronounced geographical expansion. There has been indeed a substantial diversification of destinations during the last 50 years: while in 1950 15 countries, all of them from Europe plus the USA and Canada, accounted for over 90% of total international tourist arrivals, in 2005, the market share of the top 15 countries had fallen to around 58%. In parallel, many developing countries saw their tourist arrivals increase significantly, including Northern African countries, Thailand, Indonesia, Brazil, South Africa to name but a few.

Taking into account these trends, at least three main conclusions can be drawn in connection with tourism and its potential for poverty alleviation.

1. Tourism is one of the most dynamic economic sectors in many countries, developed but also developing ones, with a wide range of upstream and downstream effects on other economic activities thanks to a very large and diversified supply chain;
2. Tourist movements towards developing and least developed countries are growing faster than in the developed world, accounting now for around 40 per cent of total international tourist arrivals;
3. Tourism in many developing and least developed countries is one of the principal, and in some countries, the main source of foreign exchange earnings and, quite often, the most viable and sustainable economic development option, with positive impacts on reducing poverty levels.

Yet, it has to be acknowledged that quite often the poor segments of the population in these countries do not fully benefit from the economic impacts of tourism. This is due mainly to a high level of leakages in the tourism economy, i.e., a high proportion of the inputs required by tour and hotel companies are provided through imports, instead of establishing linkages with other sectors of the local economy.

There is also evidence that the supply chain of tourism, and especially that of hotel companies, can be substantially improved in developing countries and LDCs in order to better contribute to poverty alleviation objectives and other Millennium Development Goals. Many inputs required by tourism companies can indeed be supplied locally, by micro, small and medium sized enterprises run by local people or employing the local poor. The employment and entrepreneurial development impacts of tourism can in fact be much higher in the supply chain (indirect effects) than in the tourism sector itself.

However, if tourism has to represent an increasingly stronger economic development opportunity for developing countries (and for those wishing to diversify their economies), such development needs to be environmentally, socially, economically and culturally sustainable. It is only when it is properly planned, developed and managed this sector can realize its strong potential to take up many challenges of our planet and our societies.

In this context, the following principles have been adopted by UNWTO and recommended to governments in order for Tourism to maximize its potential to contribute to Poverty Alleviation:

1. *Mainstreaming:* Ensure that sustainable tourism development is included in general poverty elimination programmes. Include poverty elimination measures within overall strategies for the sustainable development of tourism;
2. *Partnerships:* Develop partnerships between international, government, non-governmental and private sector bodies, with a common aim of poverty alleviation through tourism;
3. *Integration:* Adopt an integrated approach with other sectors and avoid over-dependence on tourism;
4. *Equitable distribution:* Ensure that tourism development strategies focus on more equitable distribution of wealth and services;
5. *Acting locally:* Focus action at a local/destination level, within the context of supportive national policies;
6. *Retention:* Reduce leakages from the local economy and build linkages within it, focusing on the supply chain;

7. *Viability:* Maintain sound financial discipline and assess viability of all actions taken;
8. *Empowerment:* Create conditions which empower and enable the poor to have access to information and to influence and take decisions;
9. *Human rights:* Remove all forms of discrimination and exploitation against people working in tourism, particularly against women and children;
10. *Commitment:* Plan action and the application of resources for the long term; and
11. *Monitoring:* Develop simple indicators and systems to measure the impact of tourism on poverty.

UNWTO has intensified over the last three years its efforts in the field of poverty alleviation through sustainable forms of tourism, undertaking the following main activities:

1. After the launching of the concept of "Sustainable Tourism as an effective tool for Eliminating Poverty" (ST-EP) at the Johannesburg Summit in 2002, UNWTO established the ST-EP Foundation with the sole aim to promote poverty elimination through sustainable tourism development projects. The ST-EP Foundation is located in Seoul, Korea, whose government has provided the first five million US dollars, plus the office and administrative facilities. It is currently raising further financial resources to implement poverty reduction tourism development projects, while five projects are being funded in 2006.
2. In collaboration with the Netherlands Development Organization (SNV), a multi-donor Trust Fund has been established with the objective of supporting ST-EP projects through the provision of technical assistance. SNV provided an initial contribution of 2 million euros. The Italian government has also provided a financial contribution to this Fund.
3. Technical assistance missions for identification of ST-EP pilot projects have been fielded to 19 countries so far, identifying around 150 projects for future implementation. In 2006, around 40 projects have been approved and are currently being implemented.

4. The Organization is also improving the capacity of national tourism administrations and local authorities in developing countries in this field since 2004. Nine regional capacity-building seminars have been conducted in Africa, Asia and Latin America, attended by around 600 officials from more than 60 countries. In addition, four publications were produced providing evidence of the impact of tourism in reducing poverty levels, as well as recommendations on how to maximise these impacts.

The most important of these publications, entitled "Tourism and Poverty Alleviation: Recommendations for Action", identifies seven approaches to address poverty through tourism; these are:

1. Employment of the poor in tourism enterprises
2. Supply of goods and services to tourism enterprises by the poor or by enterprises employing the poor
3. Direct sales of goods and services to visitors by the poor (informal economy)
4. Establishment and running of tourism-related enterprises by the poor – e.g. micro, small and medium sized enterprises (MSMEs), or community based enterprises (formal economy)
5. Tax or levy on tourism income or profits with proceeds benefiting the poor
6. Voluntary giving/support by tourism enterprises and tourists
7. Investment in infrastructure stimulated by tourism also benefiting the poor in the locality, directly or through support to other sectors.

The second, third and fourth of these approaches underline the strong relation between tourism and other economic activities. As a transversal sector touching upon many other economic activities that feed the hotel, catering and transport industries, or that sell goods to the tourists, tourism allows the establishment of many linkages with the local producers and sellers. Some examples of goods and services that can be supplied locally are:

1. In the hotel companies' supply chain:
   - construction materials, such as wood, stone, straw for thatching and locally made mud bricks, giving a local style to the hotels and could enhance their attractiveness;

- furniture made of local wood varieties, provided its exploitation is environmentally sustainable;
- carpets and rugs, locally woven by traditional craftsmen and women;
- decorative objects designed, painted and/or produced by local artists;
- bed linen, tablecloths, napkins and other textile items, which need to be renovated rather frequently;
- food items, especially fresh produce grown by small rural farmers, but also some processed items such as juices, bread, etc;
- laundry services, especially to replace expensive and usually imported washing equipment in small and medium sized accommodation establishments.

2. In restaurants and other catering establishments:
   - furniture, tablecloths, decorative objects, etc. as above in 1
   - local food items as above in 1
   - local drinks, freshly produced juices
   - local dishes, reflecting the local gastronomy.
3. In tour operating companies:
   - local guides
   - local, traditional means of transport
   - local cultural attractions and traditional ceremonies.

Most of the products and activities mentioned above can be produced and provided by the poor, either individually (i.e., micro-enterprises), through cooperative or community-based arrangements, or in small and medium sized enterprises employing the poor.

Some of the common problems and obstacles found in developing countries to make this happen in a substantive, massive scale are:

- unawareness of the existence of such possible local sources from large, foreign-owned hotel and tourism companies;
- absence of a corporate social responsibility commitment or practice within large and medium sized hotel and tourism companies, both foreign- and locally-owned;
- difficult access of small producers to the large hotels' senior purchasing managers;
- shortage of finance capital available in adequate terms to the small and micro-entrepreneurs, not allowing them to produce in the quantities and qualities required by hotel establishments;
- irregularity in the quality and frequency of supply of local products by local enterprises.

Generally speaking, it is possible to act upon or influence the tourism supply chain in several points, ranging from the products selected by tour operators, to the selection of suppliers by tourism companies. A first step is to gain awareness and accept that local suppliers can offer goods (such as food, furniture, etc.), as well services (guides, transport or laundry). Also, it is possible to contract local companies and poor people in the construction of the hotels (for example, for the provision of construction materials), as well as in the operation of the companies. And if it is not always easy to determine what suitable suppliers are poorest, a first step is to make sure that the suppliers are local. For poor local communities, being suppliers of hotels and other tourist companies represent numerous advantages:

- It provides a market to their productive activities and technical knowledge;
- It allows the appearance of new activities and technical abilities compatible with the local capacities and interests;
- It can complement and give support to the traditional subsistence habits in the countryside, arresting the migration towards urban zones.
- Some traditional economic activities, non-viable due to the lack of a local market, can return to be profitable, thanks to the presence of tourists in the neighbouring hotels.

- Some tourist companies have quite considerable purchasing budgets that can constitute a stable source of business for micro- or small local entrepreneurs.

Nevertheless, the commitment of the tourism sector in general, and hoteliers in particular, in favour of the poor cannot be only based on the will to contribute to poverty alleviation. Tourism entrepreneurs must also realize that this commitment can bring several advantages for their companies, among them:

- The supply of fresh and typically local foods to their clients, increasing the quality of the stay and the tourist experience, and, as a consequence of this, their willingness to prolong it, to recommend it to their friends and/or to return.
- The benefit of providing a locally rooted service allows reinforcing the authenticity of the tourism product. The personality of the lodging establishments and restaurants, by means of typical decorative and textile articles (sets of dishes, table cloths, clothes of bed, etc.), leaves a unique memory, contrary to the so-called "international" style of many chain hotels that are practically identical anywhere in the world.
- A substantive reduction in production costs as a result of lower local prices and the reduction of the cost of the transport.

For these advantages to become effective, it is necessary to act on some key points to ensure that the process is efficient and sustainable. The hotels need to be assured that the local suppliers' production capacity is sufficient to satisfy their requirements, not only in volume but also in terms of quality and reliability. If the capacity exists, it is necessary to tackle the possible problems of regularity to be able to obtain important orders with a constant quality. The time required by the tourism companies to value their sources, to look for local suppliers and to organize contacts and a suitable control of quality must also be evaluated. For the local communities and their representatives, it is important to control the transparency, and to guarantee equitable pricing and contracting policies that do not lead to abuse by the purchasing power of big companies.

In the case of the hotels, it is necessary to proceed progressively, beginning with the establishment of a few linkages carefully selected where the success seems more likely, to build on them. The hotels can give technical or commercial assistance to some of their local suppliers, including the advice on entrepreneurial management subjects and a pertinent financial support, so that they improve the quality and the capacity of their production. They can also be more tolerant with local craftsmen and traders, allowing them to sell their products or crafts in the proximity of the hotels.

The local authorities can also play a role:

- Firstly, helping to improve the information networks: often, the hotels do not know the goods and services locally available, and the suppliers do not know how to approach the companies nor with whom to put themselves in contact. It is necessary to offer assistance to the tourism companies to value their existing supply sources, and to identify the appropriate alternatives.
- Secondly, organizing specific programmes to identify new or better supply sources, for example with the intervention of the administration in charge of agriculture or helping the local farmers who work with a group of tourism companies.
- Thirdly, stimulating and supporting the cooperative agreements among small suppliers.

It is also important to know the various reasons that explain why tourism companies have difficulties in making purchases to small local, or even national, suppliers. In the case of hotels, these reasons are the following:

- The communication and information technologies, especially between big buyers and producers, are being more and more integrated. This integration tends to exclude small suppliers.
- Big hotels work mainly with recognized suppliers, often because they need to make sure that some minimum requirements about health or environmental issues, imposed to them by their chain or by public regulations, are fulfilled.
- Quite often, managers responsible for purchasing are interested simply in price reduction, and less in the maximization of benefits at destination level. In addition, commissions and personal relationships influence the purchase decisions.

- Purchasing important volumes allows individual hotels or hotel groups to receive discounts and to use their purchasing power to have better treatment in the speed of distribution and the payment conditions. The reduction in the number of suppliers means less administration of invoices and receipt of merchandise. The small producer is not prepared to work at this level.
- Storage and distribution (frozen fish and meat, distribution at the moment) are difficult for the small producer.
- Some companies do not think that the local product can be turned into a marketing tool and will not stimulate its promotion.

While the challenge is big, we firmly believe that addressing these problems in order to maximize the poverty reduction potential of the tourism supply chain is possible. It requires an organised effort and close cooperation among a number of stakeholders, including at least the following: hoteliers and hotel trade associations, incoming and outbound tour operating companies, catering establishments and their trade associations, local and external technical assistance agencies, especially those serving the rural and manufacturing sectors, financial and micro-credit institutions, among others.

It is also essential to establish a national strategy and a phased action plan in order to reduce leakages in tourism operations. At the national level, leakage avoidance can be tackled proactively through processes to enhance the abilities of the countries' regional economies to build and improve their tourism value-chain. A process for accomplishing this, at least in part, has taken shape in the form of regional cluster-based economic development. This approach to economic development is often applied across all industries in regional economies in both, developing and developed countries. The cluster approach has particular applicability to the tourism industry because of this industry's tendency to be geographically focused and organizationally fragmented. Cluster logic is affirmative in nature in that it emphasizes building domestic capacity rather than defending domestic markets. UNWTO published in 2003 a paper that offers an introduction to the application of cluster-based economic development to the challenge of avoiding or minimizing leakages from the tourism economy. This document can be consulted on-line.[1]

To conclude, I would like to recall the importance of tourism in today's economy and its potential to contribute in the fight against poverty, principally through its long supply chain. I would also recall that plenty of know-how is available for enhancing the local supply chains in developing countries, in order to make it more sustainable. By adapting all this technical information and all these guidelines to the particularities of each destination, national and local authorities, private tourism companies and local communities can find the way to increase tourism benefits and their distribution in order to reduce poverty, while protecting the natural environment and cultural heritage.

(Eugenio Yunis is a head Sustainable Development of Tourism, WTO. He can be reached at eyunis@unwto.org).

---

1 Using Cluster-Based Economic Strategy to Minimize Tourism Leakages, UNWTO, 2003: ***http://www.unwto.org/quality/E/docs/trade/trsmleaks.pdf***

SECTION III

CASES

17

Supply Chain Management in the Construction Industry: A Case Study in Spain

Josep Capó-Vicedo, José V Tomás-Miquel and M Expósito-Langa

The construction sector differs to a large extent from other productive industries. Here, supply chains are specifically configured for every construction project, where each participant is specialized in particular activities based on core competencies. Nowadays, the market is forcing the setting up of Virtual Enterprises (VE) with a customer-oriented policy to facilitate the management, and to improve the efficiency of the construction project. Based on this context, the paper analyzes the case of a Spanish construction Small and Medium Enterprise (SME), which acts as the broker of the VE corresponding to each construction project. The paper brings out the problems faced by the company acting as VE broker and suggests the appropriate solutions.

Source: The Icfai Journal of Supply Chain Management Vol. III No.4 2006. The article was published as "Virtual Supply Chains: The Case of a Spanish Construction Company".

Introduction

The construction sector presents a series of peculiarities that makes it different from other productive sectors. One of the most important is the fact that the supply chain is configured for each individual construction project. The current trend of companies participating in these supply chains is towards greater specialization, especially when referring to construction processes. Likewise, some promoter and construction companies are establishing contracts with only one supplier, who constitutes a Virtual Enterprise, containing all or part of the members of the supply chain. This implies significant savings in cost and time and other advantages, such as better control of the outsourcing processes and the possibility of focusing the organization's energy in its core competences. The paper examines a real case of a Spanish construction company. This company configured a Virtual Enterprise from the point of view of customers (promoters or property) at the first level of the Supply Chain, acting as a broker.

Construction Supply Chains

Given the particular characteristics of the sector, the supply chain is different for each construction project. London and Kenley (2000) propose a method to describe Construction Supply Chains. The main criterion to establish the relations and structure is the initial identification of each particular project. The three key factors of the model are: the project, the participants and the relationships between them.

Each project involves the demand for an infrastructure or building by the customer's organization. Figure 1 shows the structure of a construction Supply Chain, in which the customer is considered as the central organization, according to the model in Lambert *et al.* (1998). It is important to take into account that the customer may be the promoter or property owner.

According to this model, the customer (construction demand organization), as a central organization, is the equivalent to the large assembler in the traditional Supply Chain Models in the automobile sector. This challenges the general assumption of many authors that the main contractor is the equivalent to the assembler.

Figure 1: Construction Supply Chain Structure

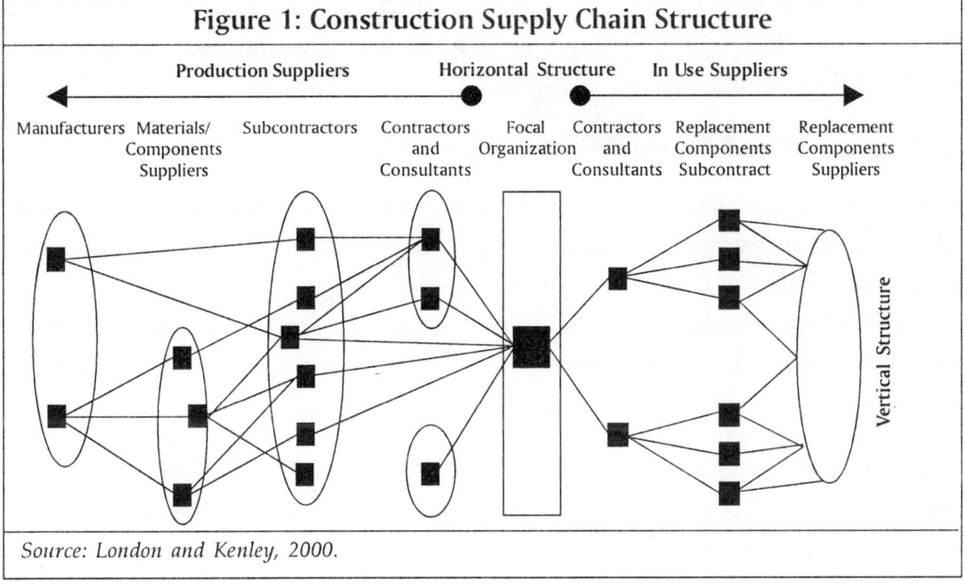

Source: London and Kenley, 2000.

In Figure 1, the horizontal structure tiers are grouped into those that supply to produce the facility/infrastructure (production suppliers), the focal demand organization, and those that supply after project completion (in use suppliers).

The model can become complicated, when there are multiple suppliers for each level and when organizations are located in more than one layer.

On the other hand, the vertical structure of each link reflects a degree of competition between suppliers. At this level, relationships between companies become one of the critical parts of the model.

Case Study

In the concrete case of the Spanish construction industries, these new alliances are being detected, mainly in the sub-sectors of residential or industrial construction, constituted by SMEs.

These alliances are constituted as networks of collaborative companies, which act as nodes of a Virtual Enterprise (VE), each of them contributing with their core competenies. All directly operate with the customer (promoter or property) as if it were dealing with a single company. Each time a market opportunity (construction project) arises, the VE is formed. Thanks to the open systems structures and the use of IT, a rapid communication is established, that produces a real time VE configuration.

Setting up of the Supply Chain Like a VE

In the paper, a representative case is studied, related to the industrial construction sub-sector and focusing a company, working under a turnkey scheme. This enterprise is located in Valencia (Spain), aims at offering the property an integral service for the construction of industrial plants. In practice, the relevance of a turnkey contract is in the fact that it is, in a simplified way, a ready-to-work wholesale contract. That means all responsibility falls upon a unique legal or physical entity.

Following the Supply Chain Model in London and Kenley (2000), corresponding to a construction project, it is possible to state the situation shown in Figure 2. There, the entire Supply Chain is perceived by the customer as a unique company (Virtual Enterprise).

Figure 2: Virtual Enterprise Configuration for Managing a Construction Project in the Industrial Construction Sub-sector

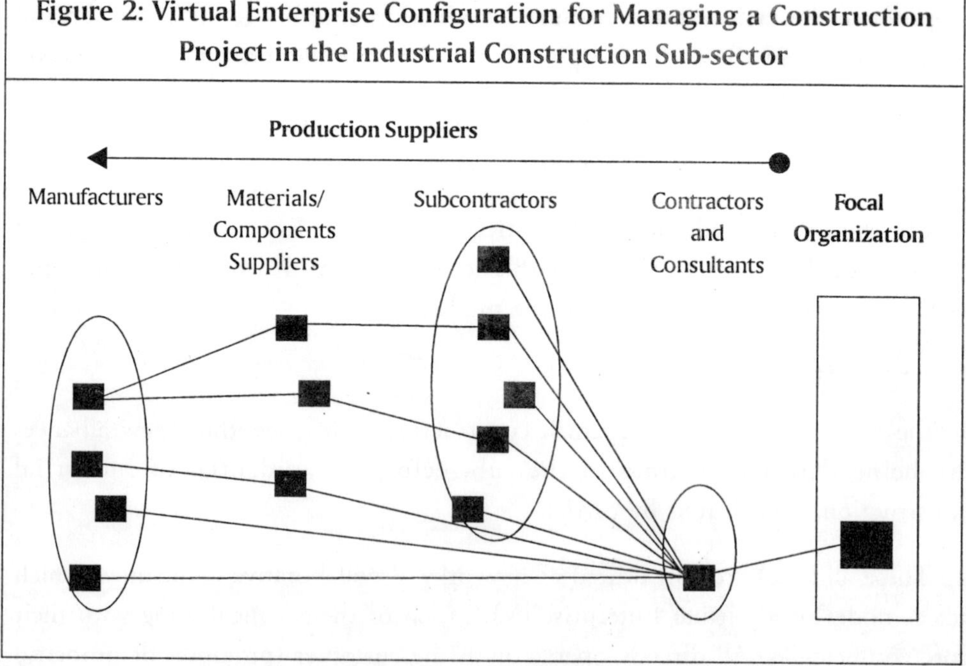

The studied company acts as the VE broker, playing various roles (Simões-Costa and Rabelo, 2002): looking for new business opportunities, managing their reception and coordinating the process of selecting the most suitable consortium of enterprises for every opportunity. The advantages for the customer are obvious:

- Communication with a single interlocutor;
- Cost reductions;
- More information available to the customer; and
- High agility in production and negotiation.

Problems Encountered

The analyzed construction firm has found various problems, while constituting the VE. The main difficulties are caused by the culture of Construction SMEs:

- The participants in the construction project are not sure about the benefits they can gain by sharing knowledge and experiences;
- Belief that they can lose competitive advantages;
- Dissimilar culture;
- Different objectives;
- Different standards and productive systems.
- Difference in language (jargon);
- Existence of a relationship among the members of the Supply Chain that present certain rivalry and lack of confidence;
- Communication and information management difficulties due to an insufficient coordination;
- The available information is incorrect or insufficient (most of the time). This can affect tasks that depend on one another;
- Low quality and failure to comply terms as a result of lack of understanding among the parts of the chain; and
- The arrangement of the companies by departments creates internal barriers.

This prevents them from having a clear vision of their own processes and makes them unable to concentrate on their customer's needs and requirements.

Need for a Cultural Change

The solution to the above mentioned problems depends mainly on the achievement of a cultural change of the participating companies in each VE.

The analyzed company operates in a well-defined geographic area. Therefore, the participants in each VE are closely located. This fact and the cooperation among them (most of them repeat in different VEs) have contributed to make this cultural change easier. A real business ecosystem (Camarinha-Matos, 2002) has been created between them.

According to this cultural change, the broker company has principally worked on three major facts, shown in Hong-Minh *et al.* (1999).

Change of Mentality

The most common problem is the rivalry that exists among the members of the chain and a low level of confidence among them. The broker, in order to solve these problems, should coordinate their efforts and try to work together, looking towards end customer satisfaction. It starts determining the customers' needs, transferring them to certain product requirements, and finally, establishing how the delivery of the final product (industrial plant) to the customer must be executed. All this must go through every construction stage. The broker promotes this relationship among the members of a chain focusing on confidence, mutual understanding, knowledge and acceptance of the particular expectations of each one and also on the information exchange. Thus, the product will be delivered on time and with the right levels of quality, satisfying the end customer and obtaining high internal contentment levels, very few conflicts, etc.

Process Management Orientation

The construction industry, especially with regard to SMEs, tends to adopt an organization by departments. This can be a problem because the companies cannot concentrate on the customer. This kind of organization is too rigid as all the activities are performed in sequence, going from one department to another, following the hierarchic lines, which makes taking decisions a slower and more complicated task.

Although the fact of focusing on the customer's requirements is not a new concept for construction companies, they do not usually pay the attention deserved to the value of the customer in their processes. A process orientation will increase the company's efficiency and the customer satisfaction will reduce terms and help to achieve high levels of quality.

The main goal must be the end customer. Therefore, they must look for ways, which offer him as much value as possible and not only according to price, quality or deadlines. If the whole company focuses on the same goal, satisfying the customer is easier than confronting several departments or sections with different goals.

Once the company is working this way, it will be easier to work together with the rest of the members of the SC.

Personnel and Knowledge Exchange

The personnel exchange between companies is a symptom of a good relationship and a process orientation.

This helps to generate confidence between a company and its suppliers, that is, between a customer and other companies. This also shows that the company wants to learn from others and is ready to share knowledge and technology.

The broker promotes the personnel exchange when a new industrial plant is being developed so that human resources, experience and knowledge can be shared.

Therefore, each company is not only focused on its own processes but it can view the global process of the entire VE working as a unique body as well. They can compete against other VE and satisfy their customers' needs.

This personnel exchange allows for personal and physical communication among people of different companies of the chain, creating thus a "social net".

A high grade of interaction will be obtained, enabling the transmission of tacit knowledge through the companies (Nonaka, 2000).

VE Life Cycle Needs

Following the VE life cycle model proposed in Camarinha-Matos and Afsarmanesh (1999), the main steps needed for each stage will be analyzed.

Creation

This stage includes all the previous activities before the start of construction. It consists of the creation of a team of designers including every professional that must take part in the project. The designer is the most important member of this team.

The contractors, depending on the contract system adopted, should participate actively in the design process.

They must define the specific points and relative calculations concerning their area, starting from the basic lines planned by the designer.

At the same time, the engineers can be integrated into each of the different contractors' organizations. This fact does not imply enlarging the structures of the contractors and/or suppliers, but it is simply a matter of integrating their own technicians at this stage.

The fact of eagerly promoting the direct hiring by different specialized companies and having them involved in the design phase leads to a more general quality, because those who participate in each part of the project have a deep knowledge of the specific technology utilized.

This methodology improves the construction process, allows a more elaborated planning and provides better overall results, in view of the fact that each contractor determines the most suitable solution in its field.

This effect is not accomplished when the designer or his team imposes on the contractor what he must do. The increasing specialization in this field turns the suppliers and contractors themselves into the ones who are better acquainted with technology and more specific products.

If the suitable conditions are achieved to increase interaction between the design team and at least the main contractors, their knowledge could be kept and shared and at the same time, a new knowledge could be developed and competitive advantages extended.

Operation

This stage should develop all the coordination tasks and the permanent control of time, costs and quality. Each construction company must be able to create an infrastructure that enables its team to have access to the organization's resources, experience and knowledge.

It is necessary to optimize to the maximum the coordination and the knowledge exchange with the rest of the members of each Virtual Supply Chain. If this objective is achieved, it would be able to slightly reduce the drawbacks that appear in the building process causing significant deviations of the terms and costs.

The studied company has proceeded in three main ways in order to achieve the mentioned objective:

- *Organization and People*—One of the goals is to create information channels for those who work on the same kind of jobs or units. In such a way, they can save the effort to solve technical problems that have been already solved by others. Both knowledge and experience at the organization should be properly organized to create a common database from which any member of the VE can have access anywhere and anytime.
- *Processes*—They analyze and design the flow of documental management that takes part in every building project. They are classified by groups (technological, legal, economic, etc.). Their specific attributes are identified as well as the different stages that each document goes through, the people who process them, etc.
- *Technology*—Some technological items help to hold this infrastructure. As an example, they have created a platform based on a web environment that allows the connectivity from any device, mobile or fixed, without the need for additional software to have access to the provided services.

One of the purposes of the above mentioned is to save time, when they search for information or documents as well as a reduction of the number of hours invested in the rework on specific construction units, due to the lack of coordination.

To conclude, it can be affirmed that the management of this stage should achieve a double goal: making easier the learning of experiences and previous errors, including the tacit knowledge with the more experienced personnel and creating a propitious environment for new techniques and ideas.

Dissolution

Once the construction process has been finished, the broker must try to organize the knowledge transfer. The main problems concerning this task are motivated by the discontinuity between the projects and their teams. Everything learned during the development of a certain project can be simply lost or forgotten when the project is over and the team is dissolved.

There are not many opportunities, when they can count on the time and space. They need to make sure that all has been learned through the project are assumed by the appropriate organization. The market causes the immediate reassignment of people to new projects, so their focus automatically changes.

In order to solve these problems, some mechanisms that promote learning in organizations have been provided. It is worthwhile mentioning the post-project review, which is becoming a part of the ordinary processes worked out by the teams. This review is a very useful tool as it maintains the generated knowledge of each project. These three facts must be complied with:

- Problems should be recognized from an impersonal point of view. People should not consider it a witch-hunt or a search for the underachieving staff;
- Videos or journals of the project could be used to help to recall the more relevant facts; and
- It must be made sure that actions are identified in the review and are rapidly implemented.

Conclusions

The paper studies a true case of a Spanish construction company, acting as a Virtual Enterprise broker in the Supply Chain, and detects the main problems and suggests the appropriate solutions.

It is necessary to establish a methodology for creating and managing this kind of Virtual Enterprises in a project environment in order to increase their potential benefits. Our research group is currently working in this direction.

(Josep Capó-Vicedo, Assistant Professor, Stategic Management, Department of Business Management, Polytechnic University of Valencia, Valencia, Spain. E-mail: pepcapo@doe.upv.es.

José V Tomás-Miquel, Assistant Professor, Stategic Management, Department of Business Management, Polytechnic University of Valencia, Valencia, Spain. E-mail: jotomi@doe.upv.es.

M Expósito-Langa, Assistant Professor, Stategic Management, Department of Business Management, Polytechnic University of Valencia, Valencia, Spain. E-mail: maexlan@omp.es.)

References

1. Camarinha-Matos L M and Afsarmanesh H (1999), "The Virtual Enterprise Concept", *Infrastructures for Virtual Enterprises: Networking Industrial Enterprises,* Kluwer Academic Publishers.
2. Camarinha-Matos L M (2002), *Collaborative Business Ecosystems and Virtual Enterprises,* Kluwer Academic Publishers.
3. Hong-Minh S M, Barker R and Naim M M (1999), *Construction Supply Chain Trend Analysis,* Seventh Annual Conference of the International Group for Lean Construction (IGLC-7), Berkeley.
4. Lambert D, Cooper M and Pugh J (1998), "Supply Chain Management", *International Journal of Logistics Management,* Vol. 9, No. 2, pp. 1-19.
5. London K and Kenley R (2000), *The Development of a Neo-industrial Organization Methodology for Describing and Comparing Construction Supply Chains,* Eighth Annual Conference of the International Group for Lean Construction (IGLC-8), Brighton, UK, July 17-19, 2000.
6. Nonaka I (1994), "A Dynamic Theory of Organisational Knowledge Creation", *Organisation Science,* Vol. 5, No. 1, pp. 14-37.
7. Simões-Costa S and Rabelo R J (2002), *Supporting the Creation of Virtual Enterprises Using Mobile Agents,* Proceedings of IFIP TC5 WG5.5. (PRO-VE'02), Kluwer Academic Publishers.

18

The Mechanics and the Method

Nasreen Taher

The case describes how dabbawallahs have evolved a unique coding system of their own which is used to track the flow of dabbas within the entire delivery network. The system relies on the hub-and-spoke concept comparable in many ways to the postal mail delivery system, where mails are sent to a central sorting facility for consolidation, subsequently being redirected to various destinations. From the customer's house to his office or factory, the dabba is handled by at least three different dabbawallahs, up to a maximum of 12 men, depending entirely on the place of pick-up and the place to which it has to be delivered.

The incredible system of the Dabbawallahs that has been in operation for 113 years thrives on enviable team work. What makes the dabbawallahs unique? And how do they work? At the simplest, the dabbawallahs deliver home cooked food to individuals at their workplaces and return empty tiffin boxes to homes and in some cases to caterers. As a team they manage to deliver nearly 175 thousand lunches daily in Mumbai, serving a total area of approximately 75 kilometers in and around the city. Given the two-way route for each dabba, the number of deliveries works out to more than 350 thousand per day.

The article also appeared in the book "Impeccable Logistics and Supply Chain Management:A Case of Mumbai Dabbawallahs".

How would one manage to move 175 thousand containers, each with its own designated origin and destination on a daily basis in an efficient and systematic fashion? Again, what sort of features are needed to be built in to the delivery system to ensure that the performance remains insulated against environmental disruptions such as break downs, no-show and the like? What makes the system even more unique is the fact that the dabbawallahs do this without using any IT or infrastructural investment and with an illiterate workforce.

The answers to all of the above depend on several factors, social, economical and regional. The system relies on the hub-and-spoke concept comparable in many ways to the postal mail delivery system, where mails are sent to a central sorting facility for consolidation, subsequently being redirected to various destinations.

The dabbawallahs operate on a zoning system approach with each zone being served by a team of 20 to 25 dabbawallahs, each serving around 30 customers per day. Each individual team operates as a separate and independent business unit and the team leader called the *Mukadam* is responsible for the efficient and well coordinated functioning of the team. The delivery takes place in four stages.

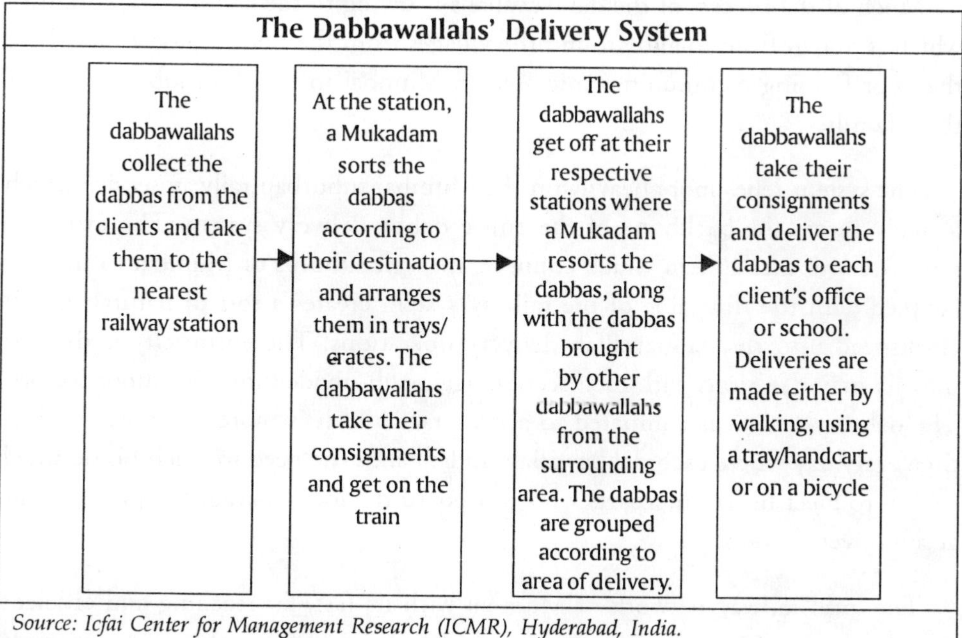

Source: Icfai Center for Management Research (ICMR), Hyderabad, India.

The teams are thus perfectly self-controlled and self-administered working units which share a common agenda. The entire system is very loosely organized as a cooperative structure with a self-regulating decentralized delivery system that has only three hierarchies of authority, thereby rendering it as a rather flat type of organization. The entire workforce comprises about 5000 workers, 800 Mukadams and a small number of executive committee members. This executive committee plays a role that mainly involves administering the welfare activities, setting the agenda, and conflict resolution. All employees are regarded as shareholders in the trust, who share in the earnings equally, irrespective of the quantum or the category of work that they are allocated. This concept of the men who form part of the organization being regarded as shareholders rather than employees results in a peaceful and well regulated working system without any room for unions or strikes. The trust collects Rs.15 from each dabbawallah every month as contribution towards a welfare fund from which loans are dispersed to the dabbawallahs for medical, educational and personal needs. Apart from this, a monthly amount is also set aside for charity purposes under which there is a 'feed the poor program.'

Much of the success of the dabbawallahs is owing to the committed workforce which is drawn from in and around the villages from the Pune region from where the poor farming communities migrated to Mumbai in search of jobs to support their families.

The system relies more heavily on the Mumbai suburban railway service which actually forms the backbone of the entire dabba delivery system. The extensive railway commuter system which connects the vast suburbs of Mumbai to the city coupled with the timetable of the railway system creates a sort of natural inbuilt clockspeed into the dabbawallah delivery operations. The entire city is divided into six major sections with each section again sub-divided into 56 minor sectors. The delivery system is compared to a relay race and it is more like a war against time every day where each dabbawallah understands the need to reach his destined station to meet his counterparts who will board the local train at the precise hour at any given station.

The local railway network of Mumbai with its fast, far-reaching and efficient trains running 365 days a year, coupled with it being a reasonably low-cost mode

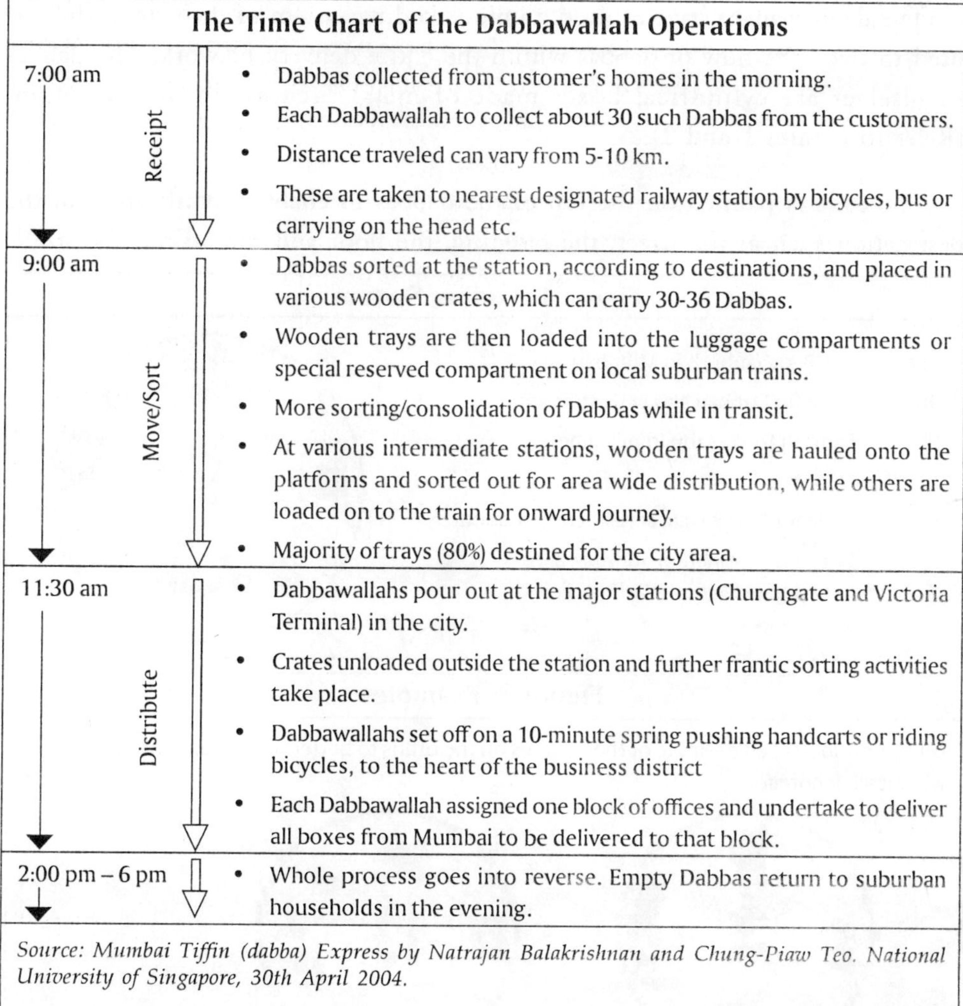

The Time Chart of the Dabbawallah Operations

Time	Stage	Activities
7:00 am	Receipt	• Dabbas collected from customer's homes in the morning. • Each Dabbawallah to collect about 30 such Dabbas from the customers. • Distance traveled can vary from 5-10 km. • These are taken to nearest designated railway station by bicycles, bus or carrying on the head etc.
9:00 am	Move/Sort	• Dabbas sorted at the station, according to destinations, and placed in various wooden crates, which can carry 30-36 Dabbas. • Wooden trays are then loaded into the luggage compartments or special reserved compartment on local suburban trains. • More sorting/consolidation of Dabbas while in transit. • At various intermediate stations, wooden trays are hauled onto the platforms and sorted out for area wide distribution, while others are loaded on to the train for onward journey. • Majority of trays (80%) destined for the city area.
11:30 am	Distribute	• Dabbawallahs pour out at the major stations (Churchgate and Victoria Terminal) in the city. • Crates unloaded outside the station and further frantic sorting activities take place. • Dabbawallahs set off on a 10-minute spring pushing handcarts or riding bicycles, to the heart of the business district • Each Dabbawallah assigned one block of offices and undertake to deliver all boxes from Mumbai to be delivered to that block.
2:00 pm – 6 pm		• Whole process goes into reverse. Empty Dabbas return to suburban households in the evening.

Source: Mumbai Tiffin (dabba) Express by Natrajan Balakrishnan and Chung-Piaw Teo. National University of Singapore, 30th April 2004.

of travel contributes in a major way towards the efficiency of the dabba delivery system, as there is at least one train in every 4 minutes.

From the customer's house to his office or factory, the dabba is handled by at least three different dabbawallahs, up to a maximum of 12 men, depending entirely on the place of pick up and the place where it has to be delivered. A dabbawallah who starts around 9 AM and has to collect around 30 dabbas will need just about one hour to complete all the collecting before he reaches the station where he gathers with the other dabbawallahs of his area.

The dabbawallahs have evolved a unique coding system of their own which is used to track the flow of dabbas within the entire delivery network. The dabbas themselves are cylindrical boxes made of metal such as tin or aluminum. (Refer to Figures 1 and 2).

The code is painted on the top of the dabbas to enable identification of the destination such as the street, the building, the floor and the office. The size is

Figure 1: Coding System

VLP	: Vile Parle (suburb in Mumbai)
9EX12	: Code for Dabbawalas at Destination
EX	: Express Towers (building name)
12	: Floor no.
E	: Code for Dabbawala at residential station
3	: Code for destination Station eg. Churchgate Station (Nariman Point)

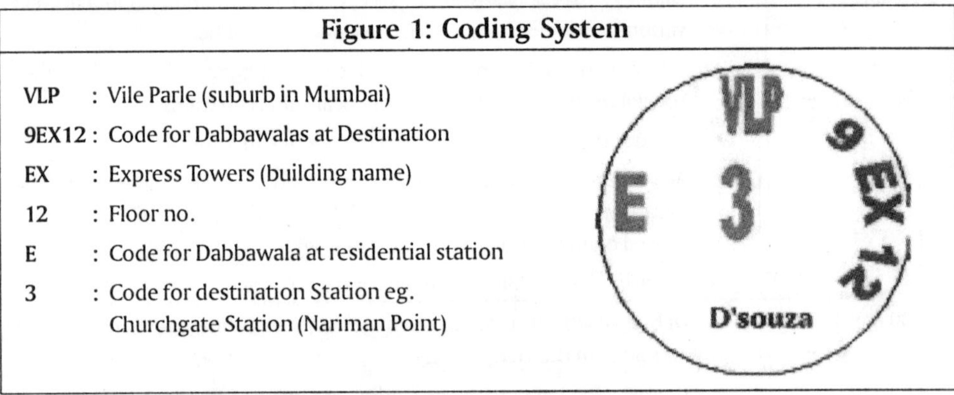

Figure 2: Examples

Let us now look at an example of these codes on the tiffins to better understand the system and what it all denotes:

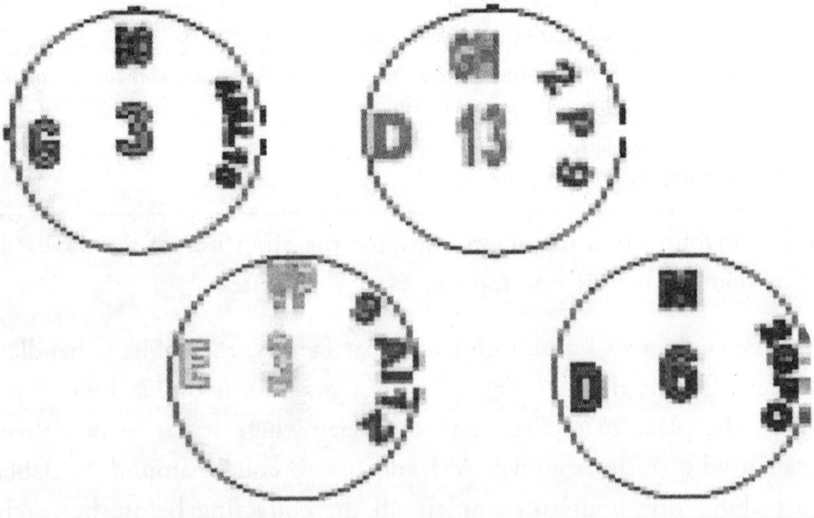

Source: www.mydabbawala.com

A Common Coding System in Use

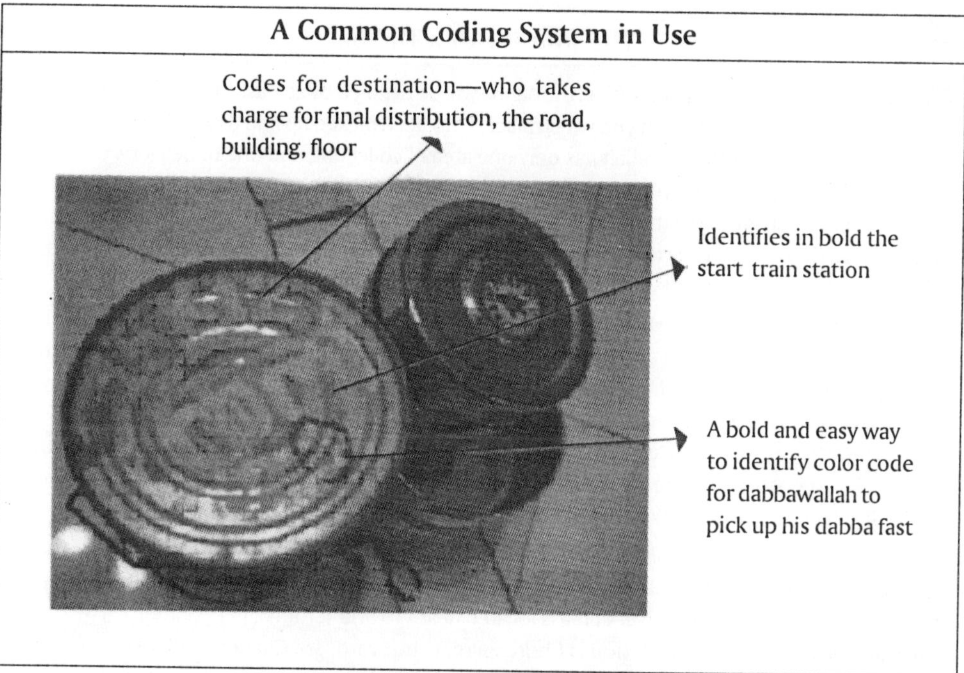

restricted to six inches which is about the size of the top of the dabba and uses colors, dashes, crosses, dots and simple symbols to indicate to the largely illiterate dabbawallahs, various details such as the originating suburb, the route to be followed and the station/destination to which it is to be delivered. The system, by its very simplicity and straight forward structure allows a smooth flow to and from the destination of the dabbas despite the fact that the dabba may have to pass through as many as six different hands in each direction of the movement each day. Over the years, the simple code of dashes and crosses has evolved into a simple text which is easy to decipher and interpret.

(Nasreen Taher was the HOD and Consulting Editor at Icfai Center for Business Research, a constituent of Icfai Business School, Bangalore.)

The Journey of a Dabba

From the customer's house to his office, the dabba will be handled by at least three different delivery men and up to 12 men, depending on which place it has been picked up and to which part of the city it has to be dropped. A Dabbawallah has only one area of collecting and one of delivery. He has to collect around 30 dabbas. He will start around 9 am and will need a little bit more than one hour to do the collecting before going to the station where he gathers with the other Dabbawallahs of this area. Of course, all the dabbas he picks up won't go to the same delivery area. At the departure station, the dabbas will thus be shared out according to the next destination of each other.

The Dabbawallahs use the train network that is roughly formed of two parallel lines oriented North-South whose terminals are Victoria Terminal and Churchgate. The two lines are connected at Dadar, a common station that allows a change of direction (Ponnuswamy, 1991:93). The train network is indeed relatively simple and that is why Dabbawallahs can operate in this city and no other (The urban network of Delhi, for example, is a lot more complicated and would not allow this system of relay). Moreover, the direction is almost always the same for the dabbas to be delivered: North-South in the morning, South-North in the afternoon.

Let's take an example by following the journey of a dabba. The dabba of Mr. Lal has been picked up by Chandra, the Dabbawallah of this city area (a part of Andheri, a suburb located on the Western line, northward). Chandra's delivery area is located near Victoria Terminal (VT), but Mr. Lal works in Nariman Point whose closest station is Churchgate, southward. So, Chandra will take care of his dabba up to Santa Cruz, a station on the same train line, where he makes a stop to gather a few dabbas to be delivered around VT and drops the dabbas to be delivered at the other terminal. Mr. Lal's dabba is then taken care of by a second Dabbawallah whose delivery area is still not Nariman Point but who is going further on the right train line. At Dadar Station, this second Dabbawallah makes another stop and exchanges tiffins with other Dabbawallahs. A third deliveryman is now in charge of Mr. Lal's dabba, this one is going up to Churchgate. Churchgate is the station for the biggest office area of Mumbai; it is thus divided in many different sectors to which different Dabbawallahs are devoted: once again, Mr. Lal's dabba will go to another Dabbawallah whose delivery sector includes the office of Mr. Lal. In that case, four men have been necessary to drop the tiffin at the right place. It will be the same for the return of the empty dabbas after lunchtime: the same Dabbawallah who delivered at the offices of a specific area will collect them again, reach the closest station and the same sharing out will start again till the Dabbawallah of the residence area has gathered his 30 customers' lot in order to begin his home to home delivery.

Excerpted from the articles titled, Dabbawallahs, Tiffin Carriers of Mumbai: Answering a Need for Specific Catering by Marie Percot.

India's Best-known and Most Efficient Networking – The Mumbai's Dabbawallah System

– Vilma D'Souza, Mumbai

Mumbai, Sep 14: Just like the saying goes, Rome was not built in a day. A similar philosophy could perhaps be applied to the Dabbawallah system and all its fame.

Although some may look down upon this business, yet its impact on the lives of the *Mumbai-vasis* cannot be ignored. *Dabba* is a Hindi word for a tiffin container and *dabbawallah* means a person who carries these containers—what is commonly known as *'bhuti'* in Konkani. The word itself brings to one's mind the home-made food and its aroma; the rest of it just follows.

I have seen them right from the time I was a kid. As I would get ready to go to school, the dabbawallah would come at the gate of the building gate and wait with his bicycle. My mom would just hurry for the only reason is that the dabbawallah would wait.

My mom is usually a person who does not bother even if her husband would wait for hours for her nor would she hurry for someone's wedding or funeral. However, the dabbawallah is the only person whom my mom was punctual towards, or would report to on time, rather.

For those who have not heard about the dabbawallahs or about their service, this topic would come as a nuance. Let me explain the whole funda of the dabbawallah and their business.

I have not studied them for long. But having seen them right from the time when I was small until I could complete my college, I can confidently say, they have all the business management qualities which are essential for an MBA to possess.

The tiffin carrier service is believed to have originated in the 19th century. These are people who pick up tiffins from homes and deliver to offices, and this practice is prominent among people travelling in the crowded trains of Mumbai, hiring the services of the dabbawallahs. Yet, for all that, the fee charged is minimal.

They start with the first team of people who go around for their pick-up rounds in the morning from the residential areas and deliver the consignment to the nearest railway station.

Thereafter, the role of the other team comes up to take it from the first railway station to the railway station closest to the destination. The next team takes charge of collecting the dabbas from that station to the exact destination.

In spite of all the dabbas being similar in their appearance, there is hardly any report of a wrong dabba being delivered. The secret behind this is a widely-used system employed to separate them with some sort of a code.

And one of the most significant incidents on my mind is that when we had shifted our residence, the change in the dabbawallah became a matter of great concern.

My dad was enjoying the freshly-packed lunch from home. Although it was being delivered to his office hot at lunchtime by the dabbawallah, he had spoken to the dabbawallahs just at one instance, that too, when he had enrolled himself on their list. And when we approached a dabbawallah in Malad, we had to go through a long round of investigation.

However, whatever may be the cause of disagreement with any dabbawallah, there is always unity among them. If one of them has some "uncch-nichh" (argument) with any of their customers then no one—mind you, absolutely no one in the whole of Mumbai Dabbawallah Committee—would agree to deliver the dabba for you.

Moreover, words of the dabbawallahs are regarded as arrows sent through the bows, which cannot be taken back. Whatever is said once cannot be changed. If a holiday is declared by the committee, no matter what happens, they would not go back on that.

Contd...

Contd...

But their story does not end here. There is a lot to learn from them. Even Prince Charles was greatly inspired by them during his visit to India, so much so that for his wedding he invited the dabbawallahs to England. The most remarkable aspect of this was that no one else from India was invited.

Let it be a news channel or other source of media and communication, they portrait the picture of these dabbawallahs as an ultimate example of unity and solidarity. The BBC has produced a documentary on dabbawallahs.

So, friends, all of you who have read this and are just concentrating on their work profile or on their community, take a cue, inspiration and get motivated by them and live united as a community.

This is where each one is concerned about the welfare of the other. Perhaps the most suitable message for the mankind.

Source: www.mydabbawala.com. Copyright © MyDabbaWala. Com. Reprinted with permission.

Pick-up point

The journey begins

Dabbas on the Move

Proforma Invoice

॥ श्री ज्ञानेश्वर प्रसन्न ॥

M : 98194 77199 / 98691 52163
O : 2682 1897

मुकादम : रघुनाथ धों. मेदगे
रोहिदास स. आढाव

१) लक्ष्मण गव्हाणे २) सुनिल मेदगे ३) आहीलू आढाव
४) मारुती यादव ५) एकनाथ बयाले ६) सचिन डोकळे
७) बबन कदम ८) एकनाथ बच्चे ९) किसन चौधरी

३, रघुनाथ पाठकचाळ, सहार रोड, विजय नगर सोसायटी समोर,
संभाजी नगर, अंधेरी (पूर्व), मुंबई - ४०० ०६९.

दिनांक ________________ माहे ________________

भोजनाचा डबा नेणे आणण्याचा हिशोब रु. ________________

वसुल करणाऱ्याची सही ________________

✦ Notice ✦

1) One months Salary is Diwali Bonus. 2) Please do not pay without Bill. 3) Please do not keep silver or stainless steel utensils in carriers. 4) If carries are lost only value will be paid in the monthly payment of half. 5) We are not responsible for carries lost in your office. 6) Delivery will depend as per train timings. 7) If train are late for 1-30 Hours of more than carrier will be return as it. 8) If any have any complaint about our servants Please let us know by post. 9) Please look carrier having single supporters hence are will not be held responsible for damage of the lunch. 10) Payment to be made in full even carrier fails to carry for 8 to 10 days in a month 11) If carriers lost we pay half from my only.

19

E-procurement Excellence – Behind the FedEx's Success

Mohammed Naved Khan

FedEx has realized major productivity gains, timesavings, cost reduction and ROI benefits as a result of the deployment of e-procurement solution. The article discusses the selection, implementation and the architecture of E-procurement solution at FedEx, while highlighting the reasons for implementation.

Industry Analysis

Fast, reliable, and time-definite delivery of documents, packages and freight is a critical success factor in the industry FedEx operates in. The major competitors of FedEx include UPS, TNT, DHL and Parcelforce. DHL is the world's largest international air express carrier, with a 40% market share, while UPS is the world's largest package distribution company.

FedEx recognized service reliability as the most important piece of the picture—believing that if the delivery did not reach its destination on time, all other issues simply faded away. The company did not necessarily strive to be the cheapest service provider, but rather emphasized on its superior quality of service, global

---

Source: Case Folio, January 2004. This article originally appeared as "E-procurement Excellence". The article also appeared in the book "The Icfai University Press on Supply Chain Management – Technology and Experiences".

coverage and easy service availability. This clearly shows how FedEx differentiated itself through strong brand building. In fact, the company's focus on the quality aspects of its services has fetched it many awards. To keep itself ahead of its competitors, FedEx invested heavily in latest IT solutions and leveraged IT as a strategic tool.

Defining Business at FedEx

Using Derek Abell's concept of business definition, we can define FedEx's business along three dimensions viz., customer group (who is being satisfied), customer function (what is being satisfied) and alternative technologies (how the need is being satisfied). Refer to Figure 1.

Figure 1

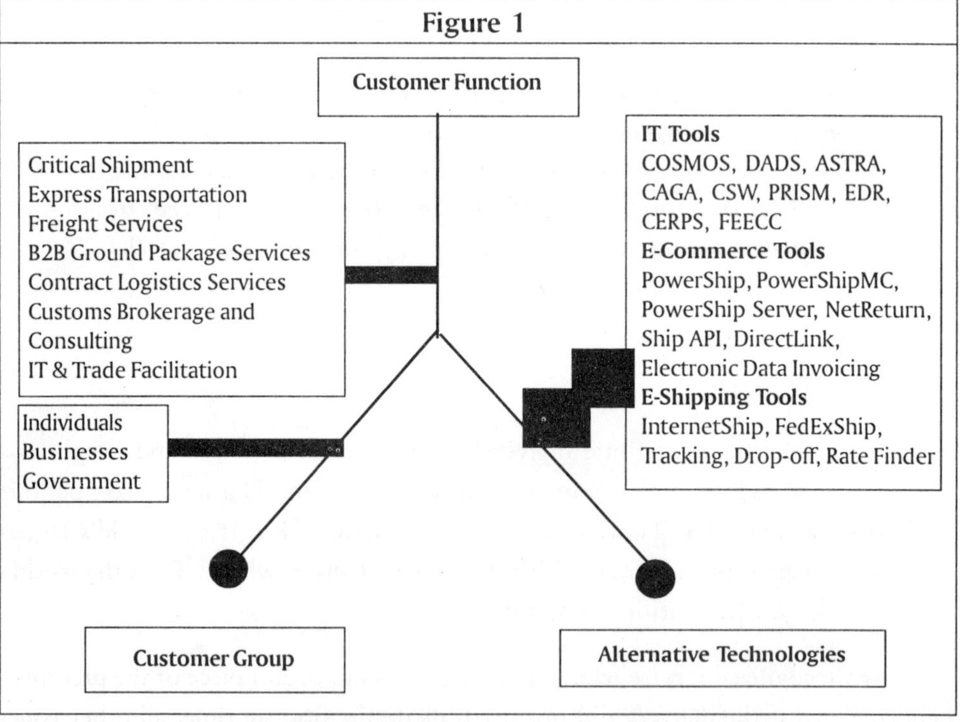

FedEx has been successful because it has been able to identify its customers' needs and used IT effectively to meet them. The company's use of innovative electronic technologies has made shipping easier, more productive, and it has been able to avoid the need to hire thousands of additional employees. All this meant that it could deliver superior customer service at considerably reduced costs.

In fact, FedEx came to be widely regarded as one of the leading strategic users and trendsetters in the use of IT. The e-procurement program implemented was another example of the effective use of alternative technologies to get an edge over the competitors. This initiative had the potential to radically redefine the rules of the game (vis-à-vis customer satisfaction).

Reasons for Implementation of E-procurement Solution

FedEx expected the e-procurement solution to emerge as a key strategy for automating and streamlining the procurement process to keep all levels of operations in working order. There was also a need to overhaul business processes and the IT infrastructure to reduce overall purchasing cycle time, consolidate purchases, gain an upper hand over suppliers, attract new suppliers and create competition for original suppliers, track spending patterns, curb unauthorized spending and administrative costs thereby leading to internal efficiency and direct cost savings.

E-procurement systems bring productivity gains by unburdening workers from tedious, time-consuming, and inefficient manual methods of processing purchase orders; employees can work more quickly and focus their attention on more strategic tasks. Most of the time savings come from the reduced need to re-enter information, from streamlining the interaction with suppliers and from having a central repository for data. Return On Investment (ROI) comes via reduction in the expense of procuring items. This is because items are cheaper when purchased through Internet marketplaces. FedEx also could reduce the cost of processing transactions by eliminating the need for paper documentation. It improved organizational effectiveness as it gained more control over what was being ordered and who was doing the ordering.

Selecting Ariba: A Strategic Decision

FedEx evaluated various e-procurement solutions available before finally selecting the Ariba platform because it matched FedEx's vision of leveraging technology to streamline operations and allowed it to turn the efficient management of operating resources into a strategic tool. Ariba's platform provided for seamless integration of FedEx's PeopleSoft financial and human resources software system running on an HP-UX, V-Class server and at the same time allowed FedEx to electronically connect to its suppliers as well as leverage network payment capabilities. It also provided buyers with the automated 'picks and shovels' they needed to integrate with ERP systems, process approvals, route invoices and perform other tasks. The Web-based user friendly front-end allowed authorized individuals to work on FedEx's behalf to order easily.

E-procurement Architecture

E-procurement systems consist of three parts:

1. **Server-based software at the buyer's end:** It is usually accessed by browser front-ends from within the organization. It automates the procurement process. In FedEx's case, it consists of Ariba's central Operating Resource Management System (ORMS) interface.
2. **The supply side is effectively a mirror image of the buyer's end:** It usually involves catalogue preparation, password access and workflow for making approved purchases, and trading history, credit agreements, discount arrangements and so on.
3. **In between these two applications is the most powerful feature of the e-procurement market—the trading portal:** The leading vendors have moved towards a portal model. The trading portal could ultimately become the place where all secure or workflow-oriented business transactions take place. FedEx is using a combination of Ariba's Market Suite, Internet Business Exchange service and the Commerce Center applications.

Implementation of E-procurement Solution at FedEx

The implementation of e-procurement solution at FedEx has been completed broadly in three phases:

- **Phase I:** Pilot implementation of Ariba's e-procurement solution that included installation of e-Commerce platform along with Ariba Buyer technology.
- **Phase II:** Rollout of 'Ariba Buyer' to around 7000 IT division employees. The managers were given charge of producing the business requirements, documents and project plans.

- **Phase III:** An over all plan was developed to bring out each commodity whose major supplier had electronic catalogs.

Critical Analysis

Ariba's ORMS showed an ROI three times the benchmark FedEx used for approving an IT project. Since at FedEx, much of the ordering process through electronic invoices and e-mail approval had already been automated, the ROI from Ariba's product came mostly from the savings generated by its online cataloging function. That function centralized and consolidated the purchase to a select few vendors, eliminating the need for employees to pick up the Yellow Pages or drive to a store to search for the items they need.

Further, due to the implementation of company-wide strategic sourcing initiatives, the number of suppliers was reduced by about 50%. Ariba enabled those suppliers (75) that represented FedEx's largest volume buys. The success of the implementation was further established when FedEx was awarded Aberdeen's 'Best e-procurement' practices award in early 2002.

Problems and Prospects

With customers in the US (as well as overseas), increasingly shopping online, analysts predict that worldwide revenues from online retailing would rise to more than $10 bn in the next few years. Further, business-to-business Internet commerce is expected to grow to an astronomical $327 bn. All this would mean explosive growth in FedEx's business (and that of competitors too) and also changing customer demands. To address these, FedEx needs to continue the initiatives in the area of human resources, systems and technology. It needs to sustain the pace of innovation and rapid growth.

FedEx needs to be cautious with respect to a number of issues. The inability to move e-procurement beyond inexpensive, indirect goods purchases can have negative implications in terms of economic viability. One of the biggest challenges could be to integrate its technology with employee competencies and their ability to deal with anonymous vendors. Another issue that needs to be addressed by FedEx is encouraging the suppliers to migrate to the e-procurement platform.

FedEx needs to note that several of its pioneering services, have been deployed with alarming regularity by competition down the line. To capitalize on the 'first mover' advantage, speed of execution is critical. And, the learning curve may help FedEx achieve scale economies faster, while competition would still be busy catching up. In an industry where saving time is essential to improve profitability, the need is to deploy new technologies (for e.g., wireless) to accelerate operations, transform customer service, and snatch market share.

(Mohammed Naved Khan is Senior Lecturer, Department of Business Administration, Faculty of Management Studies & Research, Aligarh Muslim University, Aligarh, India.)

PepsiCo's Distribution and Logistics Operations – The Wireless Way*

– K Prasanth and Vivek Gupta

Headquartered in New York, the US-based PepsiCo is one of the world's leading beverage and snack food companies. Analysts felt that one of the main reasons for the company's massive growth over the decades and the leadership status it has acquired in almost all its business segments was PepsiCo's efficient distribution and logistics management operations.

In the PepsiCo's beverages business, the bottler played an important role in ensuring the availability of the products and also in promoting them. Pepsi Americas (PAS) was the second largest Pepsi-Cola bottler with revenues of $3.2 bn in the fiscal 2002-03. PAS had to ensure the timely dispatch of goods, as well as ensure full capacity utilization of its trucks, and quicker inventory replenishment at the stores. The ultimate objective was to ensure that the stores were stocked with the required quantities of products at the right time. The aim was to continuously increase sales and productivity levels.

In order to achieve the above goals, PAS decided to make a clear distinction between its sales and delivery operations in major US territories, on an experimental basis. Under the new system (known as the pre-sell method), each day, the Account Sales Managers (ASMs) went to the retail outlets to gauge their requirements, promote products and receive orders. The following day, the Delivery Agents (DAs) delivered the orders as per the outlets' requirements.

PAS also decided to replace its various disparate business systems with an integrated ERP package developed by People Soft. The package assisted the company in its various functions, such as sales, merchandizing, CRM, procurement and so on. PAS also employed a mobile computing system using Wireless Local Area Network (WLAN) and Wireless Wide Area Network (WWAN). Under the new system, PAS replaced the previous handheld computers with PDT 8000 computers made by Symbol. The PDTs were equipped with integrated barcode scanners and a numeric keyboard. The ASMs used them to feed customer orders. Each day, the ASMs fed the order information into the sales system at the Distribution Centers (DCs) through wireless network in areas where the wireless coverage was available. In areas where wireless coverage was not available or where it was difficult to get wireless connectivity, the ASMs connected the computers to a modem to send order information through the Internet to the DCs using the traditional telephone lines. This enabled the staff at the DC to do the necessary groundwork for the next day's orders. On the next day, the DA delivered the ordered quantity of goods at the retail outlets. The method used was in contrast to the earlier one, wherein the DAs went about distributing the products depending upon their availability in the trucks rather than what the retail outlets wanted. Using the handheld computers, the ASMs could also make attractive sales pitches and show the latest Pepsi's ads, apart from transmitting order information.

(K Prashanth, Research Associate and Vivek Gupta, Senior Faculty Member, The Icfai Center for Management Research.)

* This is an excerpt from the article "PepsiCo's Distribution and Logistics Operations" by K Prasanth and Vivek Gupta, published in Marketing Mastermind, December 05.

20

Dell Inc.: Time to Discard its Direct-selling Model?

Ramamurthy Nambi

Michael Dell's innovative direct-sales strategy together with efficient supply chain management has been successful in allowing his company to sell computers at competitive prices. Dell Inc., bought components from its suppliers on credit; it sold most of the computers directly to end-users on cash payment. The case study describes how Dell has successfully implemented supply chain management to sell computers to the customer. The main idea behind this direct-sales model was to bypass the intermediary distribution network such as retail stores and system integrators, and thereby offer products at lower prices compared to competitors.

"We're not changing our strategy…we believe the market is still healthy and we don't see a whole lot changing[1]."

– Rollins,
CEO, Dell Inc.

"It would be presumptuous of me to say we have totally eliminated the advantages that they have with their direct business. I think I could say that we have negated the advantage such that it is no longer a huge strategic advantage[2]".

– David Booth,
US Country Manager and Senior Vice-President of HP.

Dell Inc., the world's largest computer manufacturer achieved a revenue of \$55.9 billion[3] in 2005 and had set itself a target of achieving a world-wide revenue of \$80 billion by 2010. Michael Dell's innovative direct-sales strategy together with efficient supply chain management had been successful in allowing his company to sell computers at competitive prices, thereby giving Dell Inc. significant market share and also comfortable profit margins. During FY 2005-06, Dell held a leading 18.2%[4] share of the world PC (personal computer) market. The Direct-selling model in particular, not only saved on margins to dealers, but also minimized the need to sell on credit, thereby resulting in a very healthy cash position. While Dell Inc. bought components from its suppliers on credit, it sold most of the computers direct to end-users on cash.

However, according to industry sources, for the fourth time (in Q4 of FY 2005-06) Dell said the company could not achieve quarterly earnings or sales forecast since the beginning of financial year 2005. Its stock price decreased by nearly 10% to \$19.91, the lowest in five years (since 2001) which also pushed down the stock prices of other computer companies bringing down NASDAQ[5] to a 14-month low[6].

Repeated missing of targets, declining sales and decreasing share prices led industry analysts to raise questions about the business model followed by Dell Inc. Was the direct-sales model struggling for survival?

Michael Dell and Dell Inc.

The founder of Dell, Inc., Michael Saul Dell was born on February 23, 1965 in Houston, Texas. When he was 15 years, he unassembed a brand new Apple II[7] computer and rebuilt it, just to see if he could. He attended Memorial High

School in Houston, Texas, where he did not perform well. Reportedly, one of his teachers told him that he "*would probably never go anywhere in life.*" After school education, he attended the University of Texas at Austin to become a physician. But, his interest was always in computers. Even while studying at the university, he started a computer company called *PC's Limited* in his room in 1984.

Realizing good growth potential and opportunities in computer sales, Michael Dell decided to quit college at the age of 19 to run his business full-time. In 1987, *PC's Limited* changed its name to Dell Computer Corporation. Despite a number of hurdles (In 1993 there was a fire accident in its laptops which caused heavy loss. In the mid 1990s Dell lost market to a competing PC selling company – Gateway), Dell managed to survive to become the most profitable PC manufacturer in the world. As Dell expanded its product line beyond computers, in 2003, the shareholders voted to rename the company *Dell, Inc.* Dell offered a range of products which mainly included servers, printing and imaging systems, workstations, notebook computers and desktop computers.

Dell Inc., overtook major players like Compaq and IBM which were dominating the PC market in the 1990s. Thereafter, Dell retained the first position in PC shipments in the US as well as in the global market and remained there right through (up to 2006).

Headquartered in Round Rock, Texas, Dell Inc, with an employee-strength of 65,200, sold a comprehensive portfolio of products and services directly to customers worldwide. Dell's direct sales operations were in 13 markets which included Australia, Brunei, China, Hong Kong, India, Japan, Korea, Macau, Malaysia, New Zealand, Singapore, Taiwan and Thailand. In addition, 38 distributors served another 31 markets (Annexure I).

Dell designed, built and delivered innovative, tailored systems that offered customers exceptional value. A sales and service operation served Dell's customers in many countries. *Fortune* magazine[8] recognized Dell as America's most admired company.

Michael Dell shared his views about his success. He said, "*I tried to surround myself with smart advisors, and I tried not to make the same mistake twice... Since we were growing so quickly, everything was constantly changing. We'd say, "What's the best way to do this?" and come up with an answer. The resulting process would work for a while, then it would stop working and we'd have to adjust it and try something else... The whole thing was one big experiment[9]."*

"We challenged ourselves constantly, to grow more or to provide better service to our customers; and each time we set a new goal, we would make it. Then we would stop for a moment, give each other a few high fives, and get started on tackling the next goal."[10]

He effectively delegated authority to subordinates, believing that the best results came from "*(turning) loose talented people who can be relied upon to do what they're supposed to do."* Business associates viewed Michael Dell as an aggressive personality and an extremely competitive risk-taker who always played close to the edge. Moreover, the people selected by Dell had similar traits, which encouraged an aggressive, intense corporate culture with a strong sense of mission and dedication. Inside Dell, Michael was known for his great attention to detail —a trait which employees termed *"Michael managing."*

Michael Dell's achievements and his phenomenal success earned many accolades for him.This included, "Entrepreneur of the Year" from *Inc.* magazine, "Man of the Year" by *PC Magazine*, "High Impact CEO" by executive search firm Hedrick and Struggles, "Top CEO in American Business" from *Worth* magazine and "CEO of the Year" by *Financial World* and *Industry Week* magazines. In 1997, 1998 and 1999, he was included in *Business Week's* list of "The Top 25 Managers of the Year."

Michael Dell, with total assets of around US$18 billion, was listed as the 4th richest man in the United States and as the 18th richest in the world by *Forbes* 400[11], 2005 publication. Dell was staying in Austin, Texas with his wife, Susan, and his four children. He owned the 15th largest home in the world, worth an estimated US$18.7 million[12].

Dell's Philosophy and Strategy

In the 15 years since the company's founding, Michael Dell viewed that working with both customers and suppliers had taught him a number of valuable lessons and formed his leadership style. He completely believed that he could learn a lot from mistakes or experiences. He said "There were obviously no classes on learning how to start and run a business in my high school, so I clearly had a lot to learn. And learn I did, mostly by experimenting and making a bunch of mistakes. One of the first things I learned, though, was that there was a relationship between screwing up and learning: The more mistakes I made, the faster I learned"[13].

His business philosophy had three main rules (Exhibit I). The company's strategy was structured around a number of main elements such as build-to-order manufacturing, just-in-time component inventories, direct sales to customers, and pioneering use of the Internet and e-commerce technology.

Exhibit I

Triangular Principle at Dell Inc.

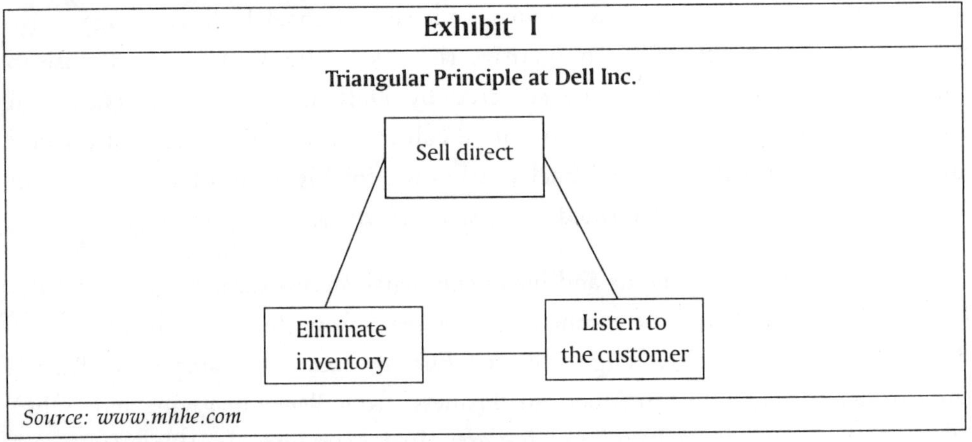

Source: www.mhhe.com

'Sell it directly'

In Dell's direct-selling method, customers directly contacted Dell for a specific product and Dell in turn shipped the products directly to them. Communication between customers and the company was mostly through the Internet or telephone[14] (Exhibit II). The main idea behind this direct-sales model was to bypass the intermediary distribution network such as retail stores and system integrators, and thereby offer products at lower prices compared to competitors.

Dell's Supply Chain

After a customer placed an order, either by phone or through the Internet on *www.dell.com*, Dell processed the order through financial evaluation (credit checking) and configuration evaluation (checking the feasibility of a specific

Exhibit II: Dell's Direct Sales Model

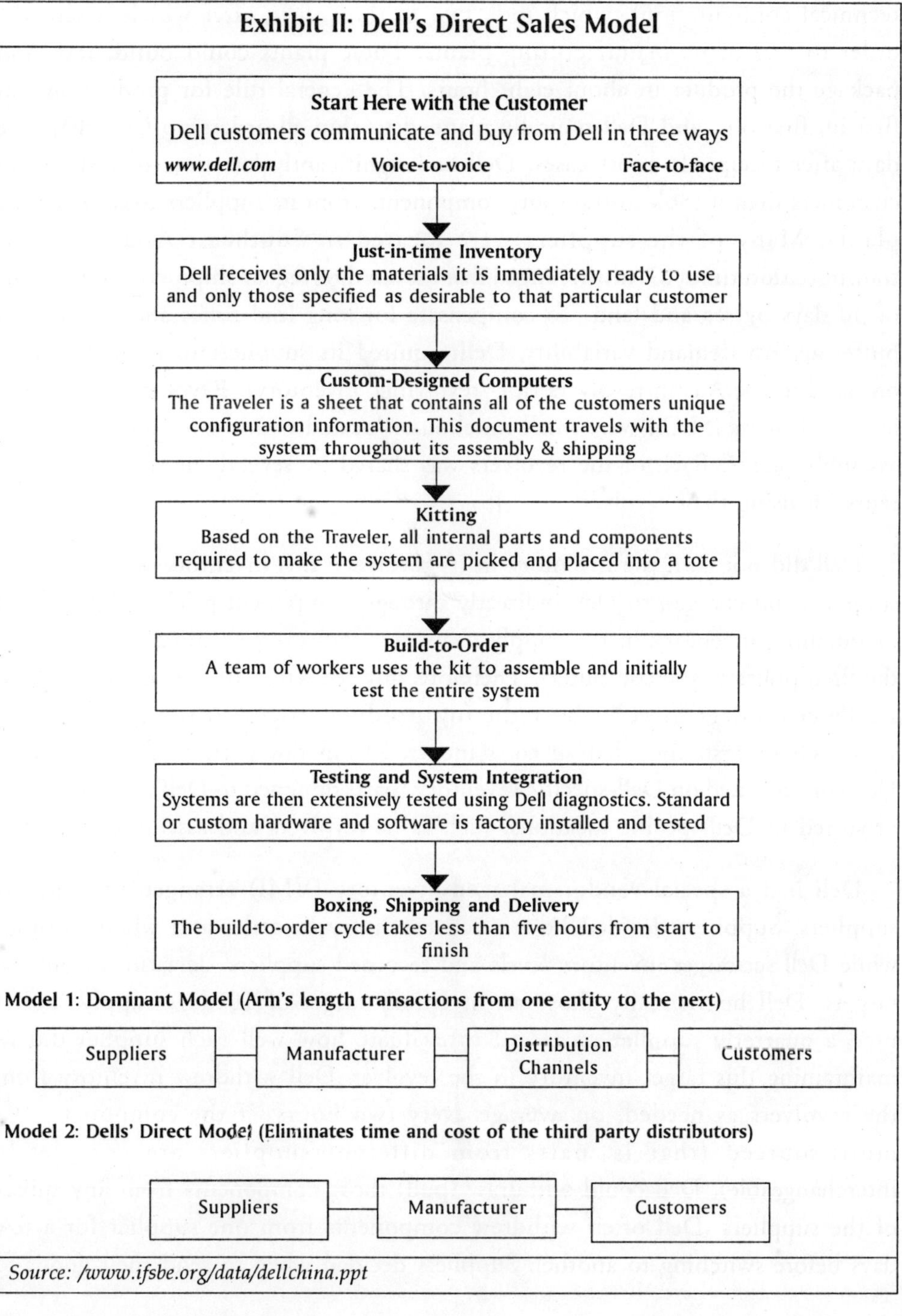

Source: /www.ifsbe.org/data/dellchina.ppt

technical configuration), which took two to three days, after which it sent the order to one of its manufacturing plants. These plants could build, test, and package the product in about eight hours. The general rule for production was first in, first out, and Dell typically planned to ship all orders no later than five days after receipt. In most cases, Dell had significantly less time to respond to customers than it took to transport components from its suppliers to its assembly plants. Many of the suppliers were located in Southeast Asia and their transportation times to Austin ranged from seven days for air shipments to upwards of 30 days by sea and land. To compensate for long lead times and also have a buffer against demand variability, Dell required its suppliers to keep inventory on hand in the Austin revolvers (for "revolving" inventory). Revolvers or supplier logistics centers (SLCs) were small warehouses located within a few miles of Dell's assembly plants. Each of the revolvers was shared by several suppliers who paid rents for using their revolver.

Dell did not own the inventory in its revolvers; this inventory was owned by suppliers and charged to Dell indirectly through component pricing. The cost of maintaining inventory in the supply chain was, however, eventually included in the final prices of the computers. Therefore, any reduction in inventory benefited Dell's customers directly by reducing product prices. Although arguably supply-chain costs included all costs incurred from raw parts to final assembly, Dell concentrated on Dell-specific inventory (parts designed to Dell's specifications or stored in Dell-specific locations, such as its revolvers and assembly plants).

Dell had a special vendor-managed-inventory (VMI) arrangement with its suppliers. Suppliers decided how much inventory to order and when to order while Dell set target inventory levels and recorded suppliers' deviations from the targets. Dell heuristically chose an inventory target of 10 days supply, and it used a quarterly supplier scorecard to evaluate how well each supplier did in maintaining this target inventory in the revolver. Dell withdrew inventory from the revolvers as needed, on average every two hours. If the component was multi-sourced (that is, parts from different suppliers are completely interchangeable), Dell could withdraw (pull) those components from any subset of the suppliers. Dell often withdrew components from one supplier for a few days before switching to another. Suppliers decided when to send their goods to their revolvers. In practice, most suppliers delivered to their revolvers on average three times a week. To help suppliers make good ordering decisions, Dell shared its forecasts with them once a month. These forecasts were generated by Dell's line of business (LOB) marketing department. In addition to product-specific trends, the forecast reflected the seasonality in sales. For home systems, Christmas was the peak time of the year. Other high-demand periods included the back-to-school season, the end of the year when the government made big purchases, and country-specific high seasons for foreign purchases (e.g., those with foreign language keyboards). Dell's sales also increased at the ends of quarters (referred to as the hockey stick).

After the center of competence (COC) checked a forecast for predicted availability of components, the forecast went to Dell's commodity teams and became the basis for a six-month rolling forecast that was updated weekly. The commodity teams made generic forecasts for systems and components and broke those forecasts down to a level of the specific parts that needed to be ordered. If the forecast was not feasible, the LOB marketing department revised it, although such revisions were very rare. The buyer-planner for each commodity received an updated rolling forecast weekly; suppliers received forecasts monthly. Dell had been setting inventory targets based on empirical data and judgment with no clear reference to any desired service levels. Dell hypothesized that it could reduce revolver inventory markedly by using a more rigorous approach and gaining better visibility of the inventory throughout the supply chain. Once it determined an optimized inventory level, Dell could collaborate with its suppliers to eliminate excess inventory. Dell emphasized that it wanted to sustain any changes over the long term, which would require integrating them into its informational infrastructure.

Value Chain was a program intended to extend Dell's successful direct-sales approach back into the supply chain with the goal of increasing the speed and quality of the information flow between Dell and its supply base. The corresponding website *valuechain.dell.com* was an extranet for sharing such information as points of contact, inventory in the supply chain, supply and demand data, component quality metrics, and new part transitions. Dell envisioned using this site to exchange with suppliers current data, forecast data, new product ideas, and other dynamic information that might help it to optimize the flow of information and materials in the supply chain.

Whether it was taking full advantages of the build-to-order supply chain (BOSC) by making suppliers partners by sharing real time information and up-to-date technologies while committing to long-term agreements, keeping no inventory, or focusing on customers' needs, Dell had put its supply chain to work for them.

This also allowed the consumers access to customized PCs and offered additional capabilities, service and content tailored to their needs together with E-Support. An important element of Dell's virtual integration with customers was identifying and customizing to finer customer segments to reap the benefits from unique opportunities and economies from increased focus and attention. Dell shared information and listened to the needs of its customers, as it did with its suppliers, which improved their relationship with customers and helped Dell to forecast demand.

Dell's Zero Time Organization and Instant Customerization Models

Dell Computer Corporation exemplified many of the principles of a Zero-Time Organization. A Zero-Time Organization had a mindset different from that of other organizations. Zero-Time Organizations designed and operated with the assumption that processes could be done instantaneously if information technology and people are creatively combined. This mindset translated into a set of organizational disciplines. A company which successfully implemented each of these disciplines was closer to achieving the organizational objective of instant customerization, which meant that the needs of any customer were fulfilled as soon as the needs were expressed. Instantaneous fulfillment of customer needs was achieved by converting knowledge into something valued by the customer. There were three models for how to achieve instant customerization (Exhibit III).

What did the Model Really Mean to Dell?

According to analysts, Dell's model was characterized by a number of elements which provided good support to the model. The direct-selling model stressed on the build-to-order principle. This build-to-order method helped the company to keep minimum inventory which again ensured quick introduction of new technology. To support its direct-selling model, the company resorted to Just-In-Time manufacturing for which regular and quick supply of components and subassemblies was critical.

Exhibit III: Summary of Zero-Time Disciplines	
Discipline	**Description**
Zero-value-gap	Core values of company are based on customers' values and these values are shared across entities.
Zero-learning-gaps	Capacity to continuously learn and create knowledge, then convert it into customer value instantly.
Zero-management-gaps	Every part of the organization is in itself a whole, complete entity with the ability and authority to function independently.
Zero-process-gaps	The property in which there are no obstacles to completing any required tasks, processes, or activities.
Zero-inclusion-gaps	All individuals and groups who need to be involved are automatically included when the process takes place.
Models of Instant Customerization	
Model	**Description**
Emergency Room Model	Everything necessary to satisfy the customers' needs and choices is waiting, accessible whenever needed.
Disneyland Model	A bounded set of choices is available, from which each customer selects whatever he or she wants.
Hybrid Model	Reasonable set of choices is available, coupled with a way to customize these choices, to meet whatever need customer has.
Source: www.flowalliance.com/Dell_Computer_A_Zero_Time_Organization.pdf	

So the company established and maintained a strong, healthy supplier management (Exhibit IV). This business model gave Dell primary intelligence about customer preferences and needs, as well as immediate feedback on design problems and quality requirements.

This strategy helped Dell Inc., to eliminate inventory of finished products and offer custom-built computers at a lower price. It also reduced the channel costs from 13.5% to 2% of product revenue. With thousands of phone and fax orders daily, $35[15] million in daily Internet sales, and daily contacts between the field sales force and customers of all types, the company was swift enough to detect shifts in sales pattern and get correct feedback on any problems with its products by observing the market trend.

Michael Dell saw his direct-sales approach as totally customer-driven system, with the flexibility to change quickly to new generations of components and PC

Exhibit IV: The Dell Supplier-Customer Model

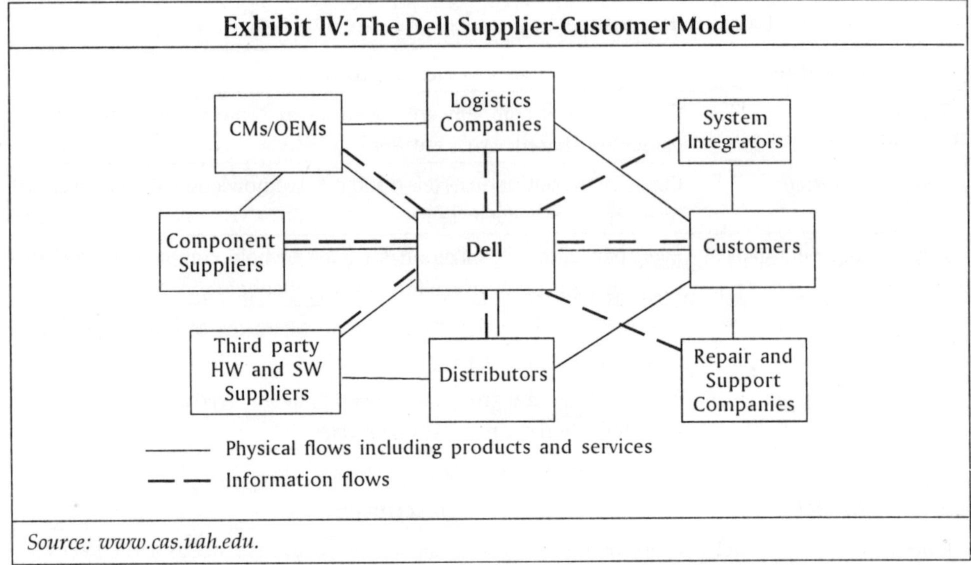

Source: www.cas.uah.edu.

models. He said "Our business model really gives us very fresh input every single day from our customers who tell us what they like or don't like and that allows us to grow very consistently[16]." Each customer order may be distinctive in terms of manufacturing, procurement, packaging, and logistics requirements but Dell's system ensured customers got what they asked for.

Industry watchers said, because of this direct-sales approach, Dell Inc., could sell computers at lower prices and hold a leading 18.2% of the world market (Annexure II).

Advantages for Dell's Model

Since the first computer was sold, two different strategies to serve customers had evolved in the computer industry. As opposed to the Dell's direct-selling approach, its main competitors (such as HP or Compaq) had opted for a vertically integrated company, offering their products through a wide range of multi-brand retail stores. Although not perfect, the Dell model still had several advantages over its competitor's strategies according to analysts. Why is it then that competitors had not adopted the Dell model in order to improve its operations?

Industry experts opined that with the emergence of Dell and its successful direct selling, certain PC manufacturers, like IBM, had exited the manufacturing industry altogether while others knew that a traditional dealer network was not as effective or efficient, but were unable to orient more sales online due to associated costs and a potential backlash from retailers stocking their products. For example, preparing to shift to online sales for Compaq would not only cost 6 to 12 months worth of sales as its dealer networks would refuse to continue selling its products, Compaq also risked losing customers for good during the change period. This negative impact to sales and stock price prevented managers from risking short-term losses in order to shift channels.

Exhibit V: Compaq's Problem in Adopting On-line Sales

- Compaq's existing processes, such as its heavy reliance on distributors, resellers and retail chains were incompatible with the processes involved in Internet retailing.
- Internet retailing involves tailoring orders for individual customers, dealing with the logistics of lean production techniques, and shipping direct-to- customers.
- Conducted its sales mainly through 44,000 distributors, resellers, and retail chains.
- Compaq attempted to launch an online catalog in 1993, but resistance from its retail channel was so fierce that the company withdrew from the effort.
- Unlike Dell, Compaq's processes and values were not compatible with those required to do business successfully on the Internet.

Source: www.lcm.csa.iisc.ernet.in

Moreover, even though certain competitors, like Compaq, had BOSC, which required large investments for internal organization design, technical processes, customer service procedures and human resources training, and communicate with their suppliers, they still lacked the direct sales downstream.

Hence as per analysts, Dell's competitors could not adopt parts of the model due to the potential pressure from their retailers and because of their existing organizational structure. On the other hand, the refusal could have been fostered by other factors, including a deliberate management decision not to adopt the model (Annexure III).

Challenges for the Business Model

According to the experts openion, things were not all green for Dell and its approach. Even though its global share of the market was high, in countries like India, China, and in some other fast-developing markets, Dell's market share was very low and had barely moved up over the past year since it started business in those markets. The main challenges before direct sales model were that the competitor's effective response to it and customer preferences in developing markets. As a reply to this Dell model, competitors, particularly HP[17], streamlined their manufacturing and distribution operations.

In past years, (from 2003 to 2006) both HP and IBM[18], competitors of Dell, performed smarter in stock prices in NASDAQ[19], USA (Exhibit VI).

Exhibit VI: Dell Comparison with its Competitors

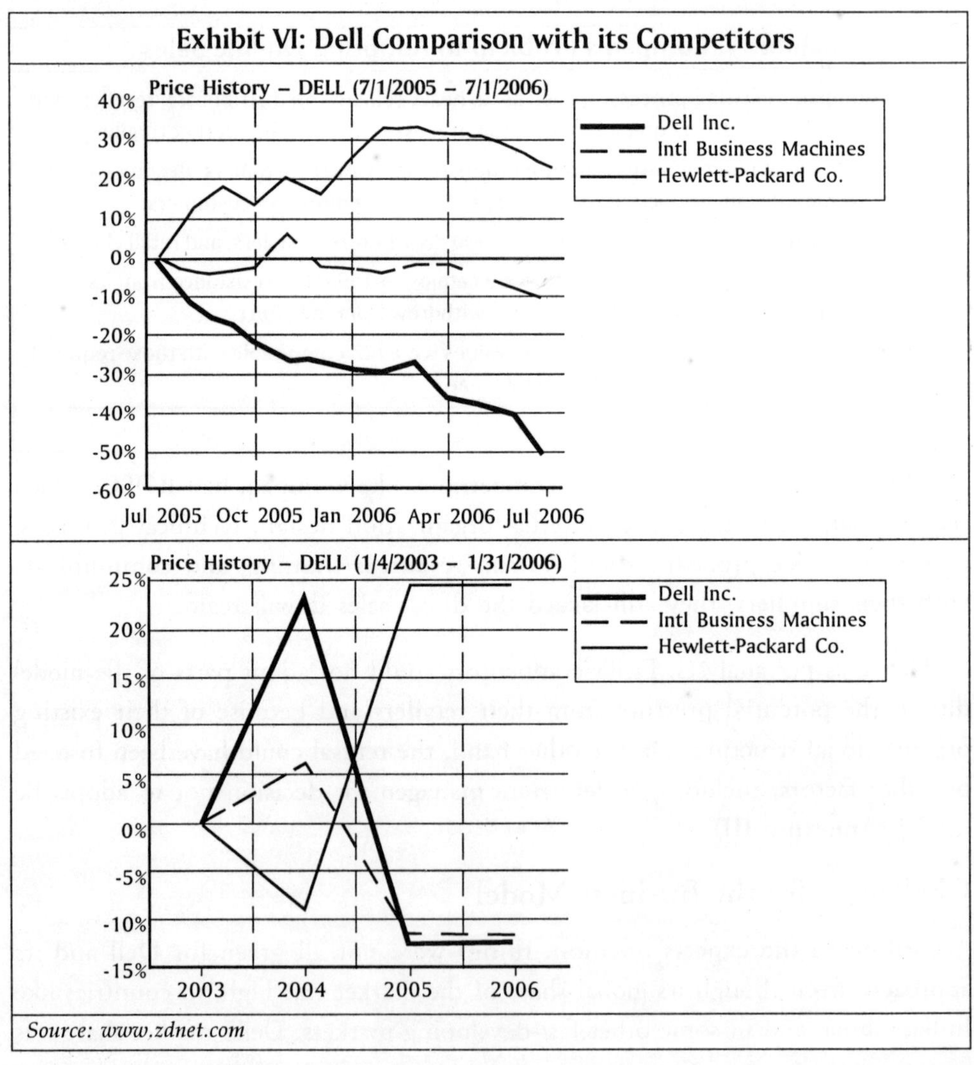

Source: www.zdnet.com

Market Share Vs. Profit

According to the company (Dell), these challenges would not move away from its basic strategy or model. But, the company's gross profit margin was consistent without any sign of improvement for a period of three years, starting from financial year 2002 to 2005, (Exhibit VII) even when their overall growth in terms of market share remained higher than their competitors.

Other manufacturers were catching up with Dell. It used to have an 8 percent to 12 percent advantage in inventory costs compared to other PC makers several years ago, but it now enjoys only a 3 percent advantage, says Richard Gardner, an analyst with Citigroup.

Exhibit VII: Dell's Market Share and Profit Margin

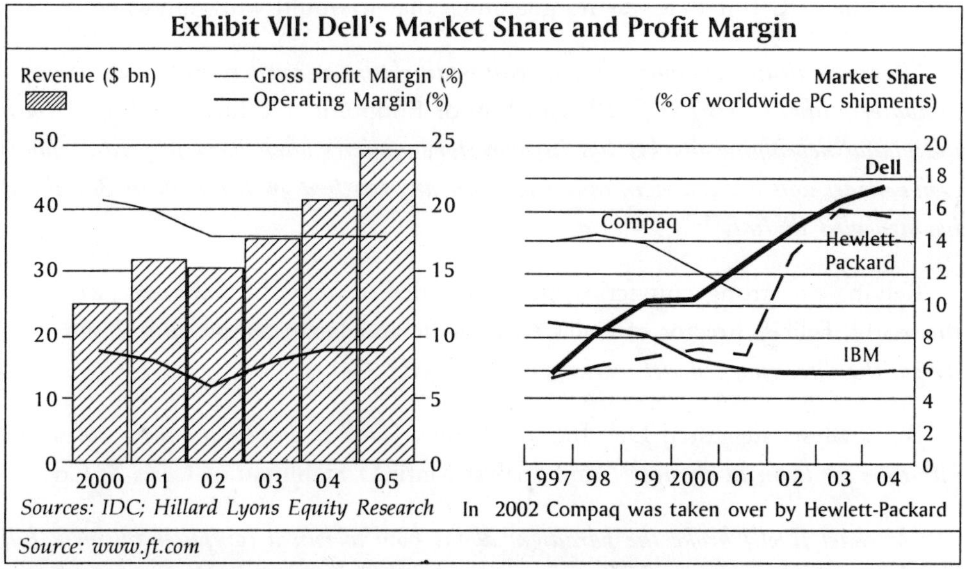

Sources: IDC; Hillard Lyons Equity Research In 2002 Compaq was taken over by Hewlett-Packard

Source: www.ft.com

Challenges in Western Countries (including USA)

It was reported that even Dell's strong market like US, started seeing rapid changes. Moreover, according to the researcher at National Purchase Diary – NPD[20] group, consumers were less interested in buying the tech-wares over the web or phone. The percentage of PC sales done through web or phone declined as the percentage of retail PC sales rose in U.S in 2005[21]. In Latin America or southern Europe, Dell's competitors often had an advantage because of their retail selling method.

Even in entire Europe, where Dell slightly increased its share of the overall PC market in 2004, its market share in fast-growing PC segment went down from 8.4% to 8.3%[22]. In desktop and notebook PCs, which contributed 80% of sales – much future growth would come from outside of Dell's US stronghold, where PC sales had slowed. About 80% of total PC unit sales from 2006 to 2010 would come from developing markets like China and India, according to tech consultancy Forrester Research.

Roger Kay, president of a research organization, Endpoint Technologies Associates said *"They're not getting their fair share of growth*[23]*."*

Many opined that Dell's direct-selling model has worked well in some countries, such as the UK. But that was no guarantee that it would work anywhere.

"In some cultures, computer buyers trust retail chains or resellers and wouldn't buy a computer without seeing it first[24], said Kay of Endpoint. He further added, *"Each individual developing market has its own story, and it's often hard to predict where Dell's model will work. For instance, the company has had great success in Brazil but has struggled in Italy*[25]*."*

Relying on strong conviction in direct-sales strategy, literally everywhere in the world, Felice, director of Dell's Asia Pacific and Japan region said "*Everywhere we go, the direct-sales model works very, very well*[26]*."*

But analysts suggested Dell Inc. to change. *"Dell is singing the same old song". "It's time for them to change*[27]*"* said analyst Mark D Stahlman of Caris & Co.

"Michael [Dell] broke the paradigm about how to run a computer business, but they haven't been so great at finding the next paradigm[28]*,"* said David Yoffie, a professor at Harvard Business School.

Dell's rivals targeted segments of the market that were growing. However, analysts viewed that Dell did not take steps to explore those opportunities. Moreover, the analysts opined, Dell's competitiveness of selling at a lower price was also at risk. Many companies in the PC market started slashing down the prices as a response to Dell's low-cost strategy, making it no longer effective. Hewlett-Packard, one of the main competitors of Dell decreased prices of its products to face the competition.

In 2002, the average selling price of a consumer PC from Dell was $1,084, according to research firm IDC. HP's average selling price for the same year was $1,009. The average for all manufacturers was $1,030. In the first three quarters of 2005, Dell's average selling price of PCs in the US was $854, more than $200 above HP's $651 average. The average selling price for the market as a whole was $744.[29] (Exhibit VIII)

Exhibit VIII: Price Comparison

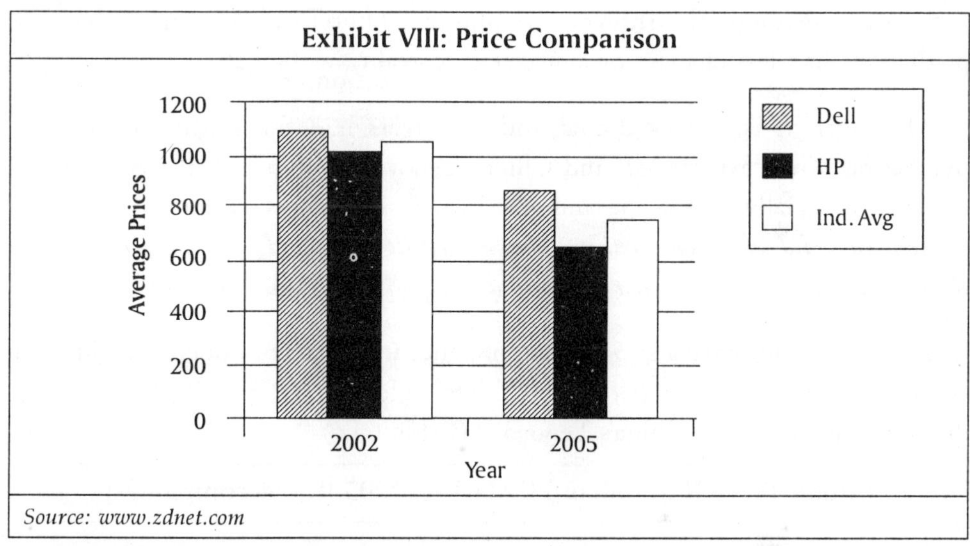

Source: www.zdnet.com

In North America, for many consumers the gains from using Dell's direct model like booking from home and delivery at door steps, were no longer worth because of significant price difference between Dell and others. Khan, Director of consulting and integration, Network service provider practice, Asia Pacific and Japan said, *"As long as (Dell) could undercut the competition, they could expand market share. But what's happened now is Dell has reached the floor... When the spread has narrowed to less than $50, it then matters how the PC is bought. Buying direct doesn't necessarily provide the type of rewards that it used to bring*[30]*."*

Challenges in India

Bob Pearson, vice president, corporate communications, Dell said, *"We believe in the potential of the India market for Dell and our customers.*[31]*"*

According to Dell, it realized India was one of its potential markets, at the same time, with some challenges. Industry sources said that poor general infrastructure was the main reason for the ineffectiveness of direct-selling model in vast, developing markets. Considering India, where PC ownership was predicted to jump from 7.9 million (2005) units to 78 million by 2010, most people didn't have internet access, many rural areas lacked phone lines, and most people knew little about computers. So people went to local stores, system integrators or computer specialists to ask for advice and to make their purchases (instead of purchasing through the internet or phone). Therefore, it seemed that the predictions had less chances of converting to reality within 2010.

Moreover, it is observed that Indian buyers had the traditional way of purchasing. Khan expects HP and China's Lenovo[32] Group Ltd. to keep gaining on Dell, especially in Europe and Asia, where retailers were more important. *"Anyone in India who buys anything, they always sit down and have a cup of tea with the store owner first. Dell is not set up to drink tea*[33]," he said.

As Dell did not have a strong retail presence in India, consumers bought their computers from other companies (HCL Technologies, HP, and IBM, whose PC division was owned by China's Lenovo)[34] (Exhibit IX).

Exhibit IX: Dell in Indian PC Market, 2005 (top 4 companies)

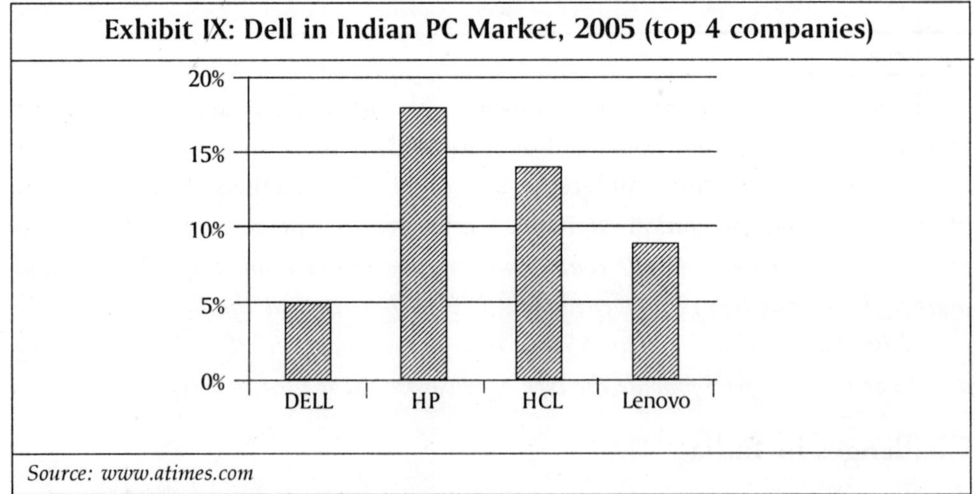

Source: www.atimes.com

Challenges in China

Similarly in China, it was reported that the lack of Dell's retail shops in China, made the market tougher for it. Most of the customers preferred to purchase in retail shops which, in turn, affected Dell's growth in such a way that it lost much market to Lenovo. According to market analysts, the difference was high between Lenovo and company Dell (Exhibit X).

Exhibit X: Market Share of PCs in China (2005)

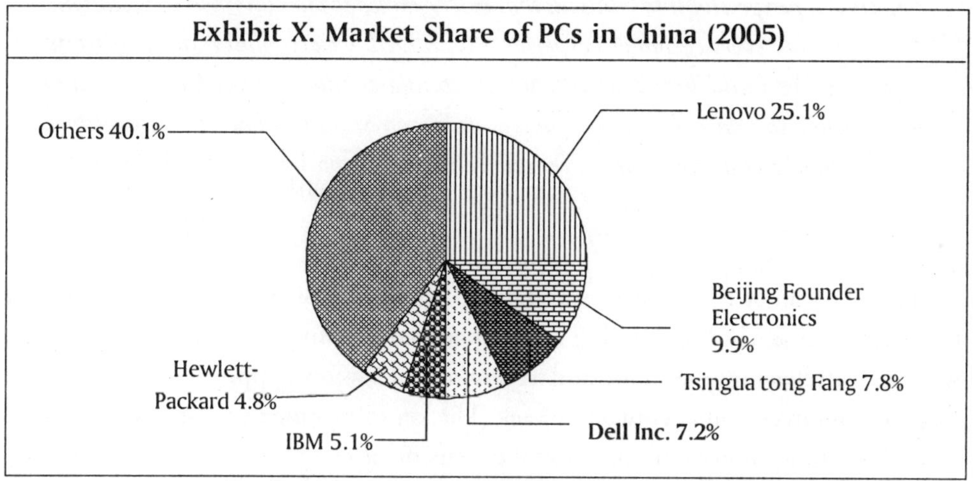

More than three-quarters of Lenovo's $13[35]-billion of sales was done through retail outlets or indirect channels, Milko Van Duijl, president of Lenovo's operations in Europe, the Middle East and Africa said. *"Customers want to see it and feel and touch the machine. And after paying for it, they want to walk away with the machine.*[36]*"* As Dell didn't have its own retail outlets and dealers, many unauthorized sales agents started spreading, particularly, in markets like China.

"The strongest evidence that Dell's model is not yet matched to the China market is the appearance of numerous unofficial 'agents' who buy its computers and sell them on for a profit,[37]*" the Financial Times*[38] noted. The market share of Dell in China was low when compared to the local players.

Customer-Centric Approach

It was observed that Dell started losing grip on customer satisfaction. In 2004, Apple had overtaken Dell Inc., and continued to be in first place till 2006 (Annexure IV). Industrialists felt the need for effective customer support from Dell to regain customer satisfaction in coming years.

"In the past we defined quality in terms of the failure rate of hardware. Hardware reliability was an essential element in satisfying our customers, but it

was not the only element. The Customer Experience was a way to challenge ourselves to expand our focus, to look at quality in all the ways the customer saw it, and to convert this perspective into solutions that met or exceeded our customers' expectations. As we improve every customer's experience with Dell, we accomplish two important objectives: we build brand loyalty, which translates into increased business; and we continue to add value, which makes us more resistant to low-cost competitors. Improving the customer experience will be the key to maintaining our success."

– Michael Dell.

The "Customer Experience" was defined as the sum of every contact a customer had with Dell, including looking at company advertising, browsing the company website, purchasing a system, and receiving follow up support. Dell had more than 16 million customer contacts a week. The key to making this initiative successful was to encourage every employee to take a customer centric view, and to encourage every department in the company to own part of the customer experience.

Michael Dell elaborated, *"There are countless stops along the way where employees behind the scenes make day-to-day decisions that affect the customer. Each of us owns part of the customer experience because everything we do ultimately touches the customer. At Dell, a complete customer experience should never end. The satisfied customer should want to call Dell for all of their hardware needs and all of their future upgrades. Strategically speaking, this affects all employees all the time in everything we do. This initiative will keep all of us focused on the most important people outside Dell—the Customers. Our customers should be treated like VIPs."*[39]

To measure the success of this initiative, performance goals were clearly set. Managers targeted three key metrics to evaluate the progress of the company, and each metric was to improve by at least 15% during the year. The metrics were:

- Order and Delivery (the percentage of orders shipped to the customer by the targeted date)
- Installation and Operation (the percentage of customer calls to technical support which require a part dispatch within 30 days of the invoice date)
- Service (the percentage of on-site service incidents resolved by a Dell Service Partner within the target time-frame).

Exhibit XI: Customers and Segmentation

- Two kinds of customer segments
  - – Transactional customers (30%)
  - – Relationship customers (40%)

  Remaining are a mix (30%)
- The customer segmentation drives the organizational structure of the company
- Dell targeted customer segments where the revenues grew faster than expenses.

Transactional Customers

- These are consumers or small businesses who make transaction-by-transaction buying decisions.
- They focus on economics of purchase and look for factors such as performance and features.
- They shop from a variety of vendors and use an array of information sources including reviews, editorials, word of mouth in making their purchasing decision.
- Dell focused on computer literate customers.
- First time buyers looked for low prices and help from sales person.

Relationship Customers

- These were consumers who treat computer purchases as Total cost of ownership over the life cycle of its use and price was a secondary consideration
- Their focus was on attributes such as service, reliability, vendor reputation and product standardization
- They were government education and business accounts
- Dell competed with resellers such as IBM, HP, Compaq etc. in this segment
- Dell competed by being more than a hardware vendor driving down the total cost of ownership with Dell Plus and Dell Financial Services
- Dell has 25% of Fortune 500 companies as exclusive accounts and was fast penetrating into small and medium segments.

Source: www.lcm.csa.iisc.ernet.in

Michael Dell summarized this initiative. *"The Customer Experience is the most important initiative we have at Dell. We monitor progress all the time in all parts of the company and tie everyone's compensation to it. I personally monitor it, and we present the results at every board meeting. It has a company-wide, world wide focus."*[40]

The Unscripted Future

According to analysts, the consequences could not only affect PC sales but also other product lines. In 2006, about 80%[41] of Dell's printers – a product line that created lots of interest among financial analysts in the past – were sold along with purchases of PCs, said Charles Lecompton, president of imaging consultancy Lira Research in Newtonville, Mass[42]. Thus, the lower the PC sales growth, the lower would be the growth of printer sales too.

Analysts opined that Dell had three options. First, it could stick with the direct-sales model, waiting for vast-markets like India and China to advance technologically. Second option was to exit the PC business, as IBM had done before[43]. Instead, Dell could concentrate on new markets for selling IT services and enhanced services rather than hardware products, where there was much growth and many opportunities.

Barry Jaruzelski, analyst at Booz Allen Hamilton[44], said, *"The market structure, their operating model and the fact that they still haven't fully exploited some other opportunities outside of PCs suggests they still have a lot of runway in front of them[45]."*

"New markets will offer more than 80 per cent of future growth," according to Dell's CEO, Rollins. Yet that didn't change the fact that, Dell was still a PC company, being termed as one of the world's toughest businesses because of the price fluctuation of the spare parts (internal components).

The third option was to create more of retail show rooms in the developing countries to ensure that it got the major portion of its PC sales in coming years. Dell could do it through a partnership with local players or purchase of a local manufacturer already keeping a strong market lead over the US companies in countries like India and China. Probably Dell could set up relationship with retailers and system integrators in these countries (Annexure V).

"Dell should probably tweak its business model in countries where it is having trouble[46]", Kay said. It should stick on to its direct sales model where it performs well and sacrifice direct-selling, where retail selling is advantageous, suggested the experts.

Yet the basic strength of its low-cost direct-sales business model should still give it an edge as pricing in the PC market was very crucial – commented the experts. The status in terms of revenue and assets were still well-reflected in its balance sheet (Annexures VI, VII).

Analysts also opined that investors would not likely be eager about any changes in the direct-sales model. After all, that could reduce Dell's margins. In 2005, with 8.6%[47] margin, it was ahead of HP's 5.4%[48]. Its consolidated revenue was also healthy across markets (Annexure VIII). However, much faster revenue growth that might come from altering that model could cover up some of that frustration created by its unachieved quarterly targets. Importantly, it would also help Dell to achieve its $80 billion mark faster. Enhanced services also offered growth as on February 3, 2006 (Annexure IX).

For the time being, Dell said it was going to continue with the present sales model. *"We're completely committed to the direct-sales model and have no plans to go retail outside of the US,"* said Dell's spokesperson. He also added, *"We're going against competitors who've been in the business there much longer... We feel good about our growth. We'll just have to expand our customer relationships*[49]*."* Dell further argued that companies that distributed through retail had no way of collecting the amount and type of information that Dell had on their clients because they lacked the direct contact. With the emphasis on customer focus, supplier partnerships, mass customization, and JIT manufacturing Dell opined that it had an edge over others.

Could the Dell approach no longer be dependent on the ultra-competitive conditions that are now emerging within the PC business and beyond? With a new wave of low-cost competitors emerging and buyers asking for much-lower prices, should Dell compromise on future growth by rigidly sticking on to its direct-sales model, accepting lower growth or exploring new ways to make a come back? After all, times were changing. With it, should Dell too need to change?

Endnotes

1 Source: *www.ft.com*

2 ibid

3 Source: *www.en.wikipedia.org*

4 Source: *www.dell.com,*

5 Stock Exchange of USA.

6 Source: What dell should do?, *www.businessworld.com.*

7 Brand name of a PC manufactured by company APPLE.

8 A business magazine published in America.

9 Source: *www.mahhe.com*

10 Arthur A Thompson, Jr., A J Strikland, Dell Computer Corporation, *www.mhhe.com*

11 An annual list published by *Forbes* magazine of the wealthiest 400 people in the United States.

12 Source: Michael Dell, *www.en.wikipedia.org*

13 ibid.

14 Dell Inc. was the 1st company to outsource customer support to India by setting up call-center in Bangalore. Later, this concept of BPO (mainly call-centers set up offshore) became a history in itself for Indian BPO industry.

15 Dell Computer Corporation, *www.mhhe.com*

16 Source: *www.kshb.com*

17 One of the main PC manufacturing companies.

18 ibid.

19 Stock Exchange in United States of America, *www.msn.com*

20 Market Research Firm providing news and information on consumer trends, sales and marketing information for a diverse range of industries.

21 "It's Dell Vs. the Dell way", *www.businessweek.com*

22 www.businessweek.com

23 Source: *www.tmcnet.com*

24 ibid.

25 Source: *www.gmtoday.com*

26 ibid.

27 Source: *www.businessworld.com*

28 ibid.

29 Source of all figures in the paragraph, *www.zdnet.com*

30 ibid.

31 Source: Sluggish Dell is bullish over India, July 24, 2006, *www.efytimes.com*

32 One of the main PC manufacturing and selling companies, *www.globeinvester.com*

33 ibid.

34 Main PC manufacturers and sellers in China.

35 *www.globeinvester.com*, July 15, 2006.

36 ibid.

37 Source: Is dell dying?, *www.slate.com*

38 An international business newspaper.

39 Source: *www.flowalliance.com/Dell_Computer_A_Zero_Time_Organization.pdf*

40 ibid.

41 *www.businessweek.com*

42 A publication company, covering printer and photography industries.

43 *www.businessweek.com*

44 Strategic management and technology consulting firm.

45 Source: *www.ft.com*

46 ibid.

47 Dell: Time for a new model?, *www.businesweek.com*

48 ibid.

49 Source: *www.businessweek.com*

References

1. About us, *www.Dell.com*
2. Dell, *www.monsterindia.com*
3. *China Daily*, Dell vows to be top PC producer in China, *www.english.people.com,* May 27, 2004.
4. Tom Krazit and Sumner Lemon, "Dell confirms disappointing Q3 results", *www.cio.co.nz,* 11/11/2005.
5. Siddharth Srivastava, "PC market heats up in India", *www.atimes.com,* Jun 21, 2006
6. Michael Dell founder of Dell Computers, *www.bga.com*
7. Arthur A Thompson, Jr., A J Strikland, Dell Computer Corporation, *www.mhhe.com*
8. Scott Morrison in San Francisco, "Slowing growth at Dell raises concerns," *www.ft.com,* August 25, 2005.
9. "Denial Gross, Dell dying?" *www.slate.com*, August 30, 2005.
10. Price history, *www.msn.com*
11. Michael Kanellos, "Dell expands lead in still-growing PC market," *www.news.com,* January 18, 2005.

12. Sumner Lemon, "Competition heats up for Dell in China's PC market," *www.infoworld.com,* March 18, 2005.

13. "Michael Dell," *www.wikipedia.org.*

14. Simon Avery, "Dell's new business model: Redemption," *www.globeinvester.com,* July 15, 2006.

15. Oliga Kharif, "Dell for a new model?," *www.businessweek.com*

16. "Dell," *www.Morningstar.com*

17. IDC, "Apple Mac attained 4.8% US market share in Q2 06," *www.macdailynews.com,* July 19, 2006.

18. Balance Sheet, *www.yahoo.com,* August.

19. Michael Kanellos, "Dell whacks prices on select note books, desktops, " *www.news.zdnet.com,* May 1, 2006.

20. "We believe in India's potential: Dell", *www.indidaily.com,* July 24, 2006.

21. "Rivals chip away at Dell: With competitors gaining, firm may need to upgrade its strategy," *www.tmcnet.com,* June10, 2006.

22. "Direct sales model puts dent in Dell's armor," *www.itbusinessedge.com,* 25 July, 2006.

23. Second quarter scores, *www.theacsi.org,* August 15, 2006.

Annexure I: Dell's Operating Centers World Over

Dell Americas

- Headquarters: Round Rock, Texas
- Manufacturing facilities: Austin, Texas; Nashville, Tennessee.; Winston-Salem, North Carolina; Eldorado Sul, Brazil
- Revenue (last four quarters): $36.8 billion
- Q1 Y/Y revenue growth: 4 percent
- Number of employees: 33,100

Dell Asia Pacific – Japan

- Headquarters: Singapore
- Manufacturing facilities: Penang, Malaysia; Xiamen, China
- Revenue (last four quarters): $6.9 billion
- Q4 Y/Y revenue growth: 17 percent
- Number of employees: A/P 21,500; Japan 1,300

Dell Europe, Middle East and Africa

- Headquarters: Bracknell, UK
- Manufacturing facilities: Limerick, Ireland
- Revenue (last four quarters): $13.1 billion
- Q1 Y/Y revenue growth: 6 percent
- Number of employees: 13,800
- The company had 49 regional offices worldwide.

Note: Market position based on Q1 –'06 IDC data

Source: www.dell.com

Annexure II: Dell's Worldwide Share of PC Shipments

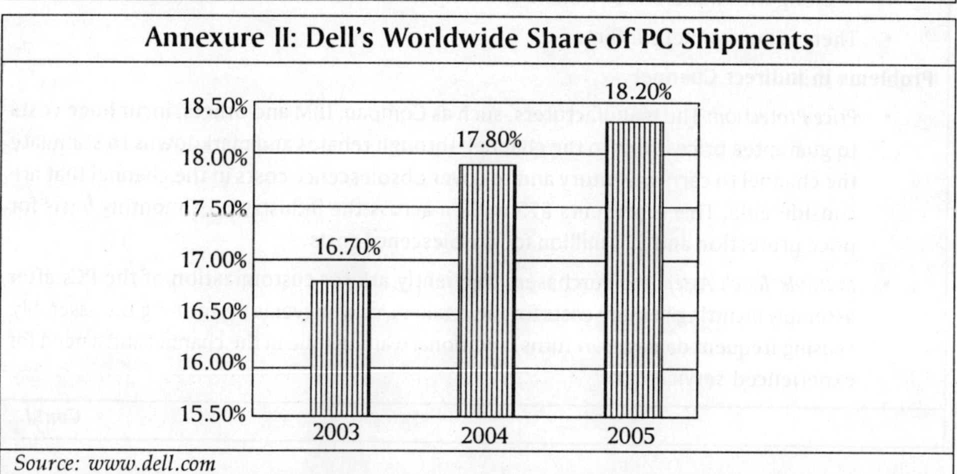

Source: www.dell.com

Annexure III: Direct Model Vs. Indirect Model

Direct Model

- The OEMs supply computers after receiving orders through their Web site or through phone calls. Direct sales force also calls on corporate customers.
- Dell has 80% of its sales volume to corporate and 20% to individual consumers.
- Dell holds very small final product inventory, forcing suppliers to keep bulk of its parts inventory on their sites.

How Dell Succeeded with the Internet?

- Dell is a prominent example of successful migration to the Internet—a success that is largely due to the company's ability to leverage pre-Internet capabilities.
- For Dell, the Internet was a sustaining force that improved upon its existing resources and processes.
- Small-to-medium size businesses and home computer users called "1–800–BUY–DELL", where trained sales representatives helped them understand the company's products and assess the compatibility of the components that they wanted.
- When the customer had arrived at a compatible system configuration, the sales representative entered the order into the company's IT system.
- By building a telephone-ordering infrastructure for its transaction clients, Dell had already invested in capabilities and processes that fit the self-help Internet model.
- Internet further reinforced the processes and values inherent in Dell-direct business model.
  - The customer can get all the information on the web and make good purchase choices and seek the help of a sales person if needed.
  - Dell's website offers hundreds of thousands of pages service and support information along with hundreds of trouble shooting scenarios.
- There is no channel conflict.

Problems in Indirect Channel

- *Price Protection:* The manufacturers, such as Compaq, IBM and others, incur huge costs to guarantee price levels to the channel, through rebates and markdowns to stimulate the channel to carry inventory and to cover obsolescence costs in the channel that are considerable. This represents $75 million across the industry on a monthly basis for price protection and $70 million for obsolescence costs.
- *Multiple Touch Assembly:* Purchasers frequently ask for customization of the PCs after assembly incurring in more costs for the retailers, or whoever is performing the assembly, causing frequent damages, returns, additional waiting time in the channel and a need for experienced service.

Contd...

Contd...

- *Inventory Financing Costs*: High costs associated with financing the operations, with parts producers financing OEMs, which finance the distributors and so on and on, as you move upwards the channel. This financing might come as stretched accounts receivables or loans. An additional cost is the cost of the money attached to the inventory stocked by the different players. This represents US$95 million across the industry in a monthly basis.
- *Price:* Companies such as Dell using the direct model normally have around 20% cost advantage over the other companies using the indirect one. These price advantages are often passed over to the customer.

Advantages of the Indirect Model

- *Service:* More and more customers are demanding services and maintenance capabilities for their purchases. Since the indirect model is spread throughout the country, it becomes easier for the indirect manufacturers to provide support through the channel than for companies such as Dell, which have to rely on a costly sales and support force or subcontract players of the indirect channel to do so.
- *Value-added services:* Some consumers are requiring more services other than maintenance, such as constant upgrades, asset management, constant visits, etc, which are more easily performed by the members of the indirect channel.

Current Initiatives Taken by Manufacturers

- Due to the disadvantages of the indirect model, manufacturers and the other channel players have focused on shifting away from Build-to-Forecast to Build-to-Order (BTO) and Channel Assembly programs (CTO). This is a shift to delivering more customized lower-cost products more quickly to the customer.

Channel Assembly

- Upon receipt of an order, OEM's ship "base units" or kits with a variety of components to a reseller or a distributor. These people then assemble and modify the machines to conform to the customer's specification.
- This system requires that the resellers and the distributors have the capability for minor assembly and that the products they produce are certified by the OEM for quality and warranty protection.
- Manufacturers have systems to handle component level deliveries and have the capability to forecast demand at the component level.

Channel Assembly: Merits

- *Improve Fulfillment:* Building a machine after order receipt, ensures that a customer will get the product of his/her choice, eliminates the cost of stock-outs for the company and provides better information to the OEM as to which machines are selling, which helps him/her in forecasting future demand.

Contd...

Contd...

- *Reduction in the cost of obsolescence:* In the old system, when manufacturers shipped preconfigured machines, the obsolescence of one component affected the value of the entire machine. In the Channel Assembly model, the obsolescence of one component does not affect the value of accompanying components.

Source: www.lcm.csa.iisc.ernet.in

Annexure IV: Customer Rating (All scores are on 100-point scale)

Year	2001	2002	2003	2004	2005	2006	% Change (from 2005)
Apple	73	73	77	81	81	83	2.5
Dell	78	76	78	79	74	78	5.4
HP	73	71	70	71	73	75	2.7
Gate Way	73	72	69	74	72	73	1.4
HP Company-Compaq	69	68	68	69	67	72	7.5

Source: www.theacsi.org

Annexure V: Key Players in the PC Supply Chain

- ***Distributors***
  - They generally supply to corporate resellers and other distributors.
  - They carry large quantities of different products, to increase their leverage when dealing with their customers.
  - They also provide specific software, peripherals, furniture, etc., as well as service.
  - Ingram Micro, Tech Data, Computer 2000, and Santech are some of the examples.
- ***Corporate Resellers/System Integrators***
  - The corporate resellers or systems integrators generally buy systems directly from manufacturers and install these systems at their corporate clients.
  - These are firms whose main purpose is to provide customization to their clients.
  - They normally integrate software, hardware, and network capabilities on a per customer basis and offer customer service after the installation as well as support for posterior updates.
- ***Retailers***
  - These are essentially the stores that sell computers to the end users. The end users are home or small office users.
  - The stores tend to supply other products, such as furniture, peripherals, and stationery.
  - Wal-Mart, Office Max, Computer City, CompUSA and Micro-Center are some of the examples.

Source: www.lcm.csa.iisc.ernet.in

Annexure VI: Asset Status of Dell Inc.

(In $ thousand)

Assets			
Period Ending	**3-Feb-06**	**28-Jan-05**	**30-Jan-04**
Current Assets			
Cash And Cash Equivalents	7,042,000	4,747,000	4,317,000
Short Term Investments	2,016,000	5,060,000	835,000
Net Receivables	5,452,000	4,414,000	3,635,000
Inventory	576,000	459,000	327,000
Other Current Assets	2,620,000	2,217,000	1,519,000
Total Current Assets	**17,706,000**	**16,897,000**	**10,633,000**
Long Term Investments	3,016,000	4,319,000	6,770,000
Property Plant and Equipment	2,005,000	1,691,000	1,517,000
Goodwill	–	–	–
Intangible Assets	–	–	–
Accumulated Amortization	–	–	–
Other Assets	382,000	308,000	391,000
Deferred Long Term Asset Charges	–	–	–
Total Assets	**23,109,000**	**23,215,000**	**19,311,000**

Source:www.finance.yahoo.com

Annexure VII: Financial Details of Dell Inc. (in million)

	2000	2001	2002	2003	2004	2005	2006
Revenue	25,265.0	31,888.0	31,168.0	35,404.0	41,444.0	49,205.0	55,908.0
COGS	20,047.0	25,445.0	25,661.0	29,055.0	33,892.0	40,190.0	45,958.0
Gross profit	5,218.0	6,443.0	5,507.0	6,349.0	7,552.0	9,015.0	9,950.0
Operating Expenses $Mil							
SGBA	2,387.0	3,193.0	2,784.0	3,050.0	3,544.0	4,298.0	5,140.0
R&D	56.0	482.0	452.0	455.0	464.0	463.0	463.0
Other	0	105.0	482.0	0	0	0	0
Operating Income	**2,263.0**	**2,663.0**	**1,789.0**	**2,844.0**	**3,544.0**	**4,254.0**	**4,347.0**
Other Income and Expenses $Mil							
Net Int Inc & others	188.0	531.0	58.0	183.0	180.0	191.0	227.0
Earnings Before Taxes	2,451.0	3,194.0	1,731.0	3,027.0	3,724.0	4,445.0	4,574.0
Income taxes	785.0	958.0	485.0	905.0	1,079.0	1,402.0	1,002.0
Earnings After Taxes	1,666.0	2,236.0	1,246.0	2,122.0	2,645.0	3,043.0	3,572.0
Acctg. Changes		59					
Disc Operations							
Ext Items							
Net Income	1,666.0	2,177.0	1,246.0	2,122.0	2,645.0	3,043.0	3,572.0
Diluted EPS, Cont Ops$	0.61	0.81	0.46	0.80	1.01	1.18	1.46
Diluted EPS$	0.61	0.79	0.46	0.80	1.01	1.18	1.46
Shares	2728	2746	2726	2644	2619	2568	2449

Source: Morningstar.com *Fiscal year end: January*

Annexure VIII: Quarterly Revenue by Region as Percentages of Consolidated Net Revenue (in $Billion)			
	Q1 FY07	Q4 FY06	Q3 FY06
Americas	63	64	64
Europe/Middle East/Africa	24	24	24
Asia Pacific-Japan	13	12	12

Source: www.dell.com

Annexure IX: What Makes Up DELL?

(in billions, except percentages)

Source of Revenue	Fiscal Year Ended					
	February 3, 2006		January 28, 2005		January 30, 2004	
	Dollars	% of Revenue	Dollars	% of Revenue	Dollars	% of Revenue
Desktop PCs	$21.1	38%	$20.8	42%	$18.7	45%
Mobility	14.1	25%	11.8	24%	9.7	23%
Software & Peripherals	8.5	15%	6.7	14%	4.9	12%
Servers & Networking	5.4	10%	4.9	10%	4.3	10%
Enhanced Services	4.9	9%	3.7	7%	2.7	7%
Storage	1.9	3%	1.3	3%	1.1	3%
Total Revenue	**$55.9**	**100%**	**549.2**	**100%**	**$41.4**	**100%**

Source: Dell's 2005 Annual Report.

Index